*Introduction to T<sub>E</sub>X*

**Other books published in this series:**

| Title | Author | ISBN |
|---|---|---|
| Using Informix-SQL | *Jonathan Leffler* | 0-201-51240-8 |
| The X Window System: A User's Guide | *Niall Mansfield* | 0-201-51341-2 |
| Getting Started with Xerox Ventura Publisher | *W. van Engelen* | 0-201-51573-3 |
| Advanced Xerox Ventura Publisher 2.0 | *Frank Peetoom* | 0-201-51574-1 |
| Turbo C 2.0 | *Arne Schäpers* | 0-201-51195-9 |
| Inside HyperCard Vol. 1 | *W. Kitza* | 0-201-51150-9 |
| Inside HyperCard Vol. 2 | *W. Kitza* | 0-201-51330-7 |

Books to be published in this series:

| | | |
|---|---|---|
| Turbo Pascal 5.5 | *Arne Schäpers* | 0-201- 51171-1 |
| SQL/Oracle | *Finkenzeller et al* | 0-201-52974-2 |
| UNIX System Management | *Thomassen* | 0-201-52950-5 |
| Introduction to SPSS/PC+ 4.0 | *Huizingh* | 0-201-52975-0 |

# Introduction to T_EX

## Jost Krieger
## Norbert Schwarz

**Addison-Wesley Publishing Company, Inc.**

Amsterdam • Reading, Massachusetts • New York • Bonn, Germany
Menlo Park, California • Don Mills, Ontario • Wokingham, England
Sydney • Singapore • Tokyo • Madrid • San Juan • Milan

Cover design: Carta, The Netherlands
Printed by: Tulp, The Netherlands

© 1989,1990 Addison-Wesley Europe
© 1989,1990 Addison-Wesley Publishing Company, Inc.

ISBN 0 201 51141 X

# Preface

This book is an experiment. The authors have lots of experience in using and teaching TeX, but much less experience in the use of the English language. As this book is based on the second edition of the German "Einführung in TeX", it would have been possible to have this book produced in the usual way, by a professional native English speaking translator. We decided not to do this for quite a few reasons: We are sure that producing the book is a lot easier for us since *we* can fit text and TeX together; it would probably be hard to find a translator who is also a TeX adept; finally we hope that the lack of expressive power will not keep us from making our intentions clear enough to be of use to the TeX user.

This book is an *introduction* to the use of the TeX system. It cannot be a replacement for Donald E. Knuth's "The TeXbook", which is the final authority in all cases of doubt and which has been a rich source of ideas for examples and applications in this book.

TeX is a big system. Hardly any person will use (or even know) all of the over 900 commands of *plain TeX*, and this book cannot possibly discuss them all. Instead, it tends more to the description of examples and useful little tricks. From the experience of the authors, it is also a bit more internationally oriented than a book of English or American origin would probably be.

Finally, we hope this book will show its readers the way to a creative use of TeX. Although it is a very powerful system in itself, TeX is most interesting in that it can be extended by anyone to his liking.

*Jost Krieger*
*Norbert Schwarz*
*Bochum, 1989*

# Contents

# 1 General Information

## 1.1 Characteristics of the TEX System

TEX (pronounced "Tech", with a German or Scottish 'ch', sometimes also spelled "TeX" or "$\tau\epsilon\chi$") is a typesetting system developed by Donald E. Knuth of Stanford University in the course of a decade. It is especially suited for the production of scientific publications containing mathematical formulae.

TEX is a *typesetting* system and *not* a word processor. The stress is here on the expression "setting type". The program offers more or less the 'state of the art' in computer-assisted typesetting. It has quite a few capabilities not present in a normal word processor.

Here is a short account of the merits of TEX:

*different typefaces*    TEX utilizes different typefaces and type sizes: in the standard case these are proportionally spaced typefaces. These fonts belong to the newly created font family of "computer modern fonts". In mathematical type, especially, the type sizes for indices, subformulae etc. are determined automatically.

*kerning*    Generally, "kerning" is performed: characters that should overlap will be put closer to one another: e.g., "voice" and "VAT" is produced instead of "voice" and "VAT".

*ligatures*    For some sequences of characters — fi, fl, ffi, ffl — TEX generates *ligatures*. A special character — fi, fl, ffi, ffl — is set for the compound characters. This is performed automatically.

*justification*    Text is exactly justified on the right margin. The characters are put below each other 'to the point'. During justification, not just one line is relevant, but the appearance of the whole paragraph is considered. There are two goals: to avoid hyphenations and, on the other hand, to make interword spacing as even as possible.

*hyphenation*    Hyphenation is performed with stored hyphenation patterns. This approach has proven itself in day-to-day use. The important point is to avoid erroneous hyphenations, which fits well with the goal of avoiding all hyphenation, if possible. Besides American hyphenation patterns, more and more foreign language patterns are available.

*mathematical type*  Mathematical formulae can be prepared in a comfortable way and are represented in a form mathematicians are used to seeing in good books. The input format mirrors the mathematical structure and contents of the different parts of the formula.

*macros*  TₑX contains a powerful macro processor — almost its own programming language. This allows users to define their own commands, to rename TₑX commands or equip them with new features. They can even produce their own command environment.

*layout*  Great importance is attached to the arrangement of the document in a general sense. Intelligent algorithms support page and line breaking and layout. Thus, with TₑX, the user can produce documents in print quality. The layout for the generated document is fully parameterized and can be customized by the user, although this is not normally necessary.

*input*  Input is more difficult for the user to write than it is with a word processor — unless she is writing formulae. The user should keep in mind that she is putting more effort in the input of her text, but the result is also **much** prettier.

*output*  Output of the TₑX results will be totally satisfying only on high-resolution laser printers or similar devices. On the other hand, with dot printers, multiple passes make satisfactory output possible.

*implementations*  TₑX has been implemented on almost all computers and operating systems. Even for many PCs, implementations are available. The TₑX System itself is almost "public domain software". It is available free of charge to each user. The only applicable costs are for generating the transport media for the sources. On the other hand, no program, even if it is written in a standardized language, will run without problems on each computer and under each operating system. This explains the availability of commercial *implementations*, especially for small machines, where the price is compensation for the implementation effort.

# 2 Operation

## 2.1 Command Structure and Command Characters

| ␣ | 0 | @ | P | ` | p | 0 |
|---|---|---|---|---|---|---|
| ! | 1 | A | Q | a | q | 1 |
| " | 2 | B | R | b | r | 2 |
| # | 3 | C | S | c | s | 3 |
| $ | 4 | D | T | d | t | 4 |
| % | 5 | E | U | e | u | 5 |
| & | 6 | F | V | f | v | 6 |
| ' | 7 | G | W | g | w | 7 |
| ( | 8 | H | X | h | x | 8 |
| ) | 9 | I | Y | i | y | 9 |
| * | : | J | Z | j | z | A |
| + | ; | K | [ | k | { | B |
| , | < | L | \ | l | \| | C |
| - | = | M | ] | m | } | D |
| . | > | N | ^ | n | ~ | E |
| / | ? | O | _ | o |  | F |
| 2 | 3 | 4 | 5 | 6 | 7 |  |

*ASCII code (without control characters)*

TEX commands and regular text input are read and processed from *one* common input file. That is, there are *no* setting instructions for an *external* text. The set of input characters that is used — typically in an input file — is based on the international ASCII character set. Thus, no computer or terminal keyboard with special code assignments is assumed, but just a computer keyboard with international key mapping. Compared to European national typewriters or keyboards with national key assignments, the one used has brackets and curly braces instead of e.g. umlauts or other national characters like 'ß', which is replaced by a tilde ' ˜ '. Other possible problems may be the paragraph sign §, which is replaced by the 'at sign' @. This leads to difficulties with the input of accented letters or diphthongs. Characters of the symbol set that occur rarely in normal text are used for the representation of TEX commands and command characters.

First, we consider the TEX commands themselves:

■ The **TEX commands** start with an introductory character before the command name. In the standard case, this is a backslash ('\'). This "escape" symbol is followed by the command name, which usually consists of letters only *(named* *command)*. It is possible, however, to use just *one* nonletter *(short command)* for the name of a command. Nonletters include digits, in this case.

The commands with names consisting of letters are terminated by a blank or the next nonletter. If a blank is intended to be *generated in the output* just after a named command, the command must be followed by the sequence \⊔ . (⊔ represents the space character.)

| examples of named commands | examples of short commands |
|---|---|
| \smallskip | \" |
| \footnote | \, |
| \par | \_ |
| \indent | \% |
| \ss | \- |

*Example of TEX input:*

```
{\bf  \narrower\narrower
   The glory and power of Printing is not
   all in the past.
   Its influence in the present makes it
   a powerful conservator of human progress.
   \par\hfill  {\it Carlyle\par}}
```

*Output:*

> **The glory and power of Printing is not all in the past. Its influence in the present makes it a powerful conservator of human progress.**
>
> *Carlyle*

Apart from the named and short commands, there are a few **command symbols** that produce their effects on their own:

**{**    **block structure braces**

**}**    Commands, especially the settings of certain parameters like typeface, type size, indentations etc., should have effects only in some restricted area, their **scope**. These scopes are introduced by the character '{' and terminated by an '}'. This is the block structure common in modern programming languages.

*All settings that are made or changed inside such a pair of braces do not exist outside this scope. All settings revert to the values that were in effect when the block was entered.*

**&**    The tabulator symbol is used for the production of tables. It is the 'TAB' character and separates the table entries.

**%**    The comment symbol: everything that follows a percent sign on the same line is a comment and will be ignored by the TEX program.

**$**    The dollar sign introduces and terminates the setting of mathematical formulae.

Here are only a few introductory remarks, for more information see the chapter on *Mathematical Typesetting*. Any information included between a pair of dollar signs or a pair of double dollar signs will be regarded as a mathematical formula and will be set to separate special rules, e.g.:

$ *typesetting information for formulae in running text* $

$$ *typesetting information for displayed formulae* $$

**#** *parameter symbol*
This character is a *replacement symbol* used during the definition of macros (shorthand notations) and in the setting of tables.

**^** *Hat* for superscripts or exponents in mathematical formulae
Example: `$x^2$` produces $x^2$. A replacement named command for this is "`\sp`".

**_** *Underbar* for subscripts and indices in mathematical formulae
Example: `$x_n$` produces $x_n$. This can be replaced by the named command "`\sb`".

**-** *Hyphen*
The simple hyphen, as it appears on a normal typewriter keyboard is not equivalent to the four different kinds of 'dashes' as the typesetter knows them. Depending on the intended sign, one, two, or three ASCII minus signs are *input* in the following example:

| | | | |
|---|---|---|---|
| the *hyphen* | `X-rays` | *for* | X-rays |
| the *en-dash* | `12--14 lbs.` | *for* | 12–14 lbs. |
| the *em-dash* | `--- think of it` | *for* | — think of it |
| the *mathematical minus sign* | `$x-y$` | *for* | $x - y$ |

If you want to print these symbols themselves, you will have to use a special representation:

`$\backslash$`     `$\{$`     `$\}$`     `\$`     `\&`     `\#`     `\_`     `\%`

The symbols ˆ and ¯ are available as *accents*.

The symbols | < > are available in the typeface "`typewriter type`". Less-than and greater-than signs, on the other hand, hardly ever show up outside of formulae. In straight text they can also be generated by a short switch to mathematics mode: `$|$`, `$<$`, and `$>$` generate the symbols |, <, and >.

## 2.2 Structure of Commands

The commands can be classified into three groups:
- commands that change settings
- commands that operate on additional information
- commands that operate on their own.

Commands that change settings, e.g., the typeface, are always used together with block structure braces to determine the scope of these settings. These braces include the commands and their scope. This is a structure equivalent to the block structure of a programming language.

An example of this:

`\rm` switches to normal typeface,

`\it` switches to *italic*,

`\bf` switches to **boldface**.

With these conditions, the input

```
This text is in normal typeface, {here it is still the same,
\bf but now it is in boldface {\it with a bit of italic}
some boldface} and back to normal at last.
```

produces the result:

> This text is in normal typeface, here it is still the same, **but now
> it is in boldface** *with a bit of italic* **some boldface** and back to
> normal at last.

The second group, of the commands that operate on something, i.e. which have parameters, consists of commands like

| | |
|---|---|
| `\matrix{...}` | to typeset matrices, |
| `\line{...}` | to typeset lines, |
| `\halign{...}` | to typeset tables. |

These commands are followed by the information that is operated upon, usually included in braces. If the parameter text consists of only *one* character or only *one* further command, the braces can be omitted.

Example: `$\widehat xyz$` for $\widehat{x}yz$ and `$\widehat {xyz}$` for $\widehat{xyz}$.

The last group of parameterless simple commands without switching effects:

| | |
|---|---|
| `\quad` | for some empty   space, |
| `\%` | for the % sign. |

## 2.3 Punctuation

Punctuation is handled in a special way by TEX. A sentence-ending period, e.g., is followed by a *somewhat* wider space. If a period follows a capital letter, TEX considers this an abbreviation and uses its normal interword space. To force normal spacing after a period, use `.\⊔` as input. This differentiation in word spacing has not been in use in all European printing. The command `\frenchspacing` globally switches the size of sentence-ending interword spaces to the same size as other spacings. This can be revoked by `\nonfrenchspacing`.

One important application is for three consecutive dots ... as an expression for "and so forth". The simple input ... generates "...". It is better to apply the command `\dots` to get the result "...".

▌  The keyboard's grave accent character produces a simple *left* quote:
   — ' —    (a replacement command is "`\lq`" — *left quote*)
   2 accent characters are collapsed to form a ligature: '' produces ".

▌  The keyboard's apostrophe character generates a simple *right* quote:
   — ' —    (a replacement command is "`\rq`" — *right quote*)
   2 apostrophes are collapsed to form a ligature: '' produces ".

▌  A double quote has as result — " —.
   In proportional typefaces, the output is the same as for 2 apostrophes.

## 2.4 A First Example

The following pages contain an example input and the corresponding TEX output. In this example the TEX commands are printed in `negative` typeface. The distinct TEX commands are separated by a tiny empty space ▌▌ for better visibility. This does *not* correspond to an empty space in the input.

The following commands are used:

| | |
|---|---|
| `\` | an empty space is forced |
| `---` | typeset an em-dash |
| `\bf` | switch to the standard typeface **boldface** |
| `\bigskip` | leave a big vertical space (blank line) |
| `\centerline` | center a line |
| `\dag` | symbol † |
| `\Delta` | mathematical symbol $\Delta$ |
| `\end` | end command to TeX |
| `\font` | definition of a new typeface |
| `\footnote` | build a footnote |
| `\large` | selection of the newly defined typeface |
| `\headline` | definition of the permanent page heading |
| `\hfill` | dynamic horizontal empty space |
| `\hrule` | horizontal black line |
| `\it` | switch to standard typeface *italic* |
| `\leftline` | typeset a left justified line |
| `\magnification` | global magnification |
| `\magstep1` | magnification factor 1.2 |
| `\magstep2` | magnification factor $1.44 = 1.2 * 1.2$ |
| `\medskip` | medium vertical spacing |
| `\medium` | selection of a private typeface |
| `\noindent` | start a paragraph *without* indentation |
| `\over` | mathematical operation for a fraction |
| `\pageno` | setting of the current page number |
| `\rightline` | typeset a right justified line |
| `\sl` | switch to standard typeface *slanted* |
| `\smallskip` | small vertical spacing |
| `\to` | mathematical operation $\rightarrow$ |
| `\vfill` | dynamic vertical empty space (fill the page) |
| `\vskip` | vertical empty space of given height |
| `$$` | start/end of mathematics |
| `{ }` | grouping braces |

```
\pageno=128
\magnification=\magstep0
\font\medium=cmbx10 scaled \magstep1
\font\large=cmbx10 scaled \magstep2
\headline={\hfill --- Example --- \hfill}
\centerline{\large Main Title}
\bigskip
\leftline{\medium Chapter Title}
\medskip
\leftline{\bf Section Title}
\medskip
\noindent This example has been set in a 10 point
typeface. The original typeface has not been
changed. The global magnification has the factor
$ f=1$. Only the intermediate titles
have been set in larger typefaces.
\smallskip
Parts of the text that should be emphasized are
written in a different typeface: {\it italic}.
Also available is one more typeface
--- {\sl slanted}---.
\bigskip
\leftline{\bf A Further New Section}
\medskip
\noindent A new paragraph is started by one or
more empty lines.
\bigskip
\rightline{\bf The Section Title on the Other Side,
    For a Change}
\medskip
Setting of formulae\footnote{\dag}{{\TeX\ was
developed with mathematical typesetting in
mind in the first place.}is easy using \TeX\ :
$$\{
f( x + \Delta x )-f(x)
\over \Delta x }\to f'(x) $$
\bigskip
\hrule height 2pt \vskip 3pt \hrule
\bigskip
\centerline{\large END}
\vfill
\end
```

*example input*

— Example — 9

# Main Title

## Chapter Title

### Section Title

This example has been set in a 10 point typeface. The original typeface has not been changed. The global magnification has the factor $f = 1$. Only the intermediate titles have been set in larger typefaces.

Parts of the text that should be emphasized are written in a different typeface: *italic*. Also available is one more typeface — *slanted* —.

### A Further New Section

A new paragraph is started by one or more empty lines.

### The Section Title on the Other Side, For a Change

Setting of formulae† is easy using TEX :

$$\frac{f(x + \Delta x) - f(x)}{\Delta x} \rightarrow f'(x)$$

## END

---

† TEX was developed with mathematical typesetting in mind in the first place.

## 2.5 Program Start and Program End

On almost every system, the TeX program is started with a "TEX" operating system command. When the program is called interactively, it first prompts the user with the question for a *format file* that contains its macro definitions.

```
This is TeX, Version 2.0 (preloaded format=plain 86.1.1)
**
```

or

```
This is TeX, Version 2.0 (no format preloaded)
**
```

The version output can, of course, differ.

When this question is answered with \relax, the standard macro package *plain TeX* is loaded. To be specific, the macro package is used that has been announced as "preloaded", or, if no macro package was preloaded, *plain TeX* will be loaded automatically. However, different macro packages can be loaded if someone has prepared them with INITEX and has then made them available. The macro package is selected by specifying the name of the file it is stored in, prefixed with an "&". Specifying &plain is thus equivalent to using the standard, preloaded package.

On the other hand, the first question can also be answered directly with the name of a file containing TeX input. In this case the standard macro package is used.

The combination of these methods is also possible, in that the specification of the macro package can be followed by the name of the input file on the same line.

```
This is TeX, Version 2.0 (preloaded format=plain 86.1.1)
**\relax
*
```
                              standard macros — dialogue following

```
This is TeX, Version 2.0 (preloaded format=plain 86.1.1)
**&latex
*
```
                    macros from the 'LATEX' format file — dialogue following

```
This is TeX, Version 2.0 (preloaded format=plain 86.1.1)
**myfile
*
```
                              standard macros — input from file 'myfile'

```
This is TeX, Version 2.0 (preloaded format=plain 86.1.1)
**&latex myfile
*
```
                    macros from the 'LATEX' format file — input from 'myfile'

When it reaches \end the program will be terminated. The preferred method, however, is specifying "\bye", because this will additionally fill up the last page with empty vertical space.

# 3 Setting Text

## 3.1 The Standard Layout

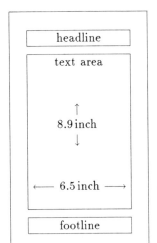

The standard page layout, as predefined by TEX, is as follows: The type area is 8.9 inch high and 6.5 inch wide. The width is represented by the internal variable \hsize *(horizontal size)* and the height by \vsize *(vertical size)*. Changing these values to get a different type area should best be done at the start of the input file. At the same time, \hsize is the dimension determining the breaking of lines into paragraphs.

Above and below the text area, headlines and footlines are set with a distance of one line (12 pt) from the text. If not changed, the headline is empty, and the footline contains a centered page number.

All standard running text (without any specialties) is broken into pages and output in the standard layout. Usually, the text is divided into paragraphs. In the input, paragraphs are separated by the command \par, or by an empty input line which is simpler and more readable. In the output, such a 'regular' paragraph is set with a bit of empty space (indentation) at the start of the first line. Indentation is deemed pleasing if it is as wide as it is high, thus forming an optical square. The default indentation in TEX is a bit wider: 20 pt. The name of the corresponding TEX variable is \parindent. The indentation can be reduced by assignments, e.g., \parindent=15pt, or enlarged by \parindent=30pt.

At the same time, the variable \parindent influences the initial indentation for itemized lists (\item, q.v. Section 3.9).

If a paragraph — like this one — should start without an indentation to the left of its first line, the input must begin with a \noindent command. That is, the input of the current paragraph starts with the following:

```
\par \noindent If a paragraph --- like this one ---
```

Alternatively, you can change `\parindent=0pt`. However, this has the additional effect that all other commands that use `\parindent` internally also use the new value '0 pt'. These are mainly `\item`, `\itemitem` and `\narrower`. By proper application of grouping with { and }, these side effects can be controlled.

One word of caution: if a very long paragraph of several pages is input — which is quite unusual — you may run into memory problems with some TeX implementations. The program stores all of the paragraph in its memory to optimize line breaks across the entire paragraph.

## 3.2 Measuring Units

Distances and sizes may be measured in several units. In its output, TeX itself uses the unit 'pt'. This is derived from the *printer's point*. Traditionally, diverse kinds of 'points' have been in use by printers in Europe and America. The following table gives an overview of the measuring units TeX knows.

| Unit | | Conversions | |
|------|------|------|------|
| **pt** | *point* † | | 1 pt = 0.0351 cm |
| **pc** | *pica* † | 1 pc = 12 pt | 1 pc = 0.422 cm |
| **in** | *inch* † | 1 in = 72.27 pt | 1 in = 2.54 cm |
| **bp** | *big point* † | 72 bp = 1 in | 1 bp = 0.0353 cm |
| **cm** | *centimetre* | | 1 cm = 28.54 pt |
| **mm** | *millimetre* | | = . |
| **dd** | *didôt point* ‡ | 1157 dd = 1238 pt | 1 dd = 0.0376 cm |
| **cc** | *cicero* ‡ | 1 cc = 12 dd | 1 cc = 0.451 cm |
| **sp** | *scaled point* * | 65536 sp = 1 pt | 1 sp < $0.6 * 10^{-6}$ cm |
| | | † anglo-american pica-(point-)system | |
| | | ‡ german typographical point system | |
| | | * internal TeX unit | |

TeX internally converts all measuring units to **sp**. The largest possible value is about 5.7583 meters. That should be enough for normal documents. Besides these *fixed* measuring units, two further units depending on the current font are available:

**em** is traditionally interpreted as the width of a capital 'M'. TeX's computer modern fonts have the attribute that all digits are 0.5 em wide.

**ex** is the height of a lowercase letter without an ascender, about the height of an 'x'. Therefore it is called x-height by a printer.

All units, distances, font sizes additionally depend on a global scaling factor called `\magnification`. This number is preset with '1000', corresponding to a factor of 1.000. This value may only be changed at the very start of the input, when no dimensions have been used. Later changes are impossible and will be refused with an error message. In principle, you can assign any value to `\magnification`, e.g., `\magnification=333` for a factor of 0.333. Problems may occur later on when the generated document has to be printed and typefaces are not available for the target output device in the requested sizes. (Photo typesetters exist which can achieve any reasonable resolution.)

A conventional solution for this problem is to restrict oneself to a set of magnification factors, which are stepped by a factor of 1.2. Typefaces for these resolutions are available for most output devices and drivers. This is supported by the \magstep command which abbreviates the common powers of 1.2.

| \magnification= | value | factor |
|---|---|---|
| \magstep0 | 1000 | 1.000 |
| \magstephalf | 1095 | 1.095 |
| \magstep1 | 1200 | 1.200 |
| \magstep2 | 1440 | 1.440 |
| \magstep3 | 1728 | 1.728 |
| \magstep4 | 2074 | 2.074 |
| \magstep5 | 2488 | 2.488 |

\magstep0 ... \magstep5 simply generate the values. One additional intermediate size \magstephalf is available, too.

If you use non-standard TEX fonts, e.g., cmff10, larger sizes may not be available in your current computer environment. This should be checked before use. All standard fonts should at least be present in sizes from \magstep0 to \magstep3.

If \magnification is changed, all sizes that are not specified as 'true' are scaled with this factor. Paragraphs are typeset with a modified skip between lines, symbols of different sizes are used, which also affects the size of paragraphs and the whole document. The height of the type area (\vsize) and the width of the type area (\hsize) are *not* changed. It is assumed that the output devices use paper of constant size. \hsize and \vsize are preset with

```
\hsize = 6.5 true in
\vsize = 8.9 true in
```

If a measuring unit is preceded by 'true', it will not be scaled by \magnification. This is very useful if pictures with fixed sizes have to be included later.

## 3.3 National Characters and Diacritical Marks

Accented letters are input by preceding them with the appropriate accenting command, e.g., German umlauts are introduced by \". There is no difference between lowercase and uppercase letters. National characters like the German eszett (double s) 'ß' or french diphthong 'œ' (oe) are input by \ss and \oe. As the input is done by named commands a space (or other nonletter) must follow, otherwise TEX cannot understand the intended commands. There is a slight complication if a word ends in such a national character. All following spaces* are only treated as a command delimiter, they generate no interword space in printing. These commands have to be followed by a '\␣'.

To get the (perfectly reasonable) statement 'Daß man großartig TEX kann' the following input is needed

```
\it Da\ss\ man gro\ss artig \TeX\ kann
```

---

* The number of spaces between two words is of no significance. Several contiguous spaces are treated as one space.

A hint: a macro definition such as \def\3{\ss} helps, as you can *always* write \3 for 'ß' without extra coding of following spaces. The nonletter symbol ('3') lets TeX identify the end of the command by itself. The last example may be rewritten as

```
\it Da\3 man gro\3artig \TeX\ kann
```

Diacritical marks are treated as accented letters by TeX. There are 14 predefined accenting commands:*

| input | output | comments |
|-------|--------|----------|
| \'o   | ò      | grave accent     (accent character) |
| \'o   | ó      | acute accent     (apostrophe) |
| \^o   | ô      | circumflex or "hat" |
| \"o   | ö      | German umlaut or diaeresis |
| \~o   | õ      | tilde or "squiggle" |
| \=o   | ō      | macron or "bar" |
| \.o   | ȯ      | dot accent |
| \u o  | ŏ      | breve accent |
| \v o  | ǒ      | háček or "check" |
| \H o  | ő      | long Hungarian umlaut |
| \t oo | o͡o     | tie-after accent |
| \c o  | ǫ      | cedilla accent |
| \d o  | ọ      | dot-under accent |
| \b o  | o̲      | underbar accent |

Note: accents may be put on arbitrary letters, e.g., ŜP̂Q̂R̂.

Apart from the accented characters that are built by a combination of two signs, there are national characters with their own typical letter form. These cannot be constructed in the same way.

| input | output | comments |
|-------|--------|----------|
| \oe   | œ      | French ligature œ |
| \OE   | Œ      | French ligature Œ |
| \ae   | æ      | Scandinavian ligature æ |
| \AE   | Æ      | Scandinavian ligature Æ |
| \aa   | å      | Scandinavian a with Angstroem |
| \AA   | Å      | Scandinavian A with Angstroem |
| \o    | ø      | Scandinavian o with sloped stem |
| \O    | Ø      | Scandinavian O with sloped stem |
| \l    | ł      | Polish suppressed-l |
| \L    | Ł      | Polish suppressed-L |
| \ss   | ß      | German "eszett" or sharp s |
| \i    | ı      | dotless "i" |
| \j    | ȷ      | dotless "j" |

---

* Accents in mathematical mode are done by separate commands.

## 3.4 Skip between Paragraphs

TEX leaves hardly any empty space between paragraphs. If you really want to have extra skip between paragraphs, you can get this automatically by changing the internal variable \parskip. This is preset to

    \parskip=0pt plus 1pt

The expression 'plus 1 pt' allows the TEX program to insert up to 1 pt of additional empty space between paragraphs during page breaking. Remaining space is distributed evenly between the paragraphs.

If a specific space, e.g., of 3 pt (this is just a \smallskip), is to be inserted between paragraphs automatically, the following input is recommended:

    \parskip=3pt plus 1pt

This automatic procedure is not very common, however. Important are the following heavily used commands:

    \smallskip
    \medskip          = 2× \smallskip
    \bigskip          = 2× \medskip
    \vskip length

These leave the following space:

for \smallskip — size: \magnification * 3 pt

for \medskip      size: \magnification * 6 pt

for \bigskip   — size: \magnification * 12 pt       (an empty line)

for \vskip 1.7 cm — This is the way to get a specific skip between paragraphs!

"pt" is the previously mentioned common unit of measurement. All distances are computed with respect to the global scaling (\magnification). The command \vskip has to be supplied with a parameter specifying the desired length.

\removelastskip is a useful command that removes a preceding skip, but only if there is one. This is usually done within macros for captions and titles, when it is not known whether any skip has already been produced.

Besides the previously mentioned instructions, there are skip commands that generate a "dynamic" kind of skip, which takes up as much space as possible. They work like springs. These are \vss, \vfil and \vfill that are described in detail in Section 8.9.

The space between two paragraphs vanishes if the page break occurs between paragraphs. This forces printing to start at the same position on each page and produces uniform pages. At the top of pages, extra space is generated that is determined by `\topskip`.

Space that does not vanish is typeset by "`\vglue` *dimension*". This may be useful for reserving room for pictures, since it is also generated at the top of pages.

The commands `\smallskip`, `\medskip`, `\bigskip` and `\vskip` finish the current paragraph and generate the space. Later on a new paragraph may be started. Another way to get space between lines but within the paragraph is shown in the following example. The paragraph lines are broken around the insertion. In the current paragraph

Here is extra space.

this is precisely what is happening. Information is stored by the command `\vadjust` and set below the *current* line. This is done after breaking the paragraph into lines. The input of this example consists of:

```
... are broken around the insertion.
\vadjust{\vskip 1cm
         \centerline{Here is extra space.}
         \vskip 1cm}
In the current paragraph ...
```

A simple "`\vadjust{\smallskip}`" gives an extra space between two paragraph lines. It is even possible to skip backwards by specifying `\vskip` with negative dimensions.

## 3.5 Spaces between Words

Horizontal skip or space between words is usually typeset in units of "em". This corresponds to the width of a capital 'M' that is also call a quad. The associated commands are `\quad` and for a doubled amount `\qquad`. The following table shows an overview:

| command | space | | unit | comments |
|---|---|---|---|---|
| `\`␣ | ‖ | | | space (font dependent) |
| `\indent` | \| | \| | 20 pt ≡ `\parindent` | paragraph indentation |
| `\enskip` | ‖ | | 0.5 em | |
| `\quad` | \| | \| | 1 em | "printer's quad" |
| `\qquad` | \| | \| | 2 em | |

Sometimes you may want to typeset a space, but also want to ensure that TEX does not break lines at this position. By specifying a "~" (tilde) a *protected space* is generated, e.g., "A.~B.~Genius". The skip generated by "~" is not a permissible line end.

Besides the command "`\hskip` *dimension*" that is used like "`\vskip`", there are some more commands to generate space and to disallow breaks.

| command | space | | unit | comments |
|---|---|---|---|---|
| ~ | ‖ | | | protected space (tilde) |
| `\enspace` | \| | \| | 0.5 em | width like `\enskip` |
| `\thinspace` | ‖ | | 1/6 em | |

`\thinspace` has a 'negative' partner "`\negthinspace`" that cancels space of the same amount.

Often space is generated that exactly matches the length of a given text. The command "`\phantom{ ... text ... }`" produces this feature:
Example:

```
\leftline{Jan Tschichold: Ausgew\"ahlte Aufs\"atze ...}
\leftline{\phantom{Jan Tschichold:} Birkh\"auser Verlag, Basel 1975}
```

yields

Jan Tschichold: Ausgewählte Aufsätze ...
        Birkhäuser Verlag, Basel 1975

These commands may be combined with instructions for aligning text within a single line: `\leftline`, `\rightline` and `\centerline`. These generate text that is flush left, flush right or centered. They should not be used within paragraphs.

The previously mentioned commands describe how to get extra space, but how will TeX justify paragraph lines to exact margins?

Each font (typeface) has four parameters that determine what can be done with an interword space in specific circumstances. They govern how much the space between words may grow or shrink. These are:

| *parameter* | *meaning* | *value in pt for* | | | |
|---|---|---|---|---|---|
| | | `\rm \sl` | `\bf` | `\ti` | `\tt` |
| `\fontdimen2` | normal interword space | 3.33 | 3.83 | 3.58 | 5.25 |
| `\fontdimen3` | possible stretch | 1.67 | 1.92 | 1.53 | 0.00 |
| `\fontdimen4` | possible shrink | 1.11 | 1.28 | 1.02 | 0.00 |
| `\fontdimen7` | additional space at punctuations | 1.11 | 1.28 | 1.02 | 5.25 |

These parameters may be changed if other behaviour is desired. To avoid changes of font parameters there are some registers that take precedence over font parameters if they are different from zero. These are `\spaceskip` and `\xspaceskip`. By

```
\spaceskip=3.33pt plus 3.34pt minus 1.11pt
```

e.g., for `\rm`, `\sl`, the value for stretching between words is doubled (compared to the original values of `\rm`). The values for spacing at punctuation may be overridden by `\xspaceskip`, e.g.,

```
\xspaceskip=3.33pt plus 2.22pt
```

doubles the additional stretchable space.

## 3.6 Skip between Lines

Lines of a paragraph are set with a distance of 12 pt. To be exact, this is the distance between the baselines of two consecutive lines.

```
. line 1
. line 2
```

The distance between baselines is governed by the internal register \baselineskip. Their positions are marked by ".". You can change this value, e.g.,

```
\baselineskip=14pt
\baselineskip=10pt
```

to get enlarged or diminished values. An incremental change is done by, e.g.,

```
\advance\baselineskip by 3pt
```

that enlarges the current value by 3 pt. The following example is typeset with enlarged \baselineskip. It is incremented by 6 pt.

```
. line 1

. line 2
```

Changes of \baselineskip also affect typesetting of mathematical formulae that consist of multiple lines.
If a line contains any large symbols, like in

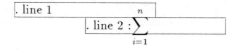

the described method of spacing would lead to overlapping lines as shown above. In reality, TeX generates the following result:

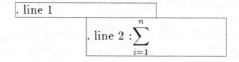

In the first picture the lower line overlaps the preceding one. To avoid this effect, TeX applies the following rule:

> If the distance between two lines (boxes) is less than \lineskiplimit, that is a threshold for line distances, a 'minimal line distance' of \lineskip is used between the two lines instead of \baselineskip. This distance is measured between the bottom edge of the first box and the top edge of the second box or line. This value may even be negative.

On the other hand, when \baselineskip is used, the distance between lines is always measured between the baselines of the lines or boxes.

The preset values for these important parameters are

```
\baselineskip=12pt
\lineskiplimit=0pt
\lineskip=1pt
```

In practice, this avoids overlapping of lines and generates a minimum skip of 1 pt between lines that are too close.

Please note that overlapping may also be generated by a preceding line if it contains symbols with large descenders, e.g., 'y' or 'g', especially if typefaces are enlarged by the use of scaling factors. Sometimes this happens if title lines are not properly generated.

Some remarks on space between lines: typefaces that have a small size need a diminished line skip, fonts with extended or boldface symbols should be used with enlarged interline skip. The following values fit for standard typefaces:

| font size | | \baselineskip |
|---|---|---|
| 10 pt | e.g. cmr10 | 12 pt |
| 9 pt | e.g. cmr9 | 11 pt |
| 8 pt | e.g. cmr8 | 9 pt |

This is demonstrated with the 'roman' typeface (\rm) and the 'boldface' fonts (\bf): After

```
\font\ninorm=cmr0
\font\eightrm=cmr8
\font\ninebf=cmbx9
\font\eightbf=cmbx8
```

fonts with diminished size are defined.

---

\ninerm                                          with \baselineskip=11pt

In the art of typography the best printing of an age is not that which copies most successfully the most approved models of another age, but that which works within a convention peculiar and necessary to itself. Design its fitness to purpose, and as every age has its own peculiar needs and characteristics, good printing will approximate to them. The design will be good as it approximates to itself. It will be excellent as it is free from pose, preciosity, or conceit. Holbrook Jackson

In the art of typography the best printing of an age is not that which copies most successfully the most approved models of another age, but that which works within a convention peculiar and necessary to itself. Design its fitness to purpose, and as every age has its own peculiar needs and characteristics, good printing will approximate to them. The design will be good as it approximates to itself. It will be excellent as it is free from pose, preciosity, or conceit. Holbrook Jackson

`\eightrm`                                with `\baselineskip=9pt`

In the art of typography the best printing of an age is not that which copies most
successfully the most approved models of
another age, but that which works within a
convention peculiar and necessary to itself.
Design its fitness to purpose, and as every
age has its own peculiar needs and characteristics, good printing will approximate to
them. The design will be good as it approximates to itself. It will be excellent as it is
free from pose, preciosity, or conceit.
Holbrook Jackson

In the art of typography the best printing of an age is not that which copies most
successfully the most approved models of
another age, but that which works within a
convention peculiar and necessary to itself.
Design its fitness to purpose, and as every
age has its own peculiar needs and characteristics, good printing will approximate to
them. The design will be good as it approximates to itself. It will be excellent as it is
free from pose, preciosity, or conceit.
Holbrook Jackson

`\ninebf`                                with `\baselineskip=11pt`

**In the art of typography the best
printing of an age is not that which
copies most successfully the most
approved models of another age,
but that which works within a convention peculiar and necessary to
itself. Design its fitness to purpose,
and as every age has its own peculiar needs and characteristics, good
printing will approximate to them.
The design will be good as it approximates to itself. It will be excellent as it is free from pose, preciosity, or conceit.
Holbrook Jackson**

**In the art of typography the best
printing of an age is not that which
copies most successfully the most
approved models of another age,
but that which works within a convention peculiar and necessary to
itself. Design its fitness to purpose,
and as every age has its own peculiar needs and characteristics, good
printing will approximate to them.
The design will be good as it approximates to itself. It will be excellent as it is free from pose, preciosity, or conceit.
Holbrook Jackson**

`\eightbf`                                with `\baselineskip=9pt`

**In the art of typography the best
printing of an age is not that which
copies most successfully the most approved models of another age, but
that which works within a convention peculiar and necessary to itself.
Design its fitness to purpose, and as
every age has its own peculiar needs
and characteristics, good printing will
approximate to them. The design will
be good as it approximates to itself.
It will be excellent as it is free from
pose, preciosity, or conceit.
Holbrook Jackson**

**In the art of typography the best
printing of an age is not that which
copies most successfully the most approved models of another age, but
that which works within a convention peculiar and necessary to itself.
Design its fitness to purpose, and as
every age has its own peculiar needs
and characteristics, good printing will
approximate to them. The design will
be good as it approximates to itself.
It will be excellent as it is free from
pose, preciosity, or conceit.
Holbrook Jackson**

## 3.7 Justification

*Justified and unjustified lines*

Usually paragraph lines are justified to the right margin by insertion or deletion
of space between words. If a text is to be typeset 'ragged right' — without justification — the command \raggedright is used. The space between words may neither be stretched nor shrunk. If need be, words may be hyphenated at line ends. By
application of grouping braces '{' and '}', the application of \raggedright may be
confined. It should be noted that the paragraph has to be finished before the scope
of \raggedright is finished, otherwise the paragraph will be typeset normally. You
have to input

```
{\raggedright ... text ... \par}
```

and not the incorrect "}\par" at the end of the section. The current paragraph is
typeset with use of \raggedright. If a text is typeset in the typewriter typeface
(\tt) the use of the special form \ttraggedright is preferable, as this will generate
spaces of equal size to text symbols.

It is even possible to generate a "\raggedleft" command to get the same effect on
the left-hand side:

```
\def\raggedleft{\leftskip=0pt plus 2em
              \spaceskip=0.333em
              \xspaceskip=.5em }
\def\ttraggedleft{\tt\leftskip=0pt plus 2em }
```

define the necessary commands. The current paragraph has been typeset by application of the command \raggedleft. These are the methods to influence the justification of lines. The unit of measure "plus 2em" that is assigned to \leftskip within
the definition of \raggedleft governs how much space may be generated at the line
margins. \raggedright is defined by changing \rightskip.

*Line oriented input, poems*

In poems the text is generated with an explicit line structure. You could do this by
a series of \leftline commands, but that would be tedious. The \obeylines command changes the interpretation of the line end of an input line. Normally a line end
is regarded as a space, but \obeylines changes this to \par. Every input line end
generates a new paragraph. Note: a paragraph starts with the usual indentation that
is determined by the current value of \parindent. The input

```
{\obeylines
Now this is what I call workmanship.
There is nothing on earth
   more exquisite than a bonny book,
with well-placed columns
of rich black writing in beautiful borders,
and illuminated pictures cunningly inset.
But nowadays, instead of looking at books,
   people read them.
\hfil G. Bernard Shaw\par}
```

results in

> Now this is what I call workmanship.
> There is nothing on earth
> more exquisite than a bonny book,
> with well-placed columns
> of rich black writing in beautiful borders,
> and illuminated pictures cunningly inset.
> But nowadays, instead of looking at books,
> people read them.
>                                    G. Bernard Shaw

With \obeylines, each input line generates a paragraph. If an input line is too long, because there are complicated TEX commands, you can inhibit the interpretation of the line end as paragraph by inserting a commentary '%' sign. The following line is interpreted as the continuation of the line that ends in a comment.

\obeylines is valid as long as the surrounding group is not closed. The typical form for input looks like this:

```
{\obeylines
      ... text ...
}
```

There are more interesting effects to be achieved in combination with \obeylines: With \everypar, commands are stored that are interpreted at the beginning of each paragraph automatically.

If the preceding example is extended by the commands "\everypar{\hfil}" and "\parindent=0pt" as in

```
{\obeylines\everypar{\hfil}\parindent=0pt
Now this is what I call workmanship.
          ...
```

you get each line centered:

> Now this is what I call workmanship.
> There is nothing on earth
> more exquisite than a bonny book,
> with well-placed columns
> of rich black writing in beautiful borders,
> and illuminated pictures cunningly inset.
> But nowadays, instead of looking at books,
> people read them.
>                                    G. Bernard Shaw

This is done by combining the effect of \parfillskip and the insertion of \hfil at the beginning of every line (paragraph). \parfillskip determines the space that is generated at the end of the last line of a paragraph. As it is preset by

```
\parfillskip=0pt plus 1fil
```

every line is surrounded with a pair of '\hfil'. This generates a centered line.

Lines may be typeset flush right by changing the '\hfil' in the \everypar command
to a stronger version, '\hfill'. The input above

```
{\obeylines\everypar{\hfill}
Now this is what I call workmanship.
            . . .
```

becomes

Now this is what I call workmanship.
There is nothing on earth
more exquisite than a bonny book,
with well-placed columns
of rich black writing in beautiful borders,
and illuminated pictures cunningly inset.
But nowadays, instead of looking at books,
people read them.
G. Bernard Shaw

The effect is the same as in the previous example. But the skip commands generate
space of different order and the stronger version overrides the weaker one.

*'verbatim mode'*

Sometimes you want to print a text *completely unchanged*, maybe a TeX or program
source. This is quite complicated at first glance, as *all* those fine mechanisms of TeX to
get properly justified paragraphs, etc., have to be abandoned. But one command must
be left to stop this form of input. The following commands do this. They modify the
way command symbols are interpreted.

```
\chardef\other=12 % other symbols
\def\ttverbatim{\begingroup
              \catcode`\\=\other \catcode`\{=\other
              \catcode`\}=\other \catcode`\$=\other
              \catcode`\&=\other \catcode`\#=\other
              \catcode`\%=\other \catcode`\~=\other
              \catcode`\_=\other \catcode`\^=\other
              \catcode`\|=\other
              \obeyspaces\obeylines\tt}
{\obeyspaces\gdef {\ }}
\outer\def\begintt{\let\par=\endgraf \ttverbatim \parskip=0pt
              \ttfinish}
{\catcode`\|=0 |catcode`\|\=\other
  |obeylines % end of line acts as  \par
  |gdef|ttfinish#1^^M#2\endtt{#1|vbox{#2}|endgroup}}
```

These commands use some features that have not been mentioned before. They can
be described here only roughly. In the beginning, all command characters like "$" and

"\" are made inactive. The result is two commands: \begintt and \endtt. \begintt starts this special form of printing and \endtt stops it if \endtt is found in the first columns of a line. There is a small problem: all the information will be read into program memory. If the source consists of several hundred lines it may be too large for the T$_E$X program. In this case, the text has to be partitioned into several pieces.

## 3.8 Justification of Paragraphs

Paragraphs are usually typeset with the width of the text area. Sometimes additional space at the sides of a paragraph is needed, maybe at the left or right side, or both.

> At the beginning of each line and after each line space is automatically generated, but the value for this space is preset to zero. The variables \leftskip and \rightskip control this space. If as in this paragraph, one of the variables has been changed, (here \leftskip=4cm) each paragraph line is indented by 4 cm. Line breaking will generate shorter lines automatically.

\leftskip

If \rightskip=6cm has been used, the paragraph lines are indented at the right side. If the effective length of paragraph lines gets smaller, it is more difficult to build paragraphs. The program can only use the space between words for justification. If there are fewer words in every line, the space to be distributed generates unsatisfactory holes. Note: a paragraph is built with the use of those parameter values that are valid when the paragraph end is detected, not the values from the very beginning.

\rightskip

\leftskip and \rightskip may also be combined. The additional command \narrower generates an incremental change of \leftskip and \rightskip by the current value of \parindent.

\parindent is the amount of indentation used at the first line of each paragraph.

> This paragraph is typeset with a single use of \narrower. It has been started by \noindent to suppress the indentation. The input looks like this:
>
> ```
> \par{\narrower\noindent This paragraph is ... \par}
> ```
>
> The command \narrower accumulates if it is used repetitively. Watch carefully for grouping braces!

> After setting \narrower 4 × you get this paragraph form with very short lines and a \leftskip and \rightskip of 4 × \parindent at both sides.

It is even possible to — very carefully — use negative values. After \leftskip= 1 cm \rightskip= -1 cm, the entire paragraph will be moved to the right side by 1 cm. The length of lines will remain unchanged. These effects always apply to the complete paragraph, as the line breaking is done when the end of the paragraph is encountered.

Besides these, the value of \voffset moves the whole output, logically the beginning of the page, when the pages are finally printed.

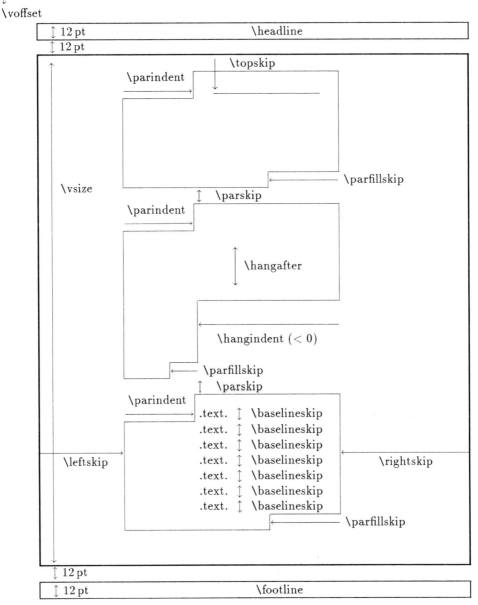

All registers are preset with zero (0 pt),except:

| | | |
|---|---|---|
| \baselineskip = 12 pt | \hsize = 6.5 in | \topskip = 10 pt |
| \parskip = 0 pt plus 1 pt | \vsize = 8.9 in | \parfillskip = 0 pt plus 1 fil |
| \parindent = 20 pt | \hangafter = 1 | |

**Table of Positioning Registers**

The vertical size of the text area is determined by \vsize; see the preceding figure. This is the initial value that is used during page breaking. It is modified if insertions or footnotes occur. The size of the headline and footline is not taken into account: these two lines are put at the top and at the bottom, when a page has been finished.

If you want to enlarge your text area height, e.g., by 1 cm, the following command will be useful:

```
\advance\vsize by 1 truecm \voffset=-0.5 truecm
```

The length of the text area is changed, but the entire page, including headline and footline, is still printed vertically centered.

The same can be done for horizontal positioning. \hsize is the width of the text area, i.e. the size that determines the length of lines when paragraphs are broken into lines. Like \voffset the new variable \hoffset determines the amount by which the whole page is moved. A typical use may be the reduction of line length and the generation of more space at the left margin for filing the document.
Example:

```
\advance\hsize by -2 truecm \advance\hoffset\by 2truecm
```

The page is moved by 2 cm to the right and the text area reduced. The dimensions are preceded by the keyword 'true', which suppresses the scaling by the factor that is given with \magnification.

## 3.9 Shape of Paragraphs

A paragraph may occur in four different shapes in practice: there may be indentation for several lines at the left and right sides and at the top or bottom lines. The generated space is mostly used for illustration. Two variables change the shape of paragraphs:

\hangindent, a dimension register, determines the amount of indentation that will be used. This value should not be mistaken for \parindent, which gives the extra paragraph indentation for the *first* line of a paragraph. If \hangindent is greater than zero, space is generated at the left side, if it is less than zero, space is generated at the right side. A change, e.g., \hangindent=3cm, can be made using all measuring units that TEX knows.

\hangafter, a counter register, determines where the indentation should occur. If \hangafter<0, the *first* |\hangafter| lines are indentated. |\hangafter| is the absolute value of \hangafter. If \hangafter≥ 0, the first \hangafter lines are *not* indented, but *all the following* lines.

---

\hangindent=3cm \hangafter=-4 gives

> TEX commands start with a "\" sign (backslash) that is followed by a name, consisting of several letters usually, or *one* other character. This may be a digit or punctuation. TEX commands with a command name (of letters) have to be recognized to be complete, i.e., the *last* letter of the command name has to be identified. Therefore they have to be followed by one or more spaces that are not printed, or any other non-letter character. If a space should be generated after a TEX command, it has to be followed by \u. "u" means a space.) Command characters, e.g., '&', must not be followed by separating text.

---

`\hangindent=3cm \hangafter=4` gives

**TEX commands** start with a "\" sign (backslash) that is followed by a name, consisting of several letters usually, or *one* other character. This may be a digit or punctuation. TEX commands with a command name (of letters) have to be recognized to be complete, i.e., the *last* letter of the command name has to be identified. Therefore they have to be followed by one or more spaces that are not
printed, or any other non-letter character. If a space should be generated after
a TEX command, it has to be followed by \ᵤ. "ᵤ" means a space.) Command
characters, e.g., '&', must not be followed by separating text.

`\hangindent=-3cm \hangafter=-4` gives

**TEX commands** start with a "\" sign (backslash) that is followed by a name,
consisting of several letters usually, or *one* other character. This may be a digit
or punctuation. TEX commands with a command name (of letters) have to be
recognized to be complete, i.e., the *last* letter of the command name has to be
identified. Therefore they have to be followed by one or more spaces that are not printed, or any other
non-letter character. If a space should be generated after a TEX command, it has to be followed by
\ᵤ. "ᵤ" means a space.) Command characters, e.g., '&', must not be followed by separating text.

`\hangindent=-3cm \hangafter=4` gives

**TEX commands** start with a "\" sign (backslash) that is followed by a name, consisting of several letters usually, or *one* other character. This may be a digit or punctuation. TEX commands with a command name (of letters) have to be recognized to be complete, i.e., the *last* letter of the command name has to be identified. Therefore they have to be followed by one or more spaces that are not
printed, or any other non-letter character. If a space should be generated after
a TEX command, it has to be followed by \ᵤ. "ᵤ" means a space.) Command
characters, e.g., '&', must not be followed by separating text.

TEX automatically resets both these values at the very beginning of every paragraph to `\hangindent=0pt` and `\hangafter=1`.

Note: there will be an extra indentation in the first line if there is no `\noindent` — in the examples above it is present — at the start of the paragraph.

There is
a further method
to determine the shape of
a paragraph. For each line you have
to specify the length of the line and the indentation at the left side. That you can do it at all
is a fine thing, but you will need to try it out in practice.
The command `\parshape` defines paragraph shapes in this way, line
by line. It is used with the following syntax $\parshape = n\,i_1\,l_1\,i_2\,l_2\ldots i_n l_n$.
The first number $n$ specifies how many definitions will follow. For each line a definition of two dimensions is needed: The first length "$i_j$" determines the indentation of
the left side and the second "$l_j$" the length of text for the current line. If the current
paragraph consists of more than $n$ lines, that is, too much information is given, the
definition of the last line will be used for all following paragraph lines. If the paragraph
text is shorter, the following definitions are ignored. As you see this has happened to

the current paragraph, where `\parshape` has been used with the following parameters:

```
\parshape=10 0.45\hsize    0.1\hsize
             0.40\hsize    0.2\hsize
             0.35\hsize    0.3\hsize
             0.30\hsize    0.4\hsize
             0.25\hsize    0.5\hsize
             0.20\hsize    0.6\hsize
             0.15\hsize    0.7\hsize
             0.10\hsize    0.8\hsize
             0.05\hsize    0.9\hsize
             0.0 \hsize    1.0\hsize
```

## 3.10 Itemization and Lists

a) Itemization and hanging indentations as used within this paragraph are made with the `\item` command. Until the current paragraph is finished, all lines are indented by the current value of `\parindent`. This is the same parameter that is used as standard indentation for every first line of any paragraph. The command `\item` gets as a parameter the text that will precede the first line of the itemized paragraph. This current paragraph was started by the text:

`\item{a)} Itemization and hanging ...`

If the parameter of `\item` is empty as in "`\item{}`", itemization is performed with an empty text. (Here: `\item{} If the parameter...`)

The command variant `\itemitem{label}` invokes the same mechanism but with doubled space as the left margin.

$a_1$ As you see in this current paragraph. Note that the text that precedes the first paragraph line may not be too long as it is inserted in "overlapping" mode. Surplus information will cross the left margin of the text area without any error message. The current paragraph is started by the text "`\itemitem{a$_1$}` As you see...". The subscript digit "$_1$" is generated by using mathematical mode. The space used for this itemization is $2 \times$ `\parindent`. There are only `\item` and `\itemitem` commands, no further steps. After a look at plain TEX macros (or by using the following example) you can get an `\itemitemitem` command:

```
\def\itemitemitem{\par\indent\indent
                  \hangindent3\parindent
                  \textindent}
```

The example input

```
\leftline{Assignments in \TeX}
\item{1.} variable assignments
\itemitem{a)} 'integer' variable
\itemitem{b)} 'dimen' variable
\itemitem{c)} 'token' variable
\itemitem{}   $\vdots$
\item{2.} Arithmetical Assignments
\itemitem{a)} {\it advance}
\itemitemitem{a$_1$)} 'integer' variable
\itemitemitem{a$_2$)} 'dimen' variable
\itemitemitem{a$_3$)} 'glue' variable
\itemitemitem{a$_4$)} 'muglue' variable
\itemitem{b)} {\it multiply}
\itemitem{c)} {\it divide}
\par
```

gives

Assignments in TeX
1. variable assignments
   a) 'integer' variable
   b) 'dimen' variable
   c) 'token' variable
     $\vdots$
2. Arithmetical Assignments
   a) *advance*
      $a_1$) 'integer' variable
      $a_2$) 'dimen' variable
      $a_3$) 'glue' variable
      $a_4$) 'muglue' variable
   b) *multiply*
   c) *divide*

The label parts, e.g., "1.", "a)", are typeset flush right with a separating space to the
text area for the current paragraph. Sometimes the author wants to get the labelling
text flush left with respect to the text area. Some macros built using the same technique
that is used by \item give the desired commands \litem and \litemitem:

```
\def\litem{\par\noindent
            \hangindent=\parindent\ltextindent}
\def\litemitem{\par\noindent
            \hangindent=2\parindent\ltextindent}
\def\ltextindent#1{\hbox to \hangindent{#1\hss}\ignorespaces}
```

Example:

```
{\parindent=4cm
\litem{\bf Humane}
        {\it Venetian Serif, Venetian Old Style} ---
        This typeface was modelled upon the humanist minuscule.
        It first appeared around 1470 in Venice.
        Characteristics are the sloped stem of the lower case 'e'
        and the slightly slanted axis of bowls. It showed
        little difference between main strokes and hairlines.
\litem{\bf Garalde}
        {\it Old Face, Old Style} ---
        Its shows a smooth transition from the stems to the serifs.
        The serifs get rounded edges.
        The cross stem of the 'e' is horizontally arranged.
\litem{\bf R\'eale}
        {\it Transitional} --- The thickness of hairlines and main
        strokes shows greater differences. The bowls axis is
        vertical. The serifs are slightly rounded.
\par}
```

gives

| | |
|---|---|
| **Humane** | *Venetian Serif, Venetian Old Style* — This typeface was modelled upon the humanist minuscule. It first appeared around 1470 in Venice. Characteristics are the sloped stem of the lower case 'e' and the slightly slanted axis of bowls. It showed little difference between main strokes and hairlines. |
| **Garalde** | *Old Face, Old Style* — Its shows a smooth transition from the stems to the serifs. The serifs get rounded edges. The cross stem of the 'e' is horizontally arranged. |
| **Réale** | *Transitional* — The thickness of hairlines and main strokes shows greater differences. The bowls axis is vertical. The serifs are slightly rounded. |

Similar to the preceding form is a variant where the labelling text is typeset to the right of the text. By changing the macros to

```
\def\ritem{\par\noindent\hangindent=-\parindent
            \hangafter=0
            \rtextindent}
\def\ritemitem{\par\noindent
                \hangafter=0
                \hangindent=-2\parindent
                \rtextindent}
\def\rtextindent#1{\hbox to 0pt{\hskip\hsize
                \hbox to 0pt{\hss#1}\hss}%
                \ignorespaces}
```

you get from this

```
{\parindent=4cm
\ritem{\bf Didone}
        {\it Modern Face, Modern Roman } ---
        The serifs are horizontal,
            ...
```

the following output:

| | |
|---|---|
| *Modern Face, Modern Roman* — The serifs are horizontal, their previous oval forms have become circles. Hairlines and main strokes differ extremely. The axis of bowls is vertical. | **Didone** |
| *Egyptian Group, Slab Serif* — All elements have the same optical stroke thickness. The characterisc elements are the slab serifs. | **Mécane** |
| *Sans Serif* — These typefaces have no serifs. Sometimes they are called "Grotesque". Crossbars and stems are optically of the same thickness. | **Lineale** |

## 3.11 Page Breaks

Page breaks are usually done automatically. If enough material for an entire page is gathered, page breaking occurs. The program searches for an optimal break position using a complex optimizing algorithm. The appendix contains information about the weighting factors employed. Usually a TeX user won't change them, as it is a very complex matter.

Sometimes you may want to get different page breaks at explicit positions. A proper input supports TeX by specifying good break positions that are also meaningful considering the contents of the text.

Specifying each page break explicitly is quite unpractical as each larger modification of the text would imply a correction of the predefined break points.

If you want to force a page break, use the command "\eject". If the current page does not contain enough material, you will get a message that TeX complains about "underfull vbox ...". Mostly you can ignore this message, but it is often not acceptable that TeX will distribute empty space between paragraphs to get a better page layout. By the combination "\vfill\eject" the current page is filled with space, if needed, and then printed.

It is preferable to support TeX in choosing good break positions. Sometimes it is even desirable to mark a position as a very bad break and to inhibit a break. The following commands mark such positions with different weights:

```
\goodbreak
\filbreak
\nobreak
```

They act as follows:
\goodbreak                    indicates a "good" break positions.
                              The current paragraph is finished.

| `\filbreak` | is described best by: start a new page if the following text up to the next `\filbreak` does not fit on the current page. |
| `\nobreak` | inhibits a page break (if it is given between paragraphs). It is useful between titles and the following text. Within paragraphs it inhibits a line break at the current position. |

Furthermore, there are three commands that combine generation of extra space between paragraphs and definition of good break positions. These are

```
\smallbreak
\medbreak
\bigbreak
```

Their spacing corresponds — at first glance — to the previously mentioned commands `\smallskip`, `\medskip` and `\bigskip`. The merits of the designated break positions are in proportions of 1 : 2 : 4, i.e., a position marked by `\bigbreak` is four times as good as one marked by `\smallbreak`.

Note that all three commands additionally remove preceding space, if this space is less than or equal to the newly generated space. That means the command 2 × `\medbreak` acts like a single `\medbreak`, but `\medskip\medskip` acts as a `\bigskip`.

## 3.12 Page Numbering

Page numbers are automatically managed by the TeX program. The page number is preset to "1". The associated counting variable is "`\count0`", normally referenced by the name "`\pageno`". You can change the current page number by assignments, e.g., "`\pageno=73`". The current page will receive the new value 73, following pages will be numbered consecutively "74, 75, ...". An incremental change can also be done by "`\advance`":

```
\advance\pageno by 4
```

The page number is referenced for printing with "`\folio`". If the page number is set to a negative value, it will be *decremented*, "$-1, -2, -3\ldots$", and the command `\folio` generates lowercase roman numerals[†] "i, ii, iii, iv, v ...".
The input

```
\centerline{\it The current page has the number \folio!}
```

generates

The current page has the number 32!

By default, the page number is generated centered within the footline. The following section discusses the layout for headlines and footlines in detail.

---

[†] Capital letters, e.g., "I, II, III", are generated by the command sequence
`\uppercase\expandafter{\folio}`
instead of "`\folio`" within the commands used for "`\footline`".

## 3.13 Headlines and Footlines

By default, the text area is preceded by a headline and followed by a footline. The headline is empty, the footline consists of the centered page number printed in roman typeface. Two associated registers, \headline and \footline, determine the layout. Their contents are preset in plain TeX by:

```
\headline={\hfil}
\footline={\hss\tenrm\folio\hss}
```

If you want to suppress the footline, simply type "\nopagenumbers". This is equivalent to "\footline={\hfil}". The range where \nopagenumbers is valid may be restricted by appropriate use of grouping braces ({...}). Note that only the printing of the footline is omitted; the page number is still incremented.

The headline and footline may be designed in a lot of forms. The following examples contain some commands previously not mentioned: they are described here very briefly, details will follow:

| | |
|---|---|
| \ifodd | tests if the following number is *odd*. This is used in the following for testing the current page number. |
| \else | precedes the alternative part of an \if... clause; within the examples it precedes the commands that are used for even numbered pages. |
| \fi | finishes an \if... clause. |
| \vbox | generates a vertical box, whose elements are typeset below one another. |
| \hss | gives dynamic — even negative — horizontal space. |

standard footline:
centered with roman numbering

```
\headline={\hfil}
\footline={\hss\tenrm\folio\hss}
```

John Baskerville & Pietro Bembo & Giambattista Bodoni & William Bulmer & William Caslon & Firmin Didot & Pierre Simon Fournier & Claude Garamond & ............ & Hermann Zapf

19

headline: centered page number

```
\headline={\hss\tenrm\folio\hss}
\footline={\hss}
```

19

John Baskerville & Pietro Bembo & Giambattista Bodoni & William Bulmer & William Caslon & Firmin Didot & Pierre Simon Fournier & Claude Garamond & ............ & Hermann Zapf

---

```
20

John Baskerville & Pietro Bembo & Gi-
ambattista Bodoni  &   William Bulmer
& William Caslon  &  Firmin Didot  &
Pierre Simon Fournier  &  Claude Gara-
mond & ............ & Hermann Zapf
```

flush left/right page numbers
— without indendation
```
\headline={\tenrm
          \ifodd\pageno
             \hss\folio
          \else
             \folio\hss
          \fi}
\footline={\hss}
```

---

```
John Baskerville & Pietro Bembo & Gi-
ambattista Bodoni  &   William Bulmer
& William Caslon  &  Firmin Didot  &
Pierre Simon Fournier  &  Claude Gara-
mond & ............ & Hermann Zapf

                                  21
```

footline: flush left/right
— with indentation
```
\headline={\hss}
\footline={\tenrm
          \ifodd\pageno
             \hss\folio\quad
          \else
             \quad\folio\hss
          \fi}
```

---

```
John Baskerville & Pietro Bembo & Gi-
ambattista Bodoni  &   William Bulmer
& William Caslon  &  Firmin Didot  &
Pierre Simon Fournier  &  Claude Gara-
mond & ............ & Hermann Zapf

              * 21 *
```

footline: page numbers with decoratives
— centered
```
\headline={\hss}
\footline={\tenrm
          \hss
          $\ast$\ \folio\
          $\ast$\hss}
```

---

```
*             Title             *

John Baskerville & Pietro Bembo & Gi-
ambattista Bodoni  &   William Bulmer
& William Caslon  &  Firmin Didot  &
Pierre Simon Fournier  &  Claude Gara-
mond & ............ & Hermann Zapf

                21
```

headline with rules
```
\def\booktitle{Title}
\headline={\vbox
   {\hrule
    \line{\strut
      $\ast$
      \hss\rm\booktitle\hss
      $\ast$}%
    \hrule}\hss}
\footline={\hss\tenrm\folio\hss}
```

```
40     A. B. Caesario: Veni, Vidi, Vici

John Baskerville & Pietro Bembo & Gi-
ambattista Bodoni  &  William Bulmer
& William Caslon  &  Firmin Didot  &
Pierre Simon Fournier  &  Claude Gara-
mond &  ............ & Hermann Zapf
```

separated author, title
and section title
```
\def\booktitle{Veni, Vidi, Vici}
\def\author{A. B. Caesario}
\def\sectiontitle{Vidi}
\headline={\ifodd\pageno
    \sectiontitle\hss\folio
 \else   \folio\hss
     \author: \booktitle \fi}
\footline={\hss}
```

```
Vidi                            41

John Baskerville & Pietro Bembo & Gi-
ambattista Bodoni  &  William Bulmer
& William Caslon  &  Firmin Didot  &
Pierre Simon Fournier  &  Claude Gara-
mond &  ............ & Hermann Zapf
```

ditto: the following page

## 3.14 Insertion of Pictures

Pictures are usually inserted afterwards in reserved places. The following commands support the reservation of space:

```
\topinsert     ... vertical material ...    \endinsert
\midinsert     ... vertical material ...    \endinsert
\pageinsert    ... vertical material ...    \endinsert
```

These commands are always paired with the closing command \endinsert. All enclosed material will be stored internally until it can be inserted at a suitable place. "Vertical material" can consist of vertical skip commands or boxes. If ordinary text is inserted it will be broken into paragraph lines as usual.
The commands act as follows:

\topinsert        tries to insert the given material at the top of the current page. If there is not enough room the information will be put at the top of the following (or a later) page.
In the example

```
\topinsert
\vskip 6 true cm
\centerline{Figure 17a: Archidiskon Imperator}
\bigskip
\endinsert
```

|                  | there is first a space of 6 cm (not scaled by magnification). Then the caption for the figure is set centered on the line, and finally, vertical space is left in the size of an empty line. |
| \midinsert       | has similar effects. It first tries to insert the information at the *current* position. If there is not enough room on the current page, the information is put at the top of the next page, exactly as with \topinsert. |
| \pageinsert      | inserts a full page. An example of this can be seen on page 35 of this book. |

There is no command "\footinsert", which might perhaps be expected. The desired effect can be achieved with footnotes, which will be described immediately.

## 3.15 Footnotes

A footnote[1] is generated by \footnote{ }{ }. The first pair of braces surrounds the labelling symbol or text, the second pair the footnote text. Raised small digits are easily generated by interim use of mathematical mode and typesetting a superscript. The first footnote of this section is generated by "\footnote{$^1$}{See also ''The \TeX{}book'' page 116!}"

If the labelling text consists only of a single symbol, e.g., "7", the first pair of braces is not needed, e.g., "\footnote7{This is remark No.~7}".

With knowledge of the plain TeX footnote macros, the generation of footnotes may be varied and adapted to special requirements. This will be demonstrated by some examples:

*maximum amount of footnotes within a page*

TeX uses a maximum area for footnotes on a page. This value is preset to 8 inches by \dimen\footins=8in. (The maximum vertical size for the text area is defined as 8.9 inch.) If only half a page may be used by footnotes this can be achieved by "\dimen\footins=4in". Footnotes that are too long will be taken over to following pages.

*footnote rules*

At the beginning of the footnote part of a page, TeX generates a separating line. This is done by the following macro:

```
\def\footnoterule{\kern-3pt
                  \hrule width 2 true in
                  \kern 2.6pt}
```

It generates a horizontal rule (line) 2 inches long. By substitution of "\hsize" for "2 true in" the line will cross the whole text area. If you want to omit any footnote rule, you can simply write "\def\footnoterule{}". \footnoterule becomes an empty macro. The footnote rule is generated without changing the vertical position. It uses the default width of 0.4 pt.

---

[1] See also "The TeXbook" page 116!

*typeface*

Note: footnote text is typeset in the current font that is active when invoking the \footnote command. It is a lot safer to set the desired font at the beginning of the footnote text.

Authors often want to set footnotes in a smaller typeface size and with diminished skip between lines. A standard recipe to achieve this is given below, for details see Chapter 7 (on macros).

```
\font\eightrm=cmr8
\long\def\FOOTNOTE#1#2{{\baselineskip=9pt
    \setbox\strutbox=\hbox{\vrule height 7pt depth 2pt width 0pt}%
    \eightrm
    \footnote{#1}{#2}}}
```

An application* of this command is demonstrated with the first footnote on the current page. The typeface design size is usually reduced only by 1 or 2 points, otherwise the text becomes barely readable.
If the last line "\footnote{#1}{#2}}}" is changed to

```
\everypar{\hangindent=\parindent}%   additionally
\footnote{#1}{#2}\everypar{}}}    %  changed
```

the value of "\hangindent" is also changed.** All lines of the footnote text are set with indentation on the left side. Further possible enhancements include automatically numbered footnotes, extra footnote registers where footnotes for a complete text section are gathered, etc.

## 3.16 Hyphenation

The TeX program hyphenates words automatically during paragraph building. It tries to minimize the number of hyphenations. In a first pass a paragraph is generated without any hyphenations. If this attempt is rejected because the result contains lines that look too bad — as measured by adding up so-called "demerits" for different events, e.g., lines with too much space in them — a second pass is performed taking possible hyphenations into account.

The hyphenation algorithm uses patterns (contained in the format file) that describe possible hyphenations. They are specific to the language the text is written in. By default American patterns are used. Patterns for, e.g., German, Portuguese, French, Dutch, and Swedish are also available.

Possible hyphenations may be specified for words that are hyphenated incorrectly or at an unsuitable position. These positions can be specified with the help of \-, as in hy\-phen\-a\-tion. Such a word can only be hyphenated at the specified points. Another possibility is to extend TeX's built-in hyphenation exception list by

---

* For the design size of 9 pt, which is just a bit smaller, the following specifications are recommended: roman font 'cmr9' and a 'baselineskip' of 11 pt, the strutbox changed to "height 8pt depth 3pt width 0pt"
** Small variations can produce a host of different footnote forms. One rather difficult possibility is setting multi-column footnotes.

applying the "\hyphenation" command, e.g., \hyphenation{Med-i-ter-ra-ne-an}.
This will fix the hyphenation points for the rest of the TeX run. If a word is specified
without any breakpoint, it will never be hyphenated. Remember that the size of the
exception list is limited (often to 307 words). You can determine the size on your current
implementation by specifying \tracingstats=1 and looking at the end of TeX's logfile.

There is a problem with hyphenating words that contain accented letters, e.g.,
umlauts in German. Building an accent, e.g., \" and \', will determine a logical end
of a word in the sense of the hyphenation algorithm. After the first accented letter the
rest of the word will not be hyphenated in any way. This is a bothering problem in
languages where accents appear often, even on the first letter of a word. A suitable
redefinition of accenting commands helps in most cases. This is done by restarting a
"new" word after the accent and inhibiting — for security reasons — a break at the
position of the accented letter. The redefinition of \" will be

```
\def\"#1{{\accent"7F #1\penalty10000\hskip 0pt plus 0pt}}
```

In foreign languages, e.g., in German, words often contain diacritical characters. The
perfectly normal word "Öffentlichkeitsarbeit" may be hyphenated in the rest of the
word, "ffentlichkeitsarbeit". The algorithm that is used by TeX usually finds possible
breaks in the rest of the word.

Another problem that usually occurs only in German is the change of spelling if
a word is hyphenated. The word "backen" becomes "bak-ken", and "Brennessel" will
be hyphenated as "Brenn-nessel".
A general purpose solution for such hyphenation problems is the "\discretionary"
instruction. The following is the applicable syntax:

```
\discretionary{ <text before the hyphenation> }
              { <text after the hyphenation>  }
              {  <text without hyphenation>   }
```

By definition of some abbreviations in

```
\def\ck{\discretionary{k-}{k}{ck}}
\def\ff{ff\discretionary{-}{f}{}}
\def\nn{nn\discretionary{-}{n}{}}
```

words may be typed as

```
ba\ck en   Schi\ff ahrt   Bre\nn essel
```

If you want to test possible hyphenations of a word that TeX may use, you can
type \showhyphens{ list of words }. TeX will log all possible break points.

Hyphenation is done while breaking paragraphs into lines. TeX uses an optimizing
algorithm that accumulates 'demerits' for unwanted events. One of these events is a
line break that leads to the hyphenation of a word. These events are weighted differently. If you change threshold values, which are described in the appendix, you can
modify this behaviour. But do this carefully! By a change of \hyphenpenalty=10000

any hyphenation will get an extremely high penalty and TEX will avoid hyphenations whenever possible. Further weighting factors are \doublehyphendemerits for hyphenation in two consecutive lines, \finalhyphendemerits for hyphenation in the last but one line of a paragraph. During page breaking \brokenpenalty is considered for a hyphenation in the last line of a page.

If you change \pretolerance=10000 no hyphenation will ever occur, as TEX will accept all paragraphs without hyphenation. No test for hyphenation positions will be done.

## 3.17 Horizontal and Vertical Rules

Horizontal and vertical rules are generated by \hrule and \vrule. If you write \hrule within a paragraph, the current paragraph will be finished and a rule will be generated across the text area. The thickness of the rule is predefined as 0.4 pt. The commands \hrule and \vrule can be used with three additional optional parameters that determine the size of the rule. A "rule" is interpreted by TEX as a black box. The box "▮", e.g., is generated by:

$$\text{\texttt{\textbackslash vrule height 4pt width3pt depth2pt}}$$

The commands \vrule and \hrule have the same optional parameters, but preset with different values:

|        | \hrule  | \vrule |
|--------|---------|--------|
| width  | *       | 0.4 pt |
| height | 0.4 pt  | *      |
| depth  | 0.0 pt  | *      |

The value "*" means that the actual size is dependent on the context. If an \hrule command is normally used between ordinary paragraphs, width will be equal to the line length \hsize. The unspecified values of \vrule will be generated from the *box* that contains the \vrule command. If a \vrule is given within an ordinary line of a paragraph, its height will be adjusted to the height of the largest character of the current line, and the depth will be set to the largest depth (caused by descenders of characters) that occurs.

Note: \hrule will finish a paragraph when given within a paragraph. \vrule may be used in a paragraph. Whether the rule that is generated by \hrule and \vrule gives the impression of a vertical or horizontal rule, depends on the parameter values that follow. This rule "████████████" is generated by the command

$$\text{\texttt{\textbackslash vrule width 1 true in height 0.3 true cm depth 0pt}}$$

The rule is adjusted to the baseline, as the depth is specified as 0 pt. If the rule should be raised and the thickness remain unchanged, you can type

$$\text{\texttt{\textbackslash vrule width 1 true in height 0.75 true cm depth -0.25 truecm}}$$

You get "████████████". The thickness of a rule can be computed as the sum of height and depth. In the following, the use of \hrule instructions is demonstrated.

```
\noindent You get an \hrule width 3 cm and want another
          \hrule width 3cm and write further text
```

produces the unsatisfying output

You get a
─────────────
    and want another
    and write further text

Typical applications of rules use extra space:

```
\medskip
\hrule
\smallskip
\leftline{New results:}
1 2 3 4 5 6 7
8 9 10 11 12 14
\smallskip
\hrule
```

that gives

New results:
    1 2 3 4 5 6 7 8 9 10 11 12 14

or another example

```
\centerline{\vrule height 4pt width 6cm}
\medskip
\centerline{\bf NOT THE END!}
\medskip
\centerline{\vrule height 4pt width 6cm}
```

**NOT THE END!**

If several \hrule commands or \vrule commands follow each other, no extra space will be generated. The rules will touch each other. That means "\hrule\hrule" is equivalent to "\hrule height 0.8pt".

The use of rules to get frames is described in Section 8.7.

## 3.18 Error Rules

Lines (or boxes that are explained later) are marked at the right margin with an error rule (a black box), if they don't fit into the current margins. The current line has received █ such a mark to demonstrate the effect. As even very slight extensions of the line into the margin are marked that would never be detected at first sight, it is necessary to suppress such rules for the final print at least. This is done by

```
\overfullrule=0pt
```

The rule width is set to zero, and it becomes invisible.

There is an internal limit (\hfuzz) that determines if an exceeding line or box should be logged. It is preset to 0.1 pt. This is quite conservative; for normal documents you can reduce the log messages by setting \hfuzz=1 pt ($\approx$ 0.3mm). The matching limit for overfull pages is "\vfuzz". It works in the same way.

# 4 List of Typefaces

## 4.1 Font Families

If you use different typefaces within the same document, these usually belong to the same *font family*. Typefaces of a specific font family have been designed with very specific characteristics, e.g., proportions of ascenders and descenders or sizes of hairlines and main strokes. A very impressive detail is the form of the serifs*. Besides the "roman" typeface, other typical variants of a font family are *an italic typeface* and **a boldface typeface**. The *slanted typeface* of the "computer modern" font family consists simply of slanted letters, while the slanted characters of the *italic typeface* show yet another shape. The form of italic serifs differs from other serif forms. TeX normally uses the computer modern font family, whose members are demonstrated below.

If fonts are used in different sizes, they will be measured in the — to the novice user at least — uncommon unit "pt" (point), which is based on use by typesetters. The use of different sizes of the same typeface does not simply generate scaled shapes, but proportions of strokes also change. Especially the widths of letters and the sizes of interword spaces are varied to achieve better readability. The letters of a 5 pt typeface are usually half as high as the same typeface in 10 pt, but the width differs as the letters and spaces are wider. This is shown by the following example where a typeface with 50 % of the height takes 70 % of the width.

10 pt typeface: Typography is a fine art.

5 pt typeface: Typography is a fine art.

## 4.2 Changes of Fonts

The typefaces of the TeX system are the members of the "computer modern" font family† developed within the TeX project. Changes between standard typefaces are

---

\* Serifs are the "hooks" at the ends of the strokes of certain letters(This typeface has no serifs!).

† They are described in Volume E of the "computer & typesetting" series of Donald E. Knuth.

predefined and are achieved by the following commands:

| | | |
|---|---|---|
| \rm | switches to "roman" (standard) | Typography is a servant — the servant of thought and language to which it gives visible existence.<br>T.M. Cleland |
| \bf | switches to "**boldface**" | **Typography is a servant — the servant of thought and language to which it gives visible existence.**<br>**T.M. Cleland** |
| \it | switches to "*italic*" | *Typography is a servant — the servant of thought and language to which it gives visible existence.*<br>*T.M. Cleland* |
| \sl | switches to "*slanted*" | *Typography is a servant — the servant of thought and language to which it gives visible existence.*<br>*T.M. Cleland* |
| \tt | switches to "`typewriter`" | `Typography is a servant --- the servant of thought and language to which it gives visible existence.`<br>`T.M. Cleland` |

Within mathematical formulae these commands have a special function: they change all fonts that are used for textstyle, scriptstyle and scriptscriptstyle. These are the fonts that are used for normal elements and subscripts or superscripts of different order. The following chapter about typesetting mathematical formulae gives details.

The ordinary commands \tenrm, \tenbf, \tenit, \tensl, and \tentt do not change the current font family for mathematical mode, they simply switch to another font for setting ordinary text. These commands are defined by "\font".
Fonts of smaller sizes can be chosen by the predefined commands

        \sevenrm        \fiverm
        \sevenbf        \fivebf

Typefaces of 7 pt and 5 pt are predefined for subscripts and superscripts.

Note: a font change doesn't apply to the skip between lines of paragraphs. If a smaller typeface is chosen, line skip may be reduced a little but not too much as readability might otherwise be lost. This is often demonstrated on the back of an insurance policy.

The reduced sizes of standard typefaces are

- By \sevenrm you get seven point roman.
- By \fiverm you get five point roman.
- By \sevenbf you get seven point boldface.

- By \fivebf you get five point boldface.

These are the standard typefaces. Besides these, there are a lot of other typefaces in different sizes. To make such a font available it has to be named by a \font command.

If you want to get portable TEX sources that may be used on any TEX implementation, it is strongly suggested that you use only standard fonts. Maybe the quite exotic font selected, e.g., cmff10, is not available in the requested size.

## 4.3 Global Magnification

Magnification of typefaces can be achieved by two different approaches:

The global scaling factor that is set by \magnification, see Section 3.2, changes all sizes (except the dimensions of the text area). The whole document will be generated in a different size. If \magnification is set to \magstep1 it is enlarged by 20 %. The fonts used are 20 % magnified, which will mean less text on each paragraph line.

This book was created using \magstep0, unscaled. The current font is "cmr10" in 10 pt. The predefined assignable values for \magstep are recapitulated:

| input \magnification= | factor |
|---|---|
| \magstep0 | 1.000 |
| \magstephalf | 1.095 |
| \magstep1 | 1.200 |
| \magstep2 | 1.440 |
| \magstep3 | 1.728 |
| \magstep4 | 2.074 |
| \magstep5 | 2.488 |

## 4.4 Fonts in Hand-Selected Magnifications

There is the additional possibility of selecting a predefined typeface with a specific magnification factor. To this end the typeface is named with the help of the \font command. For example,

\font\myfont=cmbx10 scaled \magstep2

defines the magnified boldface font with the name \myfont.

# This line is written in myfont.

The input for this is:

{\myfont This line is written in myfont.}

The magnification can be achieved either with the keyword scaled as shown, or with the keyword at. The equivalent definition in this case looks like

\font\myfont=cmbx10 at 14.4pt

In this case the explicit size is given instead of a scaling factor. The factor for the use of scaled can be calculated here as $(14.4\,pt\,/\,10\,pt) * 1000$. As everywhere in TEX input, scaling factors are specified in units of one in a thousand.

The specification of \magstep2 in the \font command is not the last word on the final typeface size, however. This factor \magstep2 will still be multiplied by the global

factor \magnification. When the global factor has a value of 1.0, this is the same
as \magstep0, i.e. the size will stay the same, but if \magnification is 1.2, that is
\magstep1, the effective scaling factor in our example will be \magstep3.

Here is one advantage of the technique with "at": By specifying "true" before the
unit in "\font\myfont=cmbx10 at 14.4truept" the scaling by \magnification can
be suppressed.

All these techniques of magnification lead to higher resolution output devices being
used with typefaces which are simply linearly scaled lower resolution typefaces. When
a typeface of size 12 pt is needed, it is always better to use, e.g., "cmr12" than simply
taking the magnified "cmr10".

For special typefaces, however, it is always necessary to check whether the desired
typeface really exists for the output device.

## 4.5 Defined Typefaces

Table of standard typefaces:

| *roman* | | *mathematical symbols* | |
|---|---|---|---|
| \tenrm (\rm) | = cmr10 | \tensy | = cmsy10 |
| \sevenrm | = cmr7 | \sevensy | = cmsy7 |
| \fiverm | = cmr5 | \fivesy | = cmsy5 |
| *bold extended* | | *mathematical text* | |
| \tenbf (\bf) | = cmbx10 | \teni (\mit) | = cmmi10 |
| \sevenbf | = cmb7 | \seveni | = cmmi7 |
| \fivebf | = cmbx5 | \fivei | = cmmi5 |
| *slanted* | | *large mathematical symbols* | |
| \tensl (\sl) | = cmsl10 | \tenex | = cmex10 |
| *italic* | | | |
| \tenit (\it) | = cmti10 | | |
| *typewriter type* | | | |
| \tentt (\tt) | | | |

This is a minimal configuration. What other typefaces are actually available depends
on the implementation and the acquired font catalogue.

In some older implementations the earlier versions of the "computer modern" font
family are still in use. In this case the font file names all start with "a" instead of "c"
— meaning "almost computer modern". The older and newer fonts are partly different
in the widths of characters. This means that line breaking will change when converting
from "am" to "cm" fonts.

## 4.6 "Computer modern" Typefaces

The following examples of computer modern typefaces demonstrate, for each font, the
original size and an enlarged variant that is magnified by 2.488 (\magstep5). The
typefaces displayed belong to the complete set of computer modern fonts that can be
generated by TEX's companion program METAFONT.

cmb10 — bold                                                    Typography is a fine art.

# Typography is a fine art.

cmbx12 — bold extended                                  Typography is a fine art.

# Typography is a fine art.

cmbx10 — bold extended                                  Typography is a fine art.

# Typography is a fine art.

cmbx9 — bold extended                                   Typography is a fine art.

# Typography is a fine art.

cmbx8 — bold extended                                   Typography is a fine art.

# Typography is a fine art.

cmbx7 — bold extended                                   Typography is a fine art.

# Typography is a fine art.

cmbx6 — bold extended                                   Typography is a fine art.

# Typography is a fine art.

cmbx5 — bold extended                                   Typography is a fine art.

# Typography is a fine art.

cmbxsl10 — bold extended slanted                        *Typography is a fine art.*

# *Typography is a fine art.*

cmbxti10 — bold extended italic                    *Typography is a fine art.*

# *Typography is a fine art.*

cmcsc10 — caps and small caps                      TYPOGRAPHY IS A FINE ART.

# TYPOGRAPHY IS A FINE ART.

cmdunh10 — dunhill roman                            Typography is a fine art.

# Typography is a fine art.

cmff10 — funny roman                                Typography is a fine art.

# Typography is a fine art.

cmfib8 — fibonacci roman                            Typography is a fine art.

# Typography is a fine art.

cmr17 — roman                                       Typography is a fine art.

# Typography

cmr12 — roman                                       Typography is a fine art.

# Typography is a fine art.

cmr10 — roman                                       Typography is a fine art.

# Typography is a fine art.

cmr9 — roman

Typography is a fine art.

Typography is a fine art.

cmr8 — roman

Typography is a fine art.

Typography is a fine art.

cmr7 — roman

Typography is a fine art.

Typography is a fine art.

cmr6 — roman

Typography is a fine art.

Typography is a fine art.

cmr5 — roman

Typography is a fine art.

Typography is a fine art.

cmsl12 — slanted

*Typography is a fine art.*

*Typography is a fine art.*

cmsl10 — slanted

*Typography is a fine art.*

*Typography is a fine art.*

cmsl9 — slanted

*Typography is a fine art.*

*Typography is a fine art.*

cmsl8 — slanted

*Typography is a fine art.*

*Typography is a fine art.*

cmss17 — sans serif                          Typography is a fine art.

# Typography is an art.

cmss12 — sans serif                              Typography is a fine art.

## Typography is a fine art.

cmss10 — sans serif                                 Typography is a fine art.

### Typography is a fine art.

cmss9 — sans serif                                    Typography is a fine art.

### Typography is a fine art.

cmss8 — sans serif                                     Typography is a fine art.

### Typography is a fine art.

cmssbx10 — sans serif bold extended              **Typography is a fine art.**

### **Typography is a fine art.**

cmssdc10 — sans serif demibold condensed           **Typography is a fine art.**

### **Typography is a fine art.**

cmssi17 — sans serif italic                     *Typography is a fine art.*

# *Typography is an art.*

cmssi12 — sans serif italic                    *Typography is a fine art.*

*Typography is a fine art.*

cmssi10 — sans serif italic                    *Typography is a fine art.*

*Typography is a fine art.*

cmssi9 — sans serif italic                    *Typography is a fine art.*

*Typography is a fine art.*

cmssi8 — sans serif italic                    *Typography is a fine art.*

*Typography is a fine art.*

cmssq8 — sans quotation                    Typography is a fine art.

Typography is a fine art.

cmssqi8 — sans quotation italic                    *Typography is a fine art.*

*Typography is a fine art.*

cmtcsc10 — typewriter caps & small caps                    TYPOGRAPHY IS A FINE ART.

TYPOGRAPHY IS A FINE ART.

cmti12 — text italic                    *Typography is a fine art.*

*Typography is a fine art.*

cmti10 — text italic                    *Typography is a fine art.*

*Typography is a fine art.*

cmti9 — text italic                                          *Typography is a fine art.*

*Typography is a fine art.*

cmti8 — text italic                                          *Typography is a fine art.*

*Typography is a fine art.*

cmti7 — text italic                                          *Typography is a fine art.*

*Typography is a fine art.*

cmtt12 — typewriter type                         Typography is a fine art.

Typography is an art.

cmtt10 — typewriter type                              Typography is a fine art.

Typography is a fine art.

cmtt9 — typewriter type                                Typography is a fine art.

Typography is a fine art.

cmtt8 — typewriter type                                 Typography is a fine art.

Typography is a fine art.

cmu10 — unslanted italic                            *Typography is a fine art.*

*Typography is a fine art.*

cmvtt10 — variable width typewriter              Typography is a fine art.

Typography is a fine art.

# 5 Mathematical Typesetting

## 5.1 Preface

Setting mathematical formulae has always been regarded as penalty work by typesetters — and with good cause. For a mathematical expression to be set aesthetically pleasingly, a minimal comprehension by the typesetter is necessary. The effort involved in formula setting has historically been exceedingly great, as mathematical typesetting is always a kind of tabular setting.

Especially for mathematical formulae, the input effort in the TeX system is extremely small. Long time usage has shown that there is no reason for the user to avoid the input of the mathematical parts of a paper. One reason for the simplicity of formula setting is the standardized layout of mathematical expressions that precludes the need for specifying special layout commands.

## 5.2 Fundamentals

For the input of mathematical formulae, a few principles are of continuous importance. If these are observed, many problems have been solved already.

— **grouping parentheses**
  To be set correctly, parts that belong together must always be grouped with '{'and '}'. E.g., `$x_ij$` gives the result $x_ij$, whereas `$x_{ij}$` yielding $x_{ij}$ was probably intended. The subscript part belonging to $x$ consists of the two symbols ij. To describe this, they have to be grouped with parentheses '{}'.

— **'above' and 'below'**
  Formula parts that have to be set *below* the line are always introduced with '_' (an underscore, or 'low line') and parts going above the line are prefixed with '^' (circumflex or 'hat').

— **the difference between form and function**
  Especially in mathematics, the various possible functions of a symbol in context are important, be it as operator, relation or anything else. Every command not only describes a printing character or symbol, but also has a mathematical function. Consequently there are some commands that generate the same graphical symbol

but have different typesetting properties, and are referred to by different names. The distances between formula elements are calculated from the functions of the components. Different functions are, e.g., operators such as $\sum$, $\int$, relations such as '=', '$\leq$', and binary operators such as '$*$' and '$-$'.

— **delimiting a formula**

The start of a formula is indicated by a $ symbol. TEX enters *mathematical mode* and stays in it up to the next '$'.

When a formula is introduced and finished with two dollar signs '$$', this mathematical formula is set with emphasis on its own line of text. The positioning of subscript signs etc. is changed as well.

— **typefaces**

In mathematical mode, all letters are set in the *math-italic* typeface, the other characters usually in the "roman" font.

Other typefaces can be selected by specifying \rm, \bf and \it.

— **structuring the input**

Blank spaces in the input have *no* consequences for the distances of formula elements. They are only needed to separate commands and symbols, as in \sin x. The distances are calculated by TEX. For a better understanding of your input, and to be able to duplicate it later on, it is recommended that you put blanks in appropriate places.

Taking these few principles into account will simplify the setting of mathematical formulae.

## 5.3 Greek Letters

Greek letters are input with their usual names as a command. The commands for lower case Greek letters start with a lower case letter, the commands for upper case Greek letters with an upper case first letter. The Greek alphabet is thus entered according to the following table:

| | | | | | |
|---|---|---|---|---|---|
| $\alpha$ | \alpha | $\iota$ | \iota | $\varrho$ | \varrho |
| $\beta$ | \beta | $\kappa$ | \kappa | $\sigma$ | \sigma |
| $\gamma$ | \gamma | $\lambda$ | \lambda | $\varsigma$ | \varsigma |
| $\delta$ | \delta | $\mu$ | \mu | $\tau$ | \tau |
| $\epsilon$ | \epsilon | $\nu$ | \nu | $\upsilon$ | \upsilon |
| $\varepsilon$ | \varepsilon | $\xi$ | \xi | $\phi$ | \phi |
| $\zeta$ | \zeta | $o$ | o | $\varphi$ | \varphi |
| $\eta$ | \eta | $\pi$ | \pi | $\chi$ | \chi |
| $\theta$ | \theta | $\varpi$ | \varpi | $\psi$ | \psi |
| $\vartheta$ | \vartheta | $\rho$ | \rho | $\omega$ | \omega |

There is no \omikron, as it looks the same as an "o". For completeness, you could define \def\omikron{o}, if you want it. Some letters have output variants, the second version is generated by prefixing the name with the string "var", e.g., \pi and \varpi.

Upper case Greek letters:

| | | | | | |
|---|---|---|---|---|---|
| A | {\rm A} | I | {\rm I} | Σ | \Sigma |
| B | {\rm B} | K | {\rm K} | T | {\rm T} |
| Γ | \Gamma | Λ | \Lambda | Υ | \Upsilon |
| Δ | \Delta | M | {\rm M} | Φ | \Phi |
| E | {\rm E} | N | {\rm N} | X | {\rm X} |
| Z | {\rm Z} | Ξ | \Xi | Ψ | \Psi |
| H | {\rm H} | Π | \Pi | Ω | \Omega |
| Θ | \Theta | R | {\rm R} | | |

There are *no* commands for Greek letters that correspond to an identically looking Roman letter. For these you can simply specify the normal letter using the font specifier '\rm'. Without this command, letters in mathematical formulae are set in *math italic font* by default. Usually Greek letters are set in a Roman typeface, but there are also variants in the 'italic' and 'bold' typefaces, lower case Greek letters are only available in 'italic'.

in italic:

| | | | | | |
|---|---|---|---|---|---|
| *A* | A | *I* | I | *Σ* | {\it\Sigma} |
| *B* | B | *K* | K | *T* | T |
| *Γ* | {\it\Gamma} | *Λ* | {\it\Lambda} | *Υ* | {\it\Upsilon} |
| *Δ* | {\it\Delta} | *M* | M | *Φ* | {\it\Phi} |
| *E* | E | *N* | N | *X* | X |
| *Z* | Z | *Ξ* | {\it\Xi} | *Ψ* | {\it\Psi} |
| *H* | H | *Π* | {\it\Pi} | *Ω* | {\it\Omega} |
| *Θ* | {\it\Theta} | *R* | R | | |

in bold:

| | | | | | |
|---|---|---|---|---|---|
| **A** | {\bf A} | **I** | {\bf I} | **Σ** | {\bf\Sigma} |
| **B** | {\bf B} | **K** | {\bf K} | **T** | {\bf T} |
| **Γ** | {\bf\Gamma} | **Λ** | {\bf\Lambda} | **Υ** | {\bf\Upsilon} |
| **Δ** | {\bf\Delta} | **M** | {\bf M} | **Φ** | {\bf\Phi} |
| **E** | {\bf E} | **N** | {\bf N} | **X** | {\bf X} |
| **Z** | {\bf Z} | **Ξ** | {\bf\Xi} | **Ψ** | {\bf\Psi} |
| **H** | {\bf H} | **Π** | {\bf\Pi} | **Ω** | {\bf\Omega} |
| **Θ** | {\bf\Theta} | **R** | {\bf R} | | |

Further variants are *typewriter type* and *slanted*. They are available via \tt and \sl. The Greek letters have been generated for use in mathematical formulae, however, and they cannot be used to set Greek text. For this you need special Greek typefaces.

This was only a short introduction. The description of all standard symbols follows in later sections. Chapter 9 deals extensively with setting mathematical formulae in diverse variants. One final note: if you want to use a mathematical symbol in normal text, you must temporarily change to mathematical mode with "$ ... $".

## 5.4 Subscripts and Superscripts

Subscripts and superscripts are built with the symbols '_' and '^', respectively. It is important to keep in mind that these symbols refer only to the next following symbol or to a following group between '{' and '}'.

$\quad$ `$x^2-y$` and `$x^{2-y}$` $\quad$ gives $\quad$ $x^2 - y$ and $x^{2-y}$.

Superscripts and subscripts of higher order are set in a smaller type, of course. They exist in two sizes, corresponding to first and second order. If there are still deeper nested structures in the formula, subscripts and superscripts are not shrunk any further. The TEX program is in the so-called *script style* when setting subscripts or superscripts of first order, and in *scriptscript style* when setting scripts of second order. With the commands \scriptstyle and \scriptscriptstyle you can force TEX into these setting modes.

The following examples illustrate the usage of subscript and superscript expressions.

$\quad$ `$x^2y^2$` $\hspace{6cm}$ $x^2y^2$

$\quad$ `$x ^  2y  ^2 $` $\hspace{6cm}$ $x^2y^2$

$\quad$ `$x_2y_2$` $\hspace{6cm}$ $x_2y_2$

$\quad$ `$_2F_3$` $\hspace{6cm}$ $_2F_3$

$\quad$ `$x^{2y}$` $\hspace{6cm}$ $x^{2y}$

$\quad$ `$x^{2^x}$` $\hspace{6cm}$ $x^{2^x}$

$\quad$ `$x^{2^{2^x}}$` $\hspace{6cm}$ $x^{2^{2^x}}$

$\quad$ `$K_n^+,K_n^-$` $\hspace{6cm}$ $K_n^+, K_n^-$

$\quad$ `$y_{x^2}$` $\hspace{6cm}$ $y_{x^2}$

$\quad$ `$z^*_{ij}$` $\hspace{6cm}$ $z^*_{ij}$

but

$\quad$ `${z^*}_{ij}$` $\hspace{6cm}$ $z^*{}_{ij}$

The following shows a minor detail: the position of subscript and superscript depends on the corresponding main term. In the following two examples the superscripts '2', '3', and '4' belong to the preceding '$x$' and the preceding ')', respectively.

$\quad$ `$((x^2)^3)^4$` $\hspace{4cm}$ $((x^2)^3)^4$

By contrast, explicit parentheses generate subformulae. These determine the positions of subscripts and superscripts. In this case not only the size of the last symbol is used for positioning, but the size of the complete subformula:

$\quad$ `${({(x^2)}^3)}^4$` $\hspace{4cm}$ $\left(\left(x^2\right)^3\right)^4$

A very common superscript is '*ı*', which is generated by the TeX command \prime.

$y_1^\prime$                                                        $y_1'$

The command sequence ^\prime can be shortened to a simple apostrophe:

$f''[g(x)]g'(x)$                                                $f''[g(x)]g'(x)$

In normal text superscripts can indicate footnotes, as in
\footnote{$^7$}{ .. text ..}

## 5.5 Root Signs

The square root sign is input as \sqrt, the root of *n*th order as \root n \of. The size of the root symbol is determined automatically. To set more than one symbol below the line of the root symbol, braces are needed as usual.

$\sqrt x$                                                $\sqrt{x}$

$\sqrt{x^3 + \sqrt\alpha}$                       $\sqrt{x^3 + \sqrt\alpha}$

$\root n+1 \of {x^n + y^n}$              $\sqrt[n+1]{x^n + y^n}$

$\root 3 \of {1 + \sqrt\alpha}$            $\sqrt[3]{1 + \sqrt\alpha}$

A large example in *display style*:

$$\sqrt{ \sqrt{ \sqrt{ \sqrt{ \sqrt{ \sqrt{x+1}}}}}}$$

gives

$$\sqrt{ \sqrt{ \sqrt{ \sqrt{ \sqrt{ \sqrt{x+1}}}}}}$$

Note: the root symbol consists of several parts. The larger variants have vertical up-strokes built from some short strokes. It is therefore possible to generate arbitrarily large roots.

## 5.6 Mathematical Accents

The commands \overline and \underline produce horizontal rules above and below an expression:

Example: $\overline{m+n}$ gives $\overline{m+n}$ and $\underline{m*n}$ gives $\underline{m*n}$.

Accents are demonstrated with the letter "*x*".

$\hat x$                                                        $\hat{x}$

$\check x$                                                      $\check{x}$

$\tilde x$                                                      $\tilde{x}$

$\acute x$                                                      $\acute{x}$

$\grave x$                                                      $\grave{x}$

$\dot x$                                                        $\dot{x}$

$\ddot x$                                                       $\ddot{x}$

$\breve x$                                                      $\breve{x}$

$\bar x$                                                        $\bar{x}$

$\vec x$                                                        $\vec{x}$

Larger tildes and hats for up to three characters are available with \widetilde and
\widehat.

$\widetilde{xyz}$          $\widetilde{xyz}$

$\widehat{xyz}$          $\widehat{xyz}$

Arrows can also be set above symbols or even complete expressions:

$\overleftarrow{A-B/C}$        $\overleftarrow{A - B/C}$

$\overrightarrow{A+B}$         $\overrightarrow{A + B}$

The accent commands for text setting \", \~, \^ ... are totally different and cannot be
interchanged with mathematical accents. Their abuse will produce an error message.

## 5.7 Displayed Formulae

Up to now we have regarded formulae that can be set in running text, because they
are not especially large. Expressions are normally set on their own separate line if
they need more space. To do this the formula has to be enclosed in double dollars
"$$". The result is centered between left and right margin and extra space is added
above and below the formula. Afterwards the text is continued without starting a new
paragraph. An example in Section 9.3 shows a way to set non-centered displayed for-
mulae. Formulae in display style are not broken across lines. The author is responsible
for arranging the formula parts in several lines. Larger mathematical expressions are
typically transformation chains, which have to be broken at significant positions.

The size of the symbols is determined automatically by TeX. Furthermore, sub-
scripts and superscripts are set to different positions. A characteristic feature of display
style is the handling of positioning in integral and sum formulae.

The commands \textstyle and \displaystyle force the mode of setting a math-
ematical formula, independent of a preceding "$" or "$$". They override the default
positioning modes.

Example: the *text style* expression $\sum_{i=1}^{n} i = \frac{n(n+1)}{2}$, converted to *display style*, produces:

$$\sum_{i=1}^{n} i = \frac{n(n+1)}{2}$$

The form of the *text style* input is $ ... $, *display style* input looks like $$ ... $$.

Obviously there are different sum symbols and the positioning of lower and upper
bounds is changed. In *text style*, the fraction is set in smaller letters.

By the way, the input for the above example is:

$$\sum_{i=1}^n i= { n(n+1)\over 2}$$

## 5.8 Fractions

In TEX, there are three different kinds of fractions:
— normal fractions with a thin standard fraction line
— 'fractions' without fraction line
— fractions for which the thickness of the fraction line is explicitly specified

\over is the command for a normal fraction. It works like a mathematical binary operator: the numerator consists of everything from the innermost enclosing opening brace to the left up to the \over command. The denominator runs up to the next enclosing closing brace to the right. If there are no such braces, the fraction contains all of the material between the dollar signs. If you have to typeset a fraction, the simplest way is to start with a '{', type the commands for the numerator, then the command '\over' for the fraction line, followed by the commands for the denominator. Finally the '}' closes the fraction. Several fractions can be nested in this way without difficulty, just by building sets of corresponding braces.

Examples (in *display style*):

```
$$ x+y^2 \over k + 1   $$
$$ a = x+y^{2 \over k+1} $$
$$ b = {x+y^2 \over k}+1 $$
$$ 1 \over { 1 + {1 \over x+1 }}$$
```

result in

$$\frac{x + y^2}{k + 1}$$

$$a = x + y^{\frac{2}{k+1}}$$

$$b = \frac{x + y^2}{k} \mid 1$$

$$\frac{1}{1 + \frac{1}{x+1}}$$

Adding a \displaystyle command in the last example will set the denominator not in script size, but in normal size. This is often required in the setting of continued fractions.

$$ 1 \over { 1 +  \displaystyle{1 \over x+1 }}$$ gives

$$\frac{1}{1 + \dfrac{1}{x + 1}}$$

Sometimes you can avoid double fractions using the slash character. The input

```
$$ a/b \over \sqrt{1+c}$$
```

yields

$$\frac{a/b}{\sqrt{1 + c}}$$

\atop is used similarly, but the output of the fraction rule is suppressed:

`$$x \atop y+2 $$` produces

$$\frac{x}{y+2}$$

If you want to determine the thickness of the fraction line, use the command `\above` instead:

`$$ \displaystyle {a \over b} \above 1pt \displaystyle {c \over d} $$`

produces the following output, where '1 pt' specifies the thickness of the middle fraction line.

$$\frac{\dfrac{a}{b}}{\dfrac{c}{d}}$$

The `\displaystyle` commands force the subfractions in the enlarged form.

## 5.9 Binomial Coefficients

Binomial coefficients are set in the same way as fractions with the command `\choose`. They look like parenthesized fractions without lines.

`$$ n \choose k+1 $$` gives

$$\binom{n}{k+1}$$

The corresponding form with brackets and curly braces results from

`$$ n \brack k+1 $$` to

$$\left[\begin{matrix} n \\ k+1 \end{matrix}\right]$$

and from `$$ n \brace k+1 $$` to

$$\left\{\begin{matrix} n \\ k+1 \end{matrix}\right\}$$

## 5.10 Integral Signs, Sums, and other Operators

Operators are mathematical functions which affect a subformula. This section describes "large" operators like sum and integral signs. These signs dominate the appearance of a mathematical formula by their sheer size. Operators often use "lower" and "upper" limits, e.g. in sum and integral signs. The limits are typeset by an underscore "_" for the lower limit and a hat "^" for the upper limit. Subformulae in these places have to be grouped by "{" and "}" in the usual way. The following table contains TEX's predefined operators. More (private) operators can be built by composition and overlaying of other symbols (see below in Section 9.2).

| text style | display style | command | example of use |
|:---:|:---:|:---|:---|
| $\Sigma$ | $\Sigma$ | \sum | summing operator |
| $\int$ | $\int$ | \int | integral operator |
| $\prod$ | $\prod$ | \prod | product operator |
| $\oint$ | $\oint$ | \oint | circuit integral |
| $\amalg$ | $\amalg$ | \coprod | coproduct |
| $\cap$ | $\cap$ | \bigcap | intersection |
| $\cup$ | $\cup$ | \bigcup | union |
| $\sqcup$ | $\sqcup$ | \bigsqcup | supremum |
| $\vee$ | $\vee$ | \bigvee | existential quantifier |
| $\wedge$ | $\wedge$ | \bigwedge | universal quantifier |
| $\odot$ | $\odot$ | \bigodot | scalar product |
| $\otimes$ | $\otimes$ | \bigotimes | tensor product |
| $\oplus$ | $\oplus$ | \bigoplus | direct sum |
| $\uplus$ | $\uplus$ | \biguplus | discriminated union |

The appearance of the large operator (sign) in a formula depends on whether it is used within a paragraph (*text style*) or in a separate formula (*display style*). The commands for operators can be combined with subscripts '_' or superscripts '^'. Depending on the current mode, style (display or text), and operator, a subscript (functioning as a lower bound) will be typeset directly below the symbol or below the baseline to the right of the operator symbol. The same mechanism is valid for superscripts (upper bounds). The following examples show the input (only for text style) and *text style* as well as *display style* output. To get display style input, left and right dollar signs have to be doubled.

Examples:

| | text style | display style |
|:---|:---:|:---:|
| `$ \sum_{n-1}^m $` | $\sum_{n-1}^m$ | $\displaystyle\sum_{n-1}^{m}$ |
| `$ \prod_{i=1}^n (i+1) $` | $\prod_{i=1}^n (i+1)$ | $\displaystyle\prod_{i=1}^{n}(i+1)$ |
| `$ \int_0^{2\pi} \sin x\, dx $` | $\int_0^{2\pi} \sin x\, dx$ | $\displaystyle\int_0^{2\pi} \sin x\, dx$ |

`$\prod_{j>0}\sum_{k>0}a_{jk}$`               $\prod_{j>0} \sum_{k>0} a_{jk}$      $\displaystyle\prod_{j>0} \sum_{k>0} a_{jk}$

`$\bigcap_{i=1}^\infty M_i=\emptyset$`        $\bigcap_{i=1}^\infty M_i = \emptyset$      $\displaystyle\bigcap_{i=1}^\infty M_i = \emptyset$

`$\sum_{\scriptstyle i<m \atop`
`         \scriptstyle j<n}  x_{ij}$`         $\sum_{i<m \atop j<n} x_{ij}$      $\displaystyle\sum_{i<m \atop j<n} x_{ij}$

In the last example, two rows of limits are put under a large operator with \atop. The
\scriptstyle commands force their sizes to the standard for limits. Otherwise, they
would have been set even smaller still.

You can change TEX's convention to set limits below and above operator signs. The $\sum$
sign receives its limits below and above it (in display style), the $\int$ beside it. Some people
prefer to change these rules. The \limits command determines that limits are typeset
below and above their symbol, \nolimits determines that limits are located beside it.
Both commands are mainly useful in display style, as in text style the usual convention
is to place the limits beside signs to conserve space. Some examples illustrate the use
of \limits and \nolimits:

`$$\sum\nolimits_{n-1}^m$$`                   $\displaystyle\sum\nolimits_{n-1}^m$

`$$\prod\nolimits_{i=1}^n (i+1)$$`            $\displaystyle\prod\nolimits_{i=1}^n (i+1)$

`$$\int\limits_0^\pi \sin x\,dx$$`            $\displaystyle\int\limits_0^\pi \sin x \, dx$

## 5.11 Parentheses and Delimiters

TEX uses 29 different kinds of parentheses and delimiters. With a few exceptions, they
can be used in arbitrary sizes as large variants can be built with repeatable extensions.
There are two possibilities to determine the size of these symbols: either automatically
by application of '\left' and '\right' to the delimiters of a subformula, or by explicitly
fixing the size of the next delimiter.

| Input | Output | Comments |
|---|---|---|
| ( | ( | left parenthesis |
| ) | ) | right parenthesis |
| [ *or* \lbrack | [ | left bracket |
| ] *or* \rbrack | ] | right bracket |
| \{ *or* \lbrace | { | left curly brace |
| \} *or* \rbrace | } | right curly brace |
| \lgroup. | ( | left parenthesis<br>This parenthesis is built<br>from parts of the left curly<br>brace without the cusp. |
| \rgroup. | ) | right parenthesis,<br>built like \lgroup |
| \rmoustache. | ⎱ | 'parenthesis',<br>built from curly brace parts |
| \lmoustache. | ⎰ | 'parenthesis',<br>built from curly brace parts |
| \lfloor | ⌊ | left floor bracket |
| \rfloor | ⌋ | right floor bracket |
| \lceil | ⌈ | left ceiling bracket |
| \rceil | ⌉ | right ceiling bracket |
| \langle *or* < | ⟨ | left angle bracket |
| \rangle *or* > | ⟩ | right angle bracket |
| / | / | slash |
| \backslash | \ | reverse slash |
| \| *or* \vert | \| | vertical bar |
| \|\| *or* \Vert | ‖ | double vertical bar (norm) |
| \arrowvert. | \| | different form of '\|'<br>built from '↓' |
| \Arrowvert. | ‖ | different form of '‖'<br>built from '⇓' |
| \bracevert. | \| | vertical bar<br>middle part of a large brace |
| \uparrow | ↑ | upward arrow |
| \downarrow | ↓ | downward arrow |
| \Uparrow | ⇑ | double upward arrow |
| \Downarrow | ⇓ | double downward arrow |
| \updownarrow | ↕ | up-and-down arrow |
| \Updownarrow | ⇕ | double up-and-down arrow |

The delimiters marked with '$_*$' can only be used combined with \left and \right or \big..., as these symbols do not have a native size.

There are 5 commands to enlarge explicitly the delimiter that follows:

| *function of* | | | | |
|---|---|---|---|---|
| *left delimiter* | *right delimiter* | *middle (relation)* | *normal sign* | *size* |
| \bigl | \bigr | \bigm | \big | slightly larger |
| \Bigl | \Bigr | \Bigm | \Big | 1.5 times the size of \bigl ... |
| \biggl | \biggr | \biggm | \bigg | 2.0 times the size of \bigl ... |
| \Biggl | \Biggr | \Biggm | \Bigg | 2.5 times the size of \bigl ... |

$$\verb|\bigl(x-s(x)\bigr)\bigl(y-s(y)\bigr)|$$

gives

$$\bigl(x - s(x)\bigr)\bigl(y - s(y)\bigr)$$

The following example compares the most common delimiters:

```
$$ \Biggl(\biggl(\Bigl(\bigl((0)\bigr)\Bigr)\biggr)\Biggr)$$
$$ \Biggl[\biggl[\Bigl[\bigl[[0]\bigr]\Bigr]\biggr]\Biggr]$$
$$ \Biggl\{\biggl\{\Bigl\{\bigl\{\{0
        \}\bigr\}\Bigr\}\biggr\}\Biggr\}$$
$$ \Biggl\lgroup\biggl\lgroup\Bigl\lgroup 0
        \Bigr\rgroup\biggr\rgroup\Biggr\rgroup$$
```

give

$$\Biggl(\biggl(\Bigl(\bigl((0)\bigr)\Bigr)\biggr)\Biggr)$$

$$\Biggl[\biggl[\Bigl[\bigl[[0]\bigr]\Bigr]\biggr]\Biggr]$$

$$\Biggl\{\biggl\{\Bigl\{\bigl\{\{0\}\bigr\}\Bigr\}\biggr\}\Biggr\}$$

$$\Biggl\lgroup\biggl\lgroup\Bigl\lgroup 0\Bigr\rgroup\biggr\rgroup\Biggr\rgroup$$

It is important to use the correct variant of \bigl, \bigr, \bigm, \big ... to specify to TEX the function of an opening, a closing, a relation or an ordinary sign, respectively, so TEX will put a bit of space on the correct side of the symbol.

## 5.12 Growing Delimiters

TEX has a built-in mechanism to enlarge a pair of delimiters in correspondence with the enclosed subformula. You can use this method for every pair of delimiters you like. The input must satisfy the following form:

\left &lt;left delimiter&gt; &lt;formula&gt; \right &lt;right delimiter&gt;

When \left and \right are used they must always appear in pairs. Any delimiter can follow them. If one of the delimiters is to be suppressed, there is a form '\left.' or '\right.' to get an empty delimiter. TEX will report an error message if a '\left' or '\right' is missing or superfluous. Additionally, \left and \right form a group just as '{' and '}' do.

Neither does \left imply that an *opening* symbol like ( { [ ... follows, nor \right that a *closing* symbol like ) } ] ... follows. Mathematicians use, e.g., ]0,1[ to denote an open interval. Remember '\left' is *to the left of the formula* and '\right' is *to the right of the formula*.

Examples:

| *input* | *text style* | *display style* |
|---|---|---|
| `$ 1+\left( 1 \over 1-x^2 \right)^3 $` | $1 + \left(\frac{1}{1-x^2}\right)^3$ | $1 + \left(\dfrac{1}{1-x^2}\right)^3$ |
| `$ 1+\left\lgroup 1\over 1-x^2`<br>`  \right\rgroup^3 $` | $1 + \left(\frac{1}{1-x^2}\right)^3$ | $1 + \left(\dfrac{1}{1-x^2}\right)^3$ |
| `$ 1+\left[ 1 \over 1-x^2 \right]^3 $` | $1 + \left[\frac{1}{1-x^2}\right]^3$ | $1 + \left[\dfrac{1}{1-x^2}\right]^3$ |
| `$ 1+\left\Vert f(x)`<br>`  \over 1+g(x) \right\Vert$` | $1 + \left\|\frac{f(x)}{1+g(x)}\right\|$ | $1 + \left\|\dfrac{f(x)}{1+g(x)}\right\|$ |
| `$ 1+\left\{ f(x) \over 1+g(x) \right\} $` | $1 + \left\{\frac{f(x)}{1+g(x)}\right\}$ | $1 + \left\{\dfrac{f(x)}{1+g(x)}\right\}$ |

Fraction-like expressions, e.g., the Eulerian number $\left\langle{n\atop k}\right\rangle$ may be defined with arbitrary delimiters. There are three primitives for 'generalized fractions':

\overwithdelims &lt;opening delimiter&gt; &lt;closing delimiter&gt;<br>\atopwithdelims &lt;opening delimiter&gt; &lt;closing delimiter&gt;<br>\abovewithdelims &lt;opening delimiter&gt; &lt;closing delimiter&gt; &lt;dimension&gt;

The command \overwithdelims builds a delimited fraction with a fraction bar of default thickness. \atopwithdelims omits any fraction line. The third command, \abovewithdelims, defines the thickness of the fraction bar explicitly as its third parameter.

Examples:

| | |
|---|---|
| `$ n\atopwithdelims\langle\rangle k$` | $\left\langle{n\atop k}\right\rangle$ |
| `$ n\overwithdelims\langle\rangle k$` | $\left\langle{n\over k}\right\rangle$ |
| `$ n\abovewithdelims\langle\rangle 1pt k$` | $\left\langle{n\over k}\right\rangle$ |

## 5.13 Mathematical Functions

There are some common mathematical functions, like 'sin' or 'cos', which are usually not typeset in italic or Greek letters, but in Roman type. TₑX has predefined a number of these functions to get this effect. They can be used like ordinary operators. Limits and subscripts are requested by '_', as usual. The positions of limits or subscripts are predefined in plain TₑX:

$$\verb|\max_{1<i<n} \log_2 a_i|$$   shows the difference in positioning

$$\max_{1<i<n} \log_2 a_i$$

The following list contains the mathematical functions. Entries which are marked with '⋆' are functions with limits placed below their names.

| | | | | | | | |
|---|---|---|---|---|---|---|---|
| \arccos | \cos  | \csc  | \exp     | \ker     | \limsup⋆ | \min⋆ | \sup⋆ |
| \arcsin | \cosh | \deg  | \gcd⋆    | \lg      | \ln      | \Pr⋆  | \tan  |
| \arctan | \cot  | \det⋆ | \hom     | \lim⋆    | \log     | \sec  | \tanh |
| \arg    | \dim  | \inf⋆ | \liminf⋆ | \max⋆    | \sin     | \sin  |       |

Some uses:

$\verb|\sin2\beta=2\sin\beta\cos\beta|$  $\sin 2\beta = 2\sin\beta\cos\beta$

$\verb|O(n\log n\log\log n)|$  $O(n\log n\log\log n)$

$\verb|\max_{1\le n}\log_2P_n)|$  $\max_{1\le n}\log_2 P_n)$

$\verb|\min_{1\le n}\log_2P_n)|$  $\min_{1\le n}\log_2 P_n)$

$\verb|\liminf_{n\to\infty}x_n=0|$  $\liminf_{n\to\infty} x_n = 0$

If you want to define your own names with similar behaviour, here are the definitions of '\min' and '\log', details are explained later:

```
\def\min{\mathop{\rm min}}
\def\log{\mathop{\rm log}\nolimits}
```

All these functions are printed with spacing like large operators.

## 5.14 Spacing within Formulae

If you are not satisfied with TₑX's automatic spacing of math formulae, you can enforce extra spacing by the commands:

| | | |
|---|---|---|
| \, | increase spacing by 3/18 "quad" | ⇔ \thinmuskip |
| \> | increase spacing by 4/18 "quad" | ⇔ \medmuskip |
| \; | increase spacing by 5/18 "quad" | ⇔ \thickmuskip |
| \! | decrease spacing by 3/18 "quad" | ⇔ -\thinmuskip |

*input*                                      *text style*          *display style*

$ \verb|\int\!\!\!\!\int_D f(x,y)\,dx\,dy| $     $\iint_D f(x,y)\,dx\,dy$   $\iint_D f(x,y)\,dx\,dy$

*compared to the unchanged version:*

$ \verb|\int\int_D f(x,y) dx  dy| $     $\int\int_D f(x,y)dxdy$   $\int\int_D f(x,y)dxdy$

For more coarse ways of obtaining extra spacing, you will often use \quad or \qquad, especially in combination with text.

    $ f(x)=\sin x \quad \hbox{for} \quad x>0$

gives

$$f(x) = \sin x \quad \text{for} \quad x > 0$$

The easiest and cleanest way to insert text into a formula is to include the text in an \hbox. Within the \hbox, math mode is suspended and the rules of text mode apply. This means all features of text setting such as ligatures, kerning, etc. are in force. Especially, accents have to be requested by the usual text mode commands. Within the '\hbox' there is no line breaking; all text is typeset in one horizontal line. After the '\hbox' is closed at its corresponding '}', math mode is restored and formula setting continues.

If you want to vary the style of mathematical spacing, see Section 9.1.

## 5.15 Matrices

Matrices are used by mathematicians in many different forms. Usually they consist of rectangular blocks of subformulae. Such an arrangement of rows and columns is usually called a *matrix*. A standard form for a matrix is, e.g.:

$$A = \begin{pmatrix} x-\lambda & 1 & 0 \\ 0 & x-\lambda & 1 \\ 0 & 0 & x-\lambda \end{pmatrix}$$

This is input as:

```
$$ A = \left(  \matrix{ x-\lambda & 1         & 0          \cr
                 0         & x-\lambda & 1          \cr
                 0         & 0         & x-\lambda \cr}
          \right) $$
```

The rows of the matrix are separated by '\cr', the '&' sign arranges the elements into columns. The size of any individual column is determined by its widest element. The left and right parentheses are produced by '\left(' and '\right)'. (All input spaces and line ends between '$$' signs are ignored by TEX. The spacing in formulae is controlled by special rules different from text setting.)

As the matrix example above is a standard form, there is a shortened form for it: '\pmatrix' (*parenthesized matrix*).

```
$$ A = \pmatrix{ x-\lambda & 1         & 0          \cr
                 0         & x-\lambda & 1          \cr
                 0         & 0         & x-\lambda \cr}$$
```

Matrices can be generated with different delimiters. It is merely necessary to precede the delimiter symbol with '\left' and '\right'. As mentioned above, \left and \right have to be paired and may not be interchanged.

One further example:

$$\det A = \begin{vmatrix} x - \lambda & 1 & 0 \\ 0 & x - \lambda & 1 \\ 0 & 0 & x - \lambda \end{vmatrix}$$

is generated by

```
$$ \det   A =
   \left\vert \matrix{ x-\lambda  & 1          & 0          \cr
                       0          & x-\lambda  & 1          \cr
                       0          & 0          & x-\lambda  \cr}
   \right\vert$$
```

Various kinds of dots are often used in combination with matrices, as follows:

| | | |
|---|---|---|
| \ldots | $\ldots$ | *low dots* |
| \vdots | $\vdots$ | *vertical dots* |
| \ddots | $\ddots$ | *diagonal dots* |
| \cdots | $\cdots$ | *centered dots* |

A typical example for this is

```
$$A=\pmatrix{ a_{11} & a_{12} & \ldots & a_{1n}  \cr
              a_{21} & a_{22} & \ldots & a_{2n}  \cr
              \vdots & \vdots & \ddots & \vdots  \cr
              a_{n1} & a_{n2} & \ldots & a_{nn}  \cr}$$
```

giving

$$A = \begin{pmatrix} a_{11} & a_{12} & \ldots & a_{1n} \\ a_{21} & a_{22} & \ldots & a_{2n} \\ \vdots & \vdots & \ddots & \vdots \\ a_{n1} & a_{n2} & \ldots & a_{nn} \end{pmatrix}$$

Sometimes matrices are partitioned by horizontal and vertical rules. This is accomplished by \hrule and \vrule. Vertical rules form a matrix column by themselves. The horizontal rule is typeset by \noalign{\hrule}. \noalign{...} gives a matrix row without arrangement in columns. The vertical rules pose a problem.

The input

```
$$  A_3 = \left[
    \matrix{ & &   & & \vrule & a_{11} & \ldots & a_{1n}  \cr
             & & C & & \vrule & a_{1n} & \ldots & a_{nn}  \cr
             & &   & & \vrule & a_{1n} & \ldots & a_{nn}  \cr
      \noalign{\hrule}
             & &   & & \vrule & \lambda&        &         \cr
             & & I & & \vrule &        & \ddots &         \cr
             & &   & & \vrule &        &        & \lambda \cr
             } \right] $$
```

gives

$$
A_3 = \left[ \begin{array}{c|ccc}
& & a_{11} & \cdots & a_{1n} \\
& C & a_{1n} & \cdots & a_{nn} \\
& & \dfrac{a_{1n}}{\lambda} & \cdots & a_{nn} \\
\hline
& I & & \ddots & \\
& & & & \lambda
\end{array} \right]
$$

The vertical rules are not continuous. The reason for this unpleasant behaviour is that matrix rows are vertically positioned depending on TeX's internal parameter '\base-lineskip'. (This is further discussed in the Chapter 'Table Alignment', see 6.6. below)

One method — more or less brute force — is demonstrated: the \vrule commands are supplemented with a specification of their *height* and *depth*. The matrix rows are concatenated by backskipping with '\noalign{\vskip - ... pt}'. ('\noalign' is further explained in Chapter 6.) The vertical lines may overlap each other. This is favourable for some output devices to avoid breaks.

The changed input

```
$$   \def\vline{\vrule height 17pt depth 5pt}
     \def\back{\noalign{\vskip-3pt}}
     \lineskip=0pt
  A_3 = \left[
       \matrix{ & &   & & \vline & a_{11} & \ldots & a_{1n}  \cr
             \back
               & & C & & \vline & a_{1n} & \ldots & a_{nn}  \cr
             \back
               & &   & & \vline & a_{1n} & \ldots & a_{nn}  \cr
             \noalign{\hrule}
               & &   & & \vline & \lambda&        &        \cr
             \back
               & & I & & \vline &        & \ddots &        \cr
             \back
               & &   & & \vline &        &        & \lambda \cr}
       \right] $$
```

yields

$$
A_3 = \left[ \begin{array}{c|ccc}
& & a_{11} & \cdots & a_{1n} \\
& C & a_{1n} & \cdots & a_{nn} \\
& & a_{1n} & \cdots & a_{nn} \\
\hline
& & \lambda & & \\
& I & & \ddots & \\
& & & & \lambda
\end{array} \right]
$$

The abbreviations

```
\def\vline{\vrule height 14pt depth 5pt}
\def\back{\noalign{\vskip-3pt}}
```

are used in anticipation of macro definitions (Chapter 7). Each command \vline or \back is just a condensed form of the text between the braces.

Usually matrices will be used as separate formulae in display style. Sometimes you may want to typeset a very small matrix within a paragraph line, e.g., $\left(\begin{smallmatrix}1&1\\0&1\end{smallmatrix}\right)$. The preceding matrix was generated with the help of the binomial operator \choose from $1\,,1\choose0\,,1$. The commands \, just give extra space to obtain a column-like appearance. An alternative way is to set up a series of ruleless fractions with \atop: $\left(\begin{smallmatrix}a&b&c\\l&m&n\end{smallmatrix}\right)$. The input for this is

$\bigl( { a\atop l} {b \atop m} {c \atop n} \bigr)$

"\bigl(" and "\bigr)" give slightly enlarged parentheses.

## 5.16 Singular Grouping Braces

Mathematicians like to use braces to indicate possible choices between alternatives. These constructs have a matrix-like structure with a 'missing' right parenthesis:

$$|x| = \begin{cases} x & \text{if } x \geq 0 \\ -x & \text{otherwise} \end{cases}$$

is produced by

$$\vert x\vert = \cases{x    & if $ x \ge 0 $ \cr
                       -x & otherwise   \cr }$$

\cases produces the enlarged brace at the left side. Lines are separated by '\cr', the tabbing symbol (column separator) '&' divides the first and second element of each matrix line. '\cases' is internally defined as a '\matrix' with a '\left\{' and a '\right.' delimiter. Furthermore, the first column is typeset in mathematical mode, the second column in text mode automatically.

Another kind of grouping braces are horizontally arranged braces, implemented by \overbrace and \underbrace.

$$\overbrace{x+\cdots+X}^{k\rm\;times}$$
$$\underbrace{x+y+z}_{>0}$$

produces

$$\overbrace{x + \cdots + X}^{k \text{ times}}$$

$$\underbrace{x + y + z}_{>0}$$

A hint for text setting: horizontal braces may be referred to by \upbracefill and \downbracefill. These are adapted to the requested width automatically (see below, Section 6.7).

## 5.17 Aligned Equations

If equations are aligned as multi-line displays, they should usually be lined up on their '=' signs or relational operators.

$$X_1 + \cdots + X_p = m$$
$$Y_1 + \cdots + Y_q = m$$

This is accomplished by the command \eqalign, which works similar to \matrix and \cases. '\cr' separates the lines, and a '&' has to be typed before the symbol at which left and right sides should be aligned. The effect is that the left side is justified flush right at the separating symbol, and the right side is justified flush left. The previous example is generated by

```
$$\eqalign{X_1 + \cdots + X_p &=m \cr
           Y_1 + \cdots + Y_q &=m \cr}$$
```

It is even possible to put more than one \eqalign expression into a single displayed formula by horizontal grouping:

```
$$\eqalign{X_1 + \cdots + X_p &=m \cr
           Y_1 + \cdots + Y_q &=m \cr}
   \qquad                                 %  spacing
   \eqalign{\alpha &= f(z) \cr
            \beta  &= f(z^2) \cr
            \gamma &= f(z^3) \cr}
$$
```

yields

$$
\begin{array}{c}
X_1 + \cdots + X_p = m \\
Y_1 + \cdots + Y_q = m
\end{array}
\qquad
\begin{array}{c}
\alpha = f(z) \\
\beta = f(z^2) \\
\gamma = f(z^3)
\end{array}
$$

The \qquad command between the two \eqalign expressions produces the extra space.

If the two parts of the formula are to be surrounded by braces, \left and \right must be used. The example, modified by '\left\{' and '\right\}'

```
$$\left\{\eqalign{X_1 + \cdots + X_p &=m \cr
                  Y_1 + \cdots + Y_q &=m \cr}\right\}
   \qquad                                       %  spacing
   \left\{\eqalign{\alpha &= f(z) \cr
                   \beta  &= f(z^2) \cr
                   \gamma &= f(z^3) \cr}\right\}
$$
```

yields

$$
\left\{
\begin{array}{c}
X_1 + \cdots + X_p = m \\
Y_1 + \cdots + Y_q = m
\end{array}
\right\}
\qquad
\left\{
\begin{array}{c}
\alpha = f(z) \\
\beta = f(z^2) \\
\gamma = f(z^3)
\end{array}
\right\}
$$

Take note of the vertical alignment of the curly braces.

## 5.18 Numbered Equations

It is common to number equations in mathematical papers for reference purposes. TeX allows these labels to appear to the left or right side of displayed formulae. The most simple form of numbering a *single* displayed formula is done on the right side by \eqno and on the left side by \leqno. After typing anything of the form

$$<formula>\eqno<numbering formula>$$

$$<formula>\leqno<numbering formula>$$

e.g.

`$$\sin 18^\circ= {1\over4} (\sqrt5-1)\eqno(1)$$`

`$$\sum_{i=1}^n i = {n(n+1) \over 2} \leqno(2')$$`

you get

$$\sin 18° = \frac{1}{4}(\sqrt{5} - 1) \tag{1}$$

$$(2') \qquad \sum_{i=1}^{n} i = \frac{n(n+1)}{2}$$

Multi-line displays are numbered by variant commands: \eqalignno with numbers on the right side and \leqalignno with numbers on the left side. The syntax of the command '\eqalign' is extended with an additional parameter separated by a '&' sign. The second '&' sign of each formula line (ending at '\cr') precedes the numbering part. The TeX input

`$$\eqalignno{ \sin^2 \alpha + \cos^2 \alpha &= 1 &(1) \cr`

`a^2 + b^2 & = c^2                  &(*) \cr}`

`$$`

will be typeset as

$$\sin^2 \alpha + \cos^2 \alpha = 1 \tag{1}$$
$$a^2 + b^2 = c^2 \tag{*}$$

There are two '&' signs on every display line. To get the numbers on the left side, only the command name has to be changed from '\eqalignno' to '\leqalignno'. A common error is to change the sequence of the parameters of '\leqalignno' also.

`$$\leqalignno{ \sin^2 \alpha + \cos^2 \alpha &= 1 &(2) \cr`

`a^2 + b^2 & = c^2                  &(**) \cr}`

`$$`

gives

$$(2) \qquad \sin^2 \alpha + \cos^2 \alpha = 1$$
$$(**) \qquad a^2 + b^2 = c^2$$

Not all lines have to be numbered:

```
$$\eqalignno{ (x+y)(x-y) &= x^2+yx-xy-y^2 &     \cr % without number
                       &= x^2-y^2              &(1) \cr
              (x+y)^2  &= x^2+2xy+y^2          &(2) \cr} $$
```

yields

$$(x + y)(x - y) = x^2 - xy - yx - y^2$$
$$= x^2 - y^2 \tag{1}$$
$$(x + y)^2 = x^2 + 2xy + y^2 \tag{2}$$

The numbering part within \eqalignno and \leqalignno is typeset in mathematical mode with math fonts. If you want to get ordinary text in a label, you have to enclose it within an '\hbox{ ... }'.

```
$$\int_{-\infty}^\infty e^{-x^2}\,dx = \pi
                        \eqno \hbox{(Formula X)}$$
```

produces

$$\int_{-\infty}^{\infty} e^{-x^2}\, dx = \pi \tag{Formula X}$$

---

*Besides the mathematical symbols already mentioned there are more,*
*which will be listed below for reference without detailed explanations.*

---

## 5.19 Mathematical Binary Operators

Mathematical binary operators are typeset with equal spacing to the left and right. In addition to the standard operators $+ - *$, these are:

| | | | | | | |
|---|---|---|---|---|---|---|
| $\pm$ | \pm | $\cap$ | \cap | $\vee$ | \vee *or* \lor |
| $\mp$ | \mp | $\cup$ | \cup | $\wedge$ | \wedge *or* \land |
| $\setminus$ | \setminus | $\uplus$ | \uplus | $\oplus$ | \oplus |
| $\cdot$ | \cdot | $\sqcap$ | \sqcap | $\ominus$ | \ominus |
| $\times$ | \times | $\sqcup$ | \sqcup | $\otimes$ | \otimes |
| $*$ | \ast | $\triangleleft$ | \triangleleft | $\oslash$ | \oslash |
| $\star$ | \star | $\triangleright$ | \triangleright | $\odot$ | \odot |
| $\diamond$ | \diamond | $\wr$ | \wr | $\dagger$ | \dagger |
| $\circ$ | \circ | $\bigcirc$ | \bigcirc | $\ddagger$ | \ddagger |
| $\bullet$ | \bullet | $\bigtriangleup$ | \bigtriangleup | $\amalg$ | \amalg |
| $\div$ | \div | $\bigtriangledown$ | \bigtriangledown | | |

## 5.20 Mathematical Relations

The most common relations $<\ >\ =$ are complemented by

| | | | | | |
|---|---|---|---|---|---|
| $\leq$ | `\leq` *or* `\le` | $\geq$ | `\geq` *or* `\ge` | $\equiv$ | `\equiv` |
| $\prec$ | `\prec` | $\succ$ | `\succ` | $\sim$ | `\sim` |
| $\preceq$ | `\preceq` | $\succeq$ | `\succeq` | $\simeq$ | `\simeq` |
| $\ll$ | `\ll` | $\gg$ | `\gg` | $\asymp$ | `\asymp` |
| $\subset$ | `\subset` | $\supset$ | `\supset` | $\approx$ | `\approx` |
| $\subseteq$ | `\subseteq` | $\supseteq$ | `\supseteq` | $\cong$ | `\cong` |
| $\sqsubseteq$ | `\sqsubseteq` | $\sqsupseteq$ | `\sqsubseteq` | $\bowtie$ | `\bowtie` |
| $\in$ | `\in` | $\ni$ | `\ni` *or* `\owns` | $\propto$ | `\propto` |
| $\vdash$ | `\vdash` | $\dashv$ | `\dashv` | $\models$ | `\models` |
| $\smile$ | `\smile` | $\mid$ | `\mid` | $\doteq$ | `\doteq` |
| $\frown$ | `\frown` | $\parallel$ | `\parallel` | $\perp$ | `\perp` |

Some relations are often used in a *negated* form:

| | | | | | |
|---|---|---|---|---|---|
| $\not<$ | `\not<` | $\not>$ | `\not>` | $\ne$ | `\ne` *or* `\not=` *or* `\neq` |
| $\not\leq$ | `\not\leq` | $\not\geq$ | `\not\geq` | $\not\equiv$ | `\not\equiv` |
| $\not\prec$ | `\not\prec` | $\not\succ$ | `\not\succ` | $\not\sim$ | `\not\sim` |
| $\not\preceq$ | `\not\preceq` | $\not\succeq$ | `\not\succeq` | $\not\simeq$ | `\not\simeq` |
| $\not\subset$ | `\not\subset` | $\not\supset$ | `\not\supset` | $\not\approx$ | `\not\approx` |
| $\not\subseteq$ | `\not\subseteq` | $\not\supseteq$ | `\not\supseteq` | $\not\cong$ | `\not\cong` |
| $\not\sqsubseteq$ | `\not\sqsubseteq` | $\not\sqsupseteq$ | `\not\sqsubseteq` | $\not\asymp$ | `\not\asymp` |
| $\not\in$ | `\not\in` | $\not\ni$ | `\not\ni` *or* `\owns` | $\not\propto$ | `\not\propto` |
| $\not\vdash$ | `\not\vdash` | $\not\dashv$ | `\not\dashv` | $\not\models$ | `\not\models` |
| $\not\smile$ | `\not\smile` | $\not\mid$ | `\not\mid` | $\not\doteq$ | `\not\doteq` |
| $\not\frown$ | `\not\frown` | $\not\parallel$ | `\not\parallel` | $\not\perp$ | `\not\perp` |

The symbol "$\notin$", generated by '`\not\in`', has an extra variant "$\notin$" (`\notin`) with corrected position of the slash (/) overprinting the "$\in$" sign.

Arrows are handled like relations:

| | | | | | |
|---|---|---|---|---|---|
| $\leftarrow$ | `\gets` | | | | |
| $\leftarrow$ | `\leftarrow` | $\longleftarrow$ | `\longleftarrow` | $\uparrow$ | `\uparrow` |
| $\Leftarrow$ | `\Leftarrow` | $\Longleftarrow$ | `\Longleftarrow` | $\Uparrow$ | `\Uparrow` |
| $\rightarrow$ | `\rightarrow` *or* `\to` | $\longrightarrow$ | `\longrightarrow` | $\downarrow$ | `\downarrow` |
| $\Rightarrow$ | `\Rightarrow` | $\Longrightarrow$ | `\Longrightarrow` | $\Downarrow$ | `\Downarrow` |
| $\leftrightarrow$ | `\leftrightarrow` | $\longleftrightarrow$ | `\longleftrightarrow` | $\updownarrow$ | `\updownarrow` |
| $\Leftrightarrow$ | `\Leftrightarrow` | $\Longleftrightarrow$ | `\Longleftrightarrow` | $\Updownarrow$ | `\Updownarrow` |
| | | $\Longleftrightarrow$ | `\iff` *with extra space !* | | |
| $\mapsto$ | `\mapsto` | $\longmapsto$ | `\longmapsto` | $\nearrow$ | `\nearrow` |
| $\hookleftarrow$ | `\hookleftarrow` | $\hookrightarrow$ | `\hookrightarrow` | $\searrow$ | `\searrow` |
| $\leftharpoonup$ | `\leftharpoonup` | $\rightharpoonup$ | `\rightharpoonup` | $\swarrow$ | `\swarrow` |
| $\leftharpoondown$ | `\leftharpoondown` | $\rightharpoondown$ | `\rightharpoondown` | $\nwarrow$ | `\nwarrow` |
| $\rightleftharpoons$ | `\rightleftharpoons` | | | | |

To systematize the many arrow commands: a capital letter at the beginning of the command means double arrows, a preceding '\long' or '\Long' the elongated variant. There are *arrows, hooks,* and *harpoons.* The directions are indicated by up, down, left, and right as well as by ne *(north east),* se *(south east),* sw *(south west),* and nw *(north west).* Vertical arrows may be combined with \left, \right, or \big... commands.

Text may be put on top of relations by \buildrel. Application of the syntactical form

$$\text{\textbackslash buildrel } \textit{upper text} \text{ \textbackslash over } \textit{relation}$$

in

```
$$ \buildrel \alpha\beta \over \longrightarrow    $$
$$ \buildrel \rm def \over = $$
```

gives

$$\buildrel \alpha\beta \over \longrightarrow$$

$$\buildrel \mathrm{def} \over =$$

## 5.21 Mathematical Symbols

| | | | | | | | |
|---|---|---|---|---|---|---|---|
| $\aleph$ | \aleph | $\prime$ | \prime | $\forall$ | \forall |
| $\hbar$ | \hbar | $\emptyset$ | \emptyset | $\exists$ | \exists |
| $\imath$ | \imath | $\nabla$ | \nabla | $\neg$ | \neg |
| $\jmath$ | \jmath | $\surd$ | \surd | $\flat$ | \flat |
| $\ell$ | \ell | $\top$ | \top | $\natural$ | \natural |
| $\wp$ | \wp | $\bot$ | \bot | $\sharp$ | \sharp |
| $\Re$ | \Re | $\Vert$ | \Vert | $\clubsuit$ | \clubsuit |
| $\Im$ | \Im | $\angle$ | \angle | $\diamondsuit$ | \diamondsuit |
| $\partial$ | \partial | $\triangle$ | \triangle | $\heartsuit$ | \heartsuit |
| $\infty$ | \infty | $\backslash$ | \backslash | $\spadesuit$ | \spadesuit |
| $\S$ | \S | $\P$ | \P | $\dag$ | \dag |
| $\ddag$ | \ddag | $\vert$ | \vert | | |

Calligraphic capital letters $\mathcal{ABCDEFGHIJKLMNOPQRSTUVWXYZ}$ are generated by ${\cal A}$ ... ${\cal Z}$.

'Oldstyle' digits 0123456789 you will get by {\oldstyle 0123456789}.

## 5.22 Empty Operators

Sometimes the author is not satisfied with any of the mathematical operators available in the mathematical fonts, not even with symbols generated by overlaying. The command '\phantom' will generate empty space for later insertion of the desired symbol — which may be hand-drawn. The input \phantom{00}7 is interpreted as '007', but instead of printing '00' only empty space is generated in the space that '00' would occupy.

The use of 'white' operators is a little bit more complicated: besides horizontal skipping, positioning of subscripts and superscripts has to be considered. As mentioned above, \sum and \lg differ in their behaviour. Notice that \sum and \lg act as 'large operators'. In

```
\mathop{\phantom\sum}
\mathop{\phantom\lg}\nolimits
```

the printout of the operators $\sum$ and lg will be suppressed but the other features will be retained. For example:

```
$$\mathop{\phantom\sum}_{i=1}^\infty x_n = \pi$$
$$\mathop{\phantom\lg}\nolimits_2 8 = 3$$
```

gives

$$\substack{\infty \\ \\ i=1} \quad x_n = \pi$$

$$_2 8 = 3$$

\mathop forces TeX — in formulae — to interpret its argument as a large operator. This is one of the eight basic elements within math mode. Other elements can be requested by

| | | | |
|---|---|---|---|
| \mathord | ordinary symbol | \mathopen | opening (bracket) |
| \mathop | large operator | \mathclose | closing (bracket) |
| \mathbin | binary operation | \mathpunct | punctuation |
| \mathrel | relation | \mathinner | subformula |

Besides \phantom, which gives the amount of space the original signs have with regard to width, height, and depth (below the baseline), there are more instructions with similar effects. The following table gives an overview:

| command | height and depth | width | output |
|---|---|---|---|
| \phantom {... *formula* ...} | as original | as original | space |
| \hphantom {... *formula* ...} | 0 | as original | space |
| \vphantom {... *formula* ...} | as original | 0 | space |
| \smash {... *formula* ...} | 0 | as original | **as original** |

## 5.23 Large Formulae — Line Breaking

The author is the best authority on deciding where his formulae may be broken into lines at meaningful positions. It is preferable to specify explicit breakpoints.

Although TeX solves some line breaking problems with text style formulae itself, it needs some help. Formulae in text mode will be broken at relations such as "$< \; = \; > \; \ldots$" or at operators like "$+ - * \ldots$" automatically, if these are outside subformulae, i.e., they do not occur within grouping braces ("{ ... }").
The formula

```
$g(x,y)=x^2+2xy+y^2=(x+y)(x+y)$
```

may be broken after the equal signs or the plus signs, however in

```
$g(x,y)={x^2+2xy+y^2}={(x+y)(x+y)}$
```

a line break may only occur at one of the equal signs.
Notice the difference between the two input lines

```
$    f(x) = x-2    $
$ { f(x) = x-2 } $
```

The second formula can not be broken at a line end.

The author may help TEX by specifying an allowed line break with \allowbreak. This command is not valid within subformulae. On the other hand, you can prohibit a possible line break by \nobreak, just as in text setting.

In formulae with multiplications you may insert a discretionary sign "\*", which acts like "\-" in text. As 'hyphenation' character a "×" sign (\times) is printed. This is useful in formulae like

```
$(x_1+1) \* (x_2+2) \* (x_3+3) ... $
```

Formulae in display style are *not* automatically broken in any way. All divisions into more than one line have to be done by the author.

An acceptable form is to break before a binary operator and to indent the following lines, e.g., with \qquad.

Example:

```
$$ \eqalign{ (a+b)^4 + (a-b)^4 &= a^4 + 4a^3b + 6a^2b^2
                                    + 4ab^3 + b^4 \cr
                              &\qquad
                                + a^4 - 4a^3b + 6a^2b^2
                                    - 4ab^3 + b^4 \cr} $$
```

gives

$$(a+b)^4 + (a-b)^4 = a^4 + 4a^3b + 6a^2b^2 + 4ab^3 + b^4$$
$$+ a^4 - 4a^3b + 6a^2b^2 - 4ab^3 + b^4$$

# 6 Tables and Alignment

## 6.1 Tabbing

Typesetting tables is one of the most interesting tasks, but also a very difficult one. To get a nice table you need suitable distances between table columns; some parts should be accentuated by a choice of different fonts, and last but not least divided by separating lines.

There are two different occasions where table setting is needed: when you have to typeset given data in the form of a table, and when a predefined format has to be typeset, e.g., a time-table.

In TeX there are two basic methods for aligning tables: by 'tabbing', which is similar to using the TAB key on many typewriters, and by producing the automatic alignment of tables with \halign — *horizontal alignment*.

Tabbing requires that the width of table columns is given *explicitly*. Defining the number of table columns is one form of starting tabbing.

"\settabs 4 \columns" defines 4 columns of equal width (that is 0.25\hsize). After defining the column sizes, tabbing is done by "\+ ... \cr". All information between "\+" and "\cr" is typeset by tabbing. The tabbing key is the well-known "&" symbol that is used within aligned mathematical formulae as demonstrated in the previous chapter.

*The input*

```
\settabs 4 \columns
\+first column &second column &third column  &fourth column \cr
\+one &two &three &four\cr
\+ eins & zwei & drei & vier \cr
```

*produces a table with 4 columns:*

| | | | |
|---|---|---|---|
| | | | |

*These are filled in with the given information:*

| first column | second column | third column | fourth column |
|---|---|---|---|
| one | two | three | four |
| eins | zwei | drei | vier |

*But:*

```
\+first column &&&& to far! \cr
```

*gives:*

first column                                                                    to far!

There is an important difference between the tabbing of a typewriter and writing "\+
... & ... \cr". The TAB key of a typewriter lets the machine go to the *next* TAB
position that is found. But in TEX *two* "&" will position to the *third* column — this is
done independently of the information in the preceding columns, so the movement can
be forward *or backward*. This can even lead to overprinting.

Tabbing may be used with different column widths by defining a template line.
The command \settabs followed by an ordinary tabbing line starting with "\+", with
"&" as position markers, and with "\cr" as line end, defines the tabbing positions.
The information between the "&" positions determines the width of the columns. Obviously, each column of the template line has to contain the elements with the longest
information. Each column should also contain some extra horizontal skip to separate
the table columns, e.g., "\quad". Remember: blanks immediately after "\+" and "&"
are ignored.

Example:

```
\settabs\+sorting algorithm\quad  &       100 elements
              &       200 elements &       500 elements &\cr
\+sorting algorithms & 100 elements & 200 elements
                      & 500 elements \cr
\+bubble sort      & 250        & 1000   & 10000 \cr
\+insertion sort   & 200        & 400    & 3000 \cr
\+selection sort   & 110        & 260    & 2000 \cr
\+shell sort       & 70         & 250    & 700 \cr
\+heap sort        & 50         & 100    & 300 \cr
\+quicksort        & 40         & 60     & 200 \cr
```

generates column widths of

| | | | |
|---|---|---|---|
| | | | |

and as printed information

| sorting algorithms | 100 elements | 200 elements | 500 elements |
|---|---|---|---|
| bubble sort | 250 | 1000 | 10000 |
| insertion sort | 200 | 400 | 3000 |
| selection sort | 110 | 260 | 2000 |
| shell sort | 70 | 250 | 700 |
| heap sort | 50 | 100 | 300 |
| quicksort | 40 | 60 | 200 |

This table is only a first approach. Aligning numbers on the right-hand side is an
improvement. By inserting \hfill (dynamic horizontal skip) you get the modified

input

```
\settabs\+sorting algorithm\quad      &   100 elements
                     & 200 elements  &   500 elements &\cr
\+sorting algorithms & 100 elements  &   200 elements
                     & 500 elements &\cr
\+bubble sort        &\hfill 250  &\hfill 1000   &\hfill 10000 &\cr
\+insertion sort     &\hfill 200  &\hfill 400    &\hfill  3000 &\cr
\+selection sort     &\hfill 110  &\hfill 260    &\hfill  2000 &\cr
\+shell sort         &\hfill  70  &\hfill 250    &\hfill   700 &\cr
\+heap sort          &\hfill  50  &\hfill 100    &\hfill   300 &\cr
\+quicksort          &\hfill  40  &\hfill  60    &\hfill   200 &\cr
```

with the printed result

| sorting algorithms | 100 elements | 200 elements | 500 elements |
|---|---|---|---|
| bubble sort | 250 | 1000 | 10000 |
| insertion sort | 200 | 400 | 3000 |
| selection sort | 110 | 260 | 2000 |
| shell sort | 70 | 250 | 700 |
| heap sort | 50 | 100 | 300 |
| quicksort | 40 | 60 | 200 |

Note: to get \hfill to work correctly in the last column, TEX has to know the start of the next column. For this reason there is an extra "&" before the \cr.

From TEX's point of view, each table element is its own *group*. Therefore changing commands like altering the current font by "\bf" are local to the current element. Flush right numbers are demonstrated above, elements may be centered within their columns by inserting \hfill on the left and right sides of the information.

The following example has been modified to get boldface column titles and centered column elements. Some extra \quad commands have been inserted within the template. The \smallskip command puts some extra vertical skip below the table headline.

```
\settabs\+\bf sorting algorithm \quad & \bf \quad 100 elements
         & \bf \quad 200 elements & \bf \quad 500 elements &\cr
\+\bf sorting algorithm\quad  & \bf 100 elements
         & \bf 200 elements & \bf 500 elements &\cr
\smallskip
\+\bf bubble sort     &\hfill 250   \hfill & \hfill 1000 \hfill &
                       \hfill 10000 \hfill & \cr
\+\bf insertion sort &\hfill 200   \hfill & \hfill 400  \hfill &
                       \hfill 3000  \hfill & \cr

...
```

This gives

| sorting algorithm | 100 elements | 200 elements | 500 elements |
|---|---|---|---|
| bubble sort | 250 | 1000 | 10000 |
| insertion sort | 200 | 400 | 3000 |
| selection sort | 110 | 260 | 2000 |
| shell sort | 70 | 250 | 700 |
| heap sort | 50 | 100 | 300 |
| quicksort | 40 | 60 | 200 |

You see the input gets rather extensive when we improve the table. A better way for typesetting such a table is described below in *Section 6.4. Automatic table alignment.*

Some general hints for building tables:

- You often want to center a table with some extra space above and below it. This is just what happens with a displayed formula. So we can use this mechanism by writing

```
$$\vbox{\settabs ...\+ ... \cr}$$
```

"$$" changes to math mode, which is immediately exited by "\vbox" — \vbox is described in detail in Chapter 8 — within the \vbox the information is typeset normally. A \vbox cannot be broken at page boundaries, but, for tables, this is quite acceptable in most cases. With this method, the last example is printed as

| sorting algorithm | 100 elements | 200 elements | 500 elements |
|---|---|---|---|
| bubble sort | 250 | 1000 | 10000 |
| insertion sort | 200 | 400 | 3000 |
| selection sort | 110 | 260 | 2000 |
| shell sort | 70 | 250 | 700 |
| heap sort | 50 | 100 | 300 |
| quicksort | 40 | 60 | 200 |

- The previously described commands \settabs, \+, and \cr use TEX's basic table building instruction \halign. Each line of a table is a table by itself, so tables are broken at page ends if they are not inserted into a \vbox.

- A table entry cannot contain a \footnote command. (You can get around this by using \vfootnote — see the appendix.)

- If you forget to type a "\cr", you will get a lot of error messages, but usually a few lines later. This can be quite confusing.

- "\+" is not allowed in a parameter for macros. If you really want to do it, substitute the command \tabalign for all occurences of \+. It does the same things without this restriction.

## 6.2 Variable Tabbing

Sometimes tables are typeset with a lot of alignment changes. A lot of \settabs commands would be needed to generate the following example:

$$
\begin{array}{c}
\textbf{tab}\text{-er-nac-le} \\
\text{-id} \\
\text{-la-ture} \\
\text{-let} \\
\text{-u-lar} \\
\text{-late} \\
\text{-la-tion} \\
\text{-tor} \\
\textbf{ta}\text{-cho-me-ter}
\end{array}
$$

There is a command "\cleartabs" to clear all tabbing positions farther to the right, as on a typewriter. On the other side a new tabbing position will be inserted by a "&" sign, if there are no more predefined tabbing positions. If there are positions remaining, TEX will, of course, go to the next such position.

The previous table is typeset by:

```
\+\cleartabs \bf tab&-er&-nac&-le&\cr
\+               &\cleartabs-id&\cr
\+               &\cleartabs-la&-ture&\cr
\+               &\cleartabs-let&\cr
\+               &\cleartabs-u&-lar&\cr
\+               &              &\cleartabs-late&\cr
\+               &              &\cleartabs-la&-tion&\cr
\+               &              &              &\cleartabs-tor&\cr
\+\cleartabs \bf  ta&-cho&-me&-ter&\cr
```

Every time a change of tabbing positions is required, a "\cleartabs" command is inserted. It kills all following positions. Afterwards new positions are defined by following "&" signs.

A simple hint: if you have defined "\def\ct{\cleartabs}", every \cleartabs can be replaced by \ct, which means much less to type.

## 6.3 Automatic Table Alignment: Template Lines

Through the use of \halign you will get best results in table typesetting, but it is a little more complicated than \settabs. TEX gets all of the information for the table into its memory and calculates the width of each column dynamically. The largest element of any column determines the width of this column.

\halign gets a lot of input, but the following rules have to be followed:

$$
\begin{array}{l}
\backslash\text{halign\{ } \textit{template line } \backslash\text{cr } \textit{line}_1 \ \backslash\text{cr} \\
\qquad\qquad\qquad \textit{line}_2 \ \backslash\text{cr} \\
\qquad\qquad\qquad \cdots \\
\qquad\qquad\quad \textit{line}_n \ \backslash\text{cr \} }
\end{array}
$$

The most important elements of the template line are "#" and "&" symbols. The "&" sign separates the columns — as with \settabs. "#" marks the positions where the elements of the rows will be filled in. All information before the "#" sign will be inserted automatically before the table information, template information after the "#" sign will be inserted after the element text. This will be demonstrated using the information of an earlier example:

```
\halign { \bf# \hfill \quad & \hfill # \quad &
                          \hfill # \quad & \hfill #        \cr
%%%%%%%
%%%%%%% <-column 1-------> <--column 2---->
%%%%%%%               <--- column 3--> <--column 4-->
%%%%%%%
sorting algorithm & 100 elements & 200 elements & 500 elements \cr
\noalign{\smallskip}
    bubble sort      &  250 &  1000 &  10000 \cr
    insertion sort   &  200 &   400 &   3000 \cr
    selection sort   &  110 &   260 &   2000 \cr
    shell sort       &   70 &   250 &    700 \cr
    heap sort        &   50 &   100 &    300 \cr
    quicksort        &   40 &    60 &    200 \cr   } % end
```

This gives:

| sorting algorithm | 100 elements | 200 elements | 500 elements |
|---|---|---|---|
| bubble sort | 250 | 1000 | 10000 |
| insertion sort | 200 | 400 | 3000 |
| selection sort | 110 | 260 | 2000 |
| shell sort | 70 | 250 | 700 |
| heap sort | 50 | 100 | 300 |
| quicksort | 40 | 60 | 200 |

Some remarks. The first column, defined by "\bf# \hfill \quad", is typeset flush left in *boldface*, after it a \quad, which means some extra space, is inserted. The following columns, all identically defined by "\hfill # \quad", are set flush right, as "#" is preceded by "\hfill", which means dynamic horizontal skip. The command "\noalign{\smallskip}" inserts information that is *not* regarded as an element of a column, but this information is printed between the rows of the table. Therefore \noalign must follow "\cr" immediately. (Spaces do not count.) In the example above \noalign inserts a \smallskip after the first table row. This is a typical application of \noalign.

Users of TEX are often discouraged by the complicated appearance of the template line. You have to get used to building your own templates. The important parts are the "#" signs and the "&" signs. The template line is finished in a fixed order: "#", possibly other information (but no "&" sign), and finally "\cr".

An additional "&" sign before the finishing "\cr" starts a new column with missing parameter sign "#". TEX will report the error message "missing #".
A very simple template line is the following:

```
\halign{#&#&#&#\cr ...}
```

This builds a table with four columns, each as wide as its largest element. All table elements are set flush left, but spaces between words may be stretched if there is no dynamic skip, e.g., \hfil, present. The columns are printed without any extra space between them. The input

```
\halign{#&#&#&#\cr
one&two&three&four\cr
five&six&seven&eight\cr
nine&ten&eleven&twelve\cr}
```

generates the table:

one twothree four
five six seven eight
nineten eleventwelve

Spaces in the input give a better result. The columns are separated by a single space (between words). The input

```
\halign{#&#&#&#\cr
one     & two   & three  & four    \cr
five    & six   & seven  & eight   \cr
nine    & ten   & eleven & twelve \cr}
```

generates the result:

one  two three  four
five  six  seven  eight
nine ten  eleven twelve

Note: spaces after a "&" and "\cr" are ignored. All empty space between the columns is generated by the spaces in the input *after* the words.

Now comes the fun part: each column gets additional information from its corresponding element in the template line. All changing commands are restricted to the current column, as each element builds a group. (\tabskip is an exception!) The following modified example generates one **boldface** column, the second is unchanged in roman, the third in *italics* and the last in typewriter type.

```
\halign{\bf #&#&\it #&\tt #\cr
%            ^^^     ^^^^  ^^^^
%         (1)      (3)   (4)
%
        one     & two   & three  & four    \cr
        five    & six   & seven  & eight   \cr
        nine    & ten   & eleven & twelve \cr}
```

gives

**one** two *three* four
**five** six *seven* eight
**nine** ten *eleven* twelve

You can build more complex tables, for example automatically entering mathematical mode with a predefined formula element within a column:

```
\halign{\it #\quad & $\sqrt{#}$ \cr
    minimum at & \pi    \cr
    maximum at & \pi+1 \cr}
```

gives

| | |
|---|---|
| *minimum at* | $\sqrt{\pi}$ |
| *maximum at* | $\sqrt{\pi+1}$ |

Sometimes a template line is not correct for all elements, because some rows have to be printed differently from other rows. \omit helps in this situation: if it is inserted at the start of a column element, the template is suppressed just for this case. The element is handled as if the template consisted of just a simple "#" sign. The last line of the following example demonstrates this:

```
\halign{\it #\quad & $#$ \cr
    minimum at & \sqrt{\pi}    \cr
    maximum at & \sqrt{\pi+1} \cr}
  incontinuity & \omit \it not found \cr} % The template
%                  ^^^^^                     element is ignored !
```

| | |
|---|---|
| *minimum at* | $\sqrt{\pi}$ |
| *maximum at* | $\sqrt{\pi+1}$ |
| *incontinuity* | *not found* |

## 6.4 Automatic Table Alignment: Column Alignment

The typical modifications that are made in a table are the following:

| | |
|---|---|
| alignment: | flush left, flush right, centered |
| font choice: | \bf, \it, \sl ... |
| column spacing: | left side, right side |
| insertion of constant text parts | |

Alignment and column spacing are the most difficult part.

Often columns of numbers have to be aligned at the decimal sign. From TEX's point of view this means that a left column has to be set flush right and a right column added flush left. The decimal sign "." may be integrated into the template line of the \halign command. In place of the decimal sign the input should contain an "&" symbol. The following example uses the "$" command in the template to force mathematical mode. This gives a mathematical "−" instead of a hyphen "-".
The input

```
$$\vbox{\halign{ #\quad &\hfill#.&#\hfill\cr
        $\sin    15^\circ$     &  $0$&&259 \cr
        $\sin    30^\circ$     &  $0$&&5    \cr
        $\sin    45^\circ$     &  $0$&&707 \cr
        $\sin {-15}^\circ$     &  $-0$&&259 \cr
        $\sin {-30}^\circ$     &  $-0$&&5    \cr}}$$
```

generates

| | |
|---|---|
| $\sin 15°$ | 0.259 |
| $\sin 30°$ | 0.5 |
| $\sin 45°$ | 0.707 |
| $\sin -15°$ | $-0.259$ |
| $\sin -30°$ | $-0.5$ |

When nearly all constant text is completely integrated into the template line (the digit "0" of the second column is still common to all rows), the input looks like

```
$$\vbox{\halign{ $\sin{#}^\circ$\quad &\hfill$#.$&$#$\hfill\cr
      15        &  0&259 \cr
      30        &  0&5    \cr
      45        &  0&707 \cr
     -15        & -0&259 \cr
     -30        & -0&5    \cr}}$$
```

## 6.5 Automatic Table Alignment: Column Spacing

To get a table with a given width, space has to be inserted between columns. TeX governs the skip between table columns by its internal register \tabskip. A table of four columns gets space at 5 positions:

(A) [          ] (1) [          ] (2) [          ] (3) [          ] ($\Omega$)

(A) gives the space skip before the first column and ($\Omega$) after the last column. In

```
    (Λ) \halign{..#..(1)&..#..(2)&..#..(3)&..#..(Ω)\cr
```

you see the positions where TeX references the current value of \tabskip. In particular, any \tabskip before the first column is generated by the value of \tabskip *before* the \halign command. The skip after the last column is determined by the current value of \tabskip at "\cr". Skip between columns is generated with respect to \tabskip at "&" positions.

The following examples demonstrate the use of \tabskip:

```
$$\vbox{\halign{#\hfil&#&#\hfil\cr  % 3 columns
         \it Name      & \it Location & \it Phone number \cr
Gorbatchev, Michail    & Moscow       & +7--095--2959051 \cr
Bush, George           & Washington   & +1--202--456111414 \cr
Elizabeth II.          & London       & +441--9304832 \cr
John Paul II.          & Vatican      & +396--6982 \cr
Dr. Vranitzky, Franz   & Vienna       & +43--222--6615 \cr
Mitterand, Francois    & Paris        & +331--26151000 \cr
Dr. Kohl, Helmut       & Bonn         & +49--228--561 \cr
Schwarz, Norbert       & Bochum       & +49--234--700--3940 \cr}}$$
```

This input generates the following table. Space between columns is determined by the blanks of the input between column data and tabbing character "&".

| Name | Location | Phone number |
|------|----------|--------------|
| Gorbatchev, Michail | Moscow | +7-095-2959051 |
| Bush, George | Washington | +1-202-456111414 |
| Elizabeth II. | London | +441-9304832 |
| John Paul II. | Vatican | +396-6982 |
| Dr. Vranitzky, Franz | Vienna | +43-222-6615 |
| Mitterand, Francois | Paris | +331-26151000 |
| Dr. Kohl, Helmut | Bonn | +49-228-561 |
| Schwarz, Norbert | Bochum | +49-234-700-3940 |

*Phone numbers (or persons) may have changed.*

This space (blanks) is considered when the column width is calculated. Blanks in the template line have the same effect. The preceding table is generated with \tabskip=0pt.

The following variant uses "\tabskip=15pt" ($\approx 5\,\mathrm{mm}$). The input data changes to

```
$$\vbox{\tabskip=15pt \halign{#\hfil&##&#\hfil\cr % 3 columns
%        ^^^^^^^^^^^^^
```

This results in

| Name | Location | Phone number |
|------|----------|--------------|
| Gorbatchev, Michail | Moscow | +7-095-2959051 |
| Bush, George | Washington | +1-202-456111414 |
| Elizabeth II. | London | +441-9304832 |
| John Paul II. | Vatican | +396-6982 |
| Dr. Vranitzky, Franz | Vienna | +43-222-6615 |
| Mitterand, Francois | Paris | +331-26151000 |
| Dr. Kohl, Helmut | Bonn | +49-228-561 |
| Schwarz, Norbert | Bochum | +49-234-700-3940 |

The value of \tabskip may be changed between columns. If it is changed at a specific column, its old value persists until the next change in the table row. The value of \tabskip is *not* grouped by the columns of an \halign like font changes.

Often you will set the width of the whole table externally. This is done by specifying "\halign to <*dimension*>". Neglecting special cases the dynamic part of horizontal skip is generated by setting \tabskip to a suitable value. Some examples:

```
\halign to 200pt{...}
\halign to 15cm{...}
\halign to 0.8\hsize{...}
```

You can even explicitly determine the *additional* width for a table. This is the extra space that will be distributed before, between, and after the table columns. Example:

```
\halign spread 4cm{..}
```

In this case, \tabskip must define the dynamic part of horizontal white space by its "plus" and "minus" parts.

The following example uses \tabskip=15pt plus 400pt to separate the table columns. Before and after the table columns, no extra space in generated. The value of "400pt" is quite arbitrary and is used to stretch the table to the requested width of \hsize. It has to be large enough.

```
$$\vbox{\halign to \hsize{%
        \tabskip=15pt plus 400pt#\hfil&#&#\hfil\tabskip=0pt\cr
  %
```

gives

| Name | Location | Phone number |
|---|---|---|
| Gorbatchev, Michail | Moscow | +7–095–2959051 |
| Bush, George | Washington | +1–202–456111414 |
| Elizabeth II. | London | +441–9304832 |
| John Paul II. | Vatican | +396–6982 |
| Dr. Vranitzky, Franz | Vienna | +43–222–6615 |
| Mitterand, Francois | Paris | +331–26151000 |
| Dr. Kohl, Helmut | Bonn | +49–228–561 |
| Schwarz, Norbert | Bochum | +49–234–700–3940 |

By specifying

```
\tabskip=0pt plus 20cm
\halign to \hsize{\tabskip=15pt#\hfil&#&#\hfil
       \tabskip=0pt plus 20cm \cr
```

you can, with a simple declaration, use \tabskip to get a centered table within any given line. The input "\tabskip=0pt plus 20cm" causes the following table to be centered with respect to \hsize. The columns are separated by 15 pt extra skip. As the table has a width of \hsize, the previously used centering commands "$$\vbox ... $$" are not necessary here. The result shows a centered table, but there is no extra space above and below it:

| Name | Location | Phone number |
|---|---|---|
| Gorbatchev, Michail | Moscow | +7–095–2959051 |
| Bush, George | Washington | +1–202–456111414 |
| Elizabeth II. | London | +441–9304832 |
| John Paul II. | Vatican | +396–6982 |
| Dr. Vranitzky, Franz | Vienna | +43–222–6615 |
| Mitterand, Francois | Paris | +331–26151000 |
| Dr. Kohl, Helmut | Bonn | +49–228–561 |
| Schwarz, Norbert | Bochum | +49–234–700–3940 |

## 6.6 Automatic Table Alignment: Rules

Often tables are typeset with rules, which give a better impression of the table data.
Although setting in this way can get a bit complicated, horizontal rules are still quite
easy. "\noalign{\hrule}" generates a horizontal rule with the width of the whole
table. Vertical rules are typeset in small parts with elements from each line. The easiest
way to get these small rules to fit together is to put them into a separate column.

Example:

```
{\offinterlineskip        % because of vertical rules, see below
 \tabskip=0pt             % because of vertical rules
 \halign{ \strut          % because of descenders
         \vrule#&         % column 1  -- vertical rule
   \quad  \bf# \quad      % column 2  -- text in boldface
             \hfil    &   %              flush left
         \vrule#&         % column 3  -- vertical rule
         \quad            % column 4  -- text flush right
         \hfil # \quad &  %
         \vrule#&         % column 5  -- vertical rule
         \quad            % column 6  -- text flush right
         \hfil # \quad &  %
         \vrule#&         % column 7  -- vertical rule
         \quad            % column 8  -- text flush right
         \hfil # \quad &  %
         \vrule#          % column 9  -- vertical rule
         \cr              % END of template
\noalign{\hrule}          %--------------------------------
& sorting algorithm && 100 elements && 200 elements
                  && 500 elements &\cr
\noalign{\hrule}          %--------------------------------
& bubble sort     && 250 && 1000 && 10000 & \cr
& insertion sort  && 200 && 400  &&  3000 & \cr
& selection sort  && 110 && 260  &&  2000 & \cr
& shell sort      &&  70 && 250  &&   700 & \cr
& heap sort       &&  50 && 100  &&   300 & \cr
& quicksort       &&  40 && 60   &&   200 & \cr
  \noalign{\hrule}        %--------------------------------
} }                       % END
```

gives

| sorting algorithm | 100 elements | 200 elements | 500 elements |
|---|---|---|---|
| bubble sort | 250 | 1000 | 10000 |
| insertion sort | 200 | 400 | 3000 |
| selection sort | 110 | 260 | 2000 |
| shell sort | 70 | 250 | 700 |
| heap sort | 50 | 100 | 300 |
| quicksort | 40 | 60 | 200 |

Some TEX commands have been used without previous explanation:

\offinterlineskip resets the extra vertical space between lines to zero. This distance that TEX usually generates between lines would otherwise cause the rules not to touch.

\strut     As \offinterlineskip inhibits the mechanism to get lines with an equal (\baselineskip) distance, \strut is necessary to force lines to have equal height and depth. In practice, \strut gives an invisible rule (of width zero) that has the usual height of a line (8.5 pt) and the usual depth of a line (3.5 pt).

Otherwise each line would be generated with the height of its highest element and the depth of the element with the largest extension below the baseline. A line may contain only letters like "x", "u", and "n". Without letters with ascenders and descenders, this line will be too small.

\hidewidth    If this command is preceding a column element, the width of this element will not be considered in calculation of the column width. The information of the current table element may overprint its left and right neighbours that should be empty. In contrast to \multispan the contents of the template is used.

\omit     You can use \omit only at the first position of a table entry. \omit forces TEX to, for once, forget the information of the template line for this column. The template may be thought of as a simple "#" for this element. With this method you can omit standard text that is needed in most table rows, but not in a few special cases.

\multispan n    is similar to \omit. It is like an \omit for more than one column, with the additional effect that one table element is set across $n$ columns. The information will spread over several columns. The template information for all these $n$ columns will be ignored. As with \omit, if you want to, e.g., center information spanning several columns, you have to explicitly specify the "\hfil" command in suitable places.

&&     If a template element starts with a "&&", TEX will repeat the following template information as often as it is needed to get templates for additional columns. If all template elements of a table have to be the same, the template can look like "\halign ... {&& ... # ... \cr}".

There is a technical problem with tables containing rules, with respect to \noalign. Tables without rules may easily be enlarged, e.g., with "\noalign{\smallskip}" or something similar. This will give interrupted vertical rules if you are not very careful. There are two possible solutions.

The first method is to simply insert rows of the form " & & & \cr". This will generate an empty table row with just the rules in it (assuming no constant text is present in the template line). In case the generated skip is too big, you can skip back by something like "\noalign{\vskip -0.5 \baselineskip}" to get only half a line distance. The vertical rules overlap now, but that is not a problem: on the contrary sometimes it is an advantage, e.g., when an output driver does not fit rules exactly end to end.

The second method is based upon a \strut technique with an enlarged vertical rule. Plain TEX defines a normal line with a height of 8.5 pt and a depth of 3.5 pt. You can simulate a \smallskip before the current table row by inserting

```
\vrule height 11.5 pt width 0pt
```

Should the "\smallskip" effect be typeset after the current row

```
\vrule depth 6.5pt width 0pt
```

will help.

## Typical Errors

There are two typical errors in typesetting a table with rules:

| one  | two | three  | four   |   | one  | two | three  | four   |
|------|-----|--------|--------|---|------|-----|--------|--------|
| five | six | seven  | eight  |   | five | six | seven  | eight  |
| nine | ten | eleven | twelve |   | nine | ten | eleven | twelve |

1. The left table is not typeset with "\tabskip=0pt" at the beginning and the end of the template line. The table grows in width and gets skip on the left and right-hand sides. But the commands "\noalign{\hrule}" generate horizontal rules with the width of the complete table.
2. The right table lacks the \offinterlineskip and \strut commands. Therefore TEX generates vertical skip between the rows, which causes broken vertical rules. (The generated vertical skip is based on \baselineskip.

Here at last is an enhanced version of the last example:

| sorting algorithm | number of sorted elements | | |
|---|---|---|---|
| | 100 | 200 | 500 |
| bubble sort | 250 | 1000 | 10000 |
| insertion sort | 200 | 400 | 3000 |
| selection sort | 110 | 260 | 2000 |
| shell sort | 70 | 250 | 700 |
| heap sort ⎫ acceptable | 50 | 100 | 300 |
| quicksort ⎭ | 40 | 60 | 200 |

This table is typeset using some special features. The outer rules are thicker than the inner rules. A shadowing effect is achieved by generating very thick rules. The title is spread across several columns. The first column is typeset in italics automatically, the other columns are set flush right. The overlapping brace is generated by using \smash which generates an output with a logical height and depth of zero.
This example is generated by:

```
$$\offinterlineskip \tabskip=0pt      % centering, outer tabskip=0
 \vbox{                               % enter vertical mode !!!
                                      %-----------------------------
 \halign to 0.8\hsize                 % table width is 80 %
                                      %     of a line
   {\strut                            % equalize line heights
    \vrule width 0.8pt\quad#          % col. 1: thick line, allow
    \tabskip= 0pt plus 100pt          %         skip between columns
 & \it#  \quad \hfil                  % col. 2: italic, flush left
 & \vrule##&                          % col. 3: line
 & \quad \hfil # \quad                % col. 4: flush right
 & \vrule#                            % col. 5: line
 & \quad \hfil # \quad                % col. 6: flush right
 & \vrule#                            % col. 7: line
 & \quad \hfil # \quad  \tabskip=0pt  % col. 8: flush right
 & \vrule width 6.0pt#                % col. 9: extra thick line
   \cr                                % END OF TEMPLATE %%%%%%%%
                                      %-----------------------------
 \multispan9\leaders\hrule            % shorted thick horizontal line
   height0.8pt\hfill\hskip5.2pt\cr    %    (\leaders, see 6.7)
                                      %-----------------------------
 & \bf sorting algorithm              % title
       \vrule height 11.5pt           %    enlarged height
             width 0pt                %    (by an invisible rule)
       &&\multispan 5 \hfill          %    multispan 5
       number of sorted elements      %    => 5 columns
             \hfill &                  %       (centered)
     \omit \vrule width0.8pt          % indented rule block
     \vrule width 5.2pt height        %    to get shadowing effect
       7.5pt depth 3.5pt \cr          %
                                      %-----------------------------
    &&&      100 &\omit& 200          % 2.title row
             &\omit&500 & \cr         %    \omit => without rules
                                      %-----------------------------
 \noalign{\hrule\hrule}               % 2 x horizontal rule (thick)
                                      %-----------------------------
 & bubble sort     && 250 && 1000 && 10000 & \cr      %
 & insertion sort  && 200 && 400  && 3000  & \cr      %
 & selection sort  && 110 && 260  && 2000  & \cr      %
 & shell sort      && 70  && 250  && 700   & \cr      %
 & heap sort \smash{$\left.\vrule height 17pt depth 9pt   % that is
                 width 0pt\right\}$} acceptable      % a brace
             && 50  && 100  && 300   & \cr            %
 & quicksort       && 40  && 60   && 200   & \cr      %
                                      %-----------------------------
 \noalign{\hrule height 0.8pt}        % thick horizontal rule
 \multispan9\hskip 4pt                % generate indented thick rule
   \leaders\hrule height3.2pt         %    (\leaders, see 6.7)
                 \hfill\cr            %
}}$$                                  % end of \halign, vbox, math.
```

## 6.7 Auxiliary Commands for Table Generation

*column rules*

Some further commands provide still more features for the design of pleasing tables. They can be used for fine-structuring the information in the table. The first group consists of commands to fill one column (or some consecutive columns) with a pattern:

| | | | |
|---|---|---|---|
| \hrulefill | ──────── | \dotfill | ············ |
| \downbracefill | ⏝ | \leftarrowfill | ←──────── |
| \upbracefill | ⏜ | \rightarrowfill | ────────→ |

This is demonstrated by an example with \dotfill. The column is filled with dots up to its width, determined by its largest element.

```
$$\vbox{\tabskip=40pt   \halign{#\dotfill\quad&(#\unskip) \cr
        Use                        &  13    \cr
        Ordinary Text              &  21    \cr
        Mathematical Typesetting & 61    \cr}}$$
```

gives the following output. There is a little trick in the template line, which is worth mentioning. "\unskip" removes the skip otherwise generated by the blanks between the numbers and the following \cr. Without \unskip you would get "(13 )".

$$
\begin{array}{ll}
\text{Use} \dotfill & (13) \\
\text{Ordinary Text} \dotfill & (21) \\
\text{Mathematical Typesetting} & (61)
\end{array}
$$

The command \hrulefill, defined by "\def\hrulefill{\leaders\hrule\hfill}" generates a rule of predefined width. A new command to generate thicker rules may be defined by

```
\def\thickhrulefill{\leaders\hrule height 0.8pt\hfill}
```

The command \leaders repeats the following element as often as determined by the next element but one. If that is a dynamic skip, the repetition is governed by the surrounding box or element size.

A quite complex example

```
$$\vbox{\offinterlineskip  \tabskip=0pt
        \halign{\vrule\vrule\strut\quad $#^\circ$ \quad &
                \vrule#&
                \quad\hfill$#,$&
                #\hfill\quad\vrule\vrule\cr
        \noalign{\hrule\hrule}
        \sin{-15} && -0&259 \cr
        \omit\vrule\vrule&&\multispan2\dotfill\vrule\vrule \cr
        \sin{0}   && 0&0    \cr
        \omit\vrule&&\multispan2\hrulefill \cr
        \cos{0}   && 1&0    \cr
        \omit\vrule\vrule&&\multispan2\dotfill\vrule\vrule \cr
        \cos{15}  && 0&966 \cr
        \noalign{\hrule\hrule}}}$$
```

gives

| $\sin -15°$ | $-0{,}259$ |
|---|---|
| $\sin 0°$ | $0{,}0$ |
| $\cos 0°$ | $1{,}0$ |
| $\cos 15°$ | $0{,}966$ |

By duplicating the \hrule and vrule commands, thick rules are built. The same effect can be produced by

```
\vrule width 0.8pt
\hrule height 0.8pt
```

This is based upon the fact that 0.4 pt is the standard width of TEX's rules.

*dynamic repeating template lines*

If you put a "&&" into a template line in place of a simple "&", TEX will repeat the template information as often as needed. In

```
\halign{#&&#\cr
%         ^ ^
```

the element "&#" will be repeated indefinitely. In

```
\halign{#&&\quad\hfill#&#\quad\cr
```

the periodic element consists of "&\quad\hfill#&#\quad", which is just the description of two columns. If a template starts with a "&" like "\halign{& ...}", the whole template will be repeated.

The following example demonstrates that this feature is sometimes quite useful:

```
$$\vbox{\halign{&\hfill#\unskip\hfill\quad\cr
    $ x = $ &  1 &  2 &  3 & 4 &  5  & 6   & \dots \cr
$\Gamma(x)=$ &  1 &  2 &  6 & 24 & 120 & 720 & \dots \cr}}$$
```

yields

$$
\begin{array}{rccccccc}
x = & 1 & 2 & 3 & 4 & 5 & 6 & \ldots \\
\Gamma(x) = & 1 & 2 & 6 & 24 & 120 & 720 & \ldots
\end{array}
$$

*extending the width of the table*

By \halign spread <*dimension*> {...} the whole table will be stretched by the value of dimension. The amount of stretch will be divided according to the actual values of \tabskip. Note: the simultaneous use of "spread" and "rules" within the same table may be complicated.

*spanning columns*

If a tabbing command "&" is substituted by the command \span, the left and right element are treated as *one* element, including the value of \tabskip for the space

between these two columns. In contrast to \multispan template information is used
and *not* omitted. This is demonstrated below:

```
$$\vbox{\tabskip=15pt plus 200pt
        \halign spread 4cm{\hfill#&##&\hfill#\cr
        % element 1 flush right
        % element 2 normal (left)
        % element 3 flush right
      left      &    middle  &    right   \cr
      1000      &      2000  &    3000    \cr
      100   \span     200    &     300    \cr
       10      &       20 \span   30      \cr
        1   \span       2 \span    3    \cr}}$$
```

gives

| left | middle | right |
|------|--------|-------|
| 1000 | 2000 | 3000 |
|  | 100 200 | 300 |
| 10 | 20 | 30 |
|  | 1 2 | 3 |

In this case, elements are contracted in the last three rows:

| 1: | left | middle | right |
|----|------|--------|-------|
| 2: |  |  |  |
| 3: |  |  |  |
| 4: |  |  |  |
| 5: |  |  |  |

```
\hfill 100 200            % line 3   element: 1 + 2
    20 \hfill 30          % line 4   element:     2 + 3
\hfill 1 2 \hfill 3       % line 5   element: 1 + 2 + 3
```

This means that for the third row the input is set flush right, separated by a space in
the first two columns.

In line 4 the second and third columns are joined by \span. This generates a
combined element "20 \hfill 30", which forces "20" to be flush left and "30" to be
flush right.

The last line is a combination of the material of all three columns: "\hfill 1
2 \hfill 3". This centers "1 2" within the rest of the columns not used by the "3"
typeset on the right.

If you use \span in the template, it will have a different effect: a following macro
command will be expanded while defining the template and not delayed until generation
of each table row. This allows you to predefine template elements by macros.

# 7 Definition of New Commands — Macros

## 7.1 Simple Macros

You can make your input a lot easier by using abbreviations for parts of text that occur repeatedly. This is done by definition of a *macro*. If you want to typeset the vector $(x_1, \ldots, x_n)$ frequently, it will be tedious to always type `$(x_1,\ldots,x_n)$`. TEX's `\def` command will help:

```
\def\XV{(x_1,\ldots,x_n)}
```

turns the new command "`\XV`" into an abbreviation for the long input "`$(x_1, \ldots,x_n)$`". The savings in typing are demonstrated by the formula:

$$\sum_{(x_1,\ldots,x_n)\neq 0} (f(x_1,\ldots,x_n) + g(x_1,\ldots,x_n))$$

To get this, you need the input

```
\def\XV{(x_1,\ldots,x_n)}
$$\sum_{\XV\ne0}\bigl(f\XV+g\XV\bigr)$$
```

whereas the direct input — without macro use — would have been

```
$$\sum_{(x_1,\ldots,x_n)\ne0}
    \bigl(f(x_1,\ldots,x_n)+g(x_1,\ldots,x_n)\bigr)$$
```

Whenever TEX finds the command `\XV` in the input data, it will substitute it with "`(x_1,\ldots,x_n)`". The result is exactly the same.

> *Very important: the braces* — "`{`" *and* "`}`" — *which appear in the definition of the macro, will not be reinserted into the text. They are only needed to delimit the definition.*

There is an important difference between the two definitions

```
\def\eg{\bf for example}
\def\EG{{\bf for example}}
```

Both macros will generate the output "**for example**", but the first one will not reset
the font to the previously selected font, so the following text will be typeset in boldface,
too. If you look closely, you will see that `\eg`, when called, will expand to "`\bf for`
`example`", while `\EG` will expand to "`{\bf for example}`". The additional pair of
braces is very important.

> *Remember: when in doubt, use an additional pair of braces to group
> the input. A superfluous pair of braces rarely has an adverse effect..*

## 7.2 Macros with Parameters

The most frequently used macros are macros with parameters. If you want to develop
a universal macro for $x,y,z$-vectors, you can input

```
\def\vector#1{(#1_1,\ldots,#1_n)}
```

The use of `$\vector y$` gives $(y_1, \ldots, y_n)$
and `$\vector \lambda$` results in $(\lambda_1, \ldots, \lambda_n)$.

Macros may have up to 9 parameters. They must be numbered consecutively and
accessed as #1, #2, #3 ... #9. TEX has to decide how much of the following text will
be represented by a parameter. If a macro is defined without special text separating
the parameters — which is the normal way — TEX will associate the next *token* with
a parameter. This may be the command for another macro call. In the preceding
example the call "`\vector\lambda`" contains the additional macro name "`\lambda`" in
the parameter position. A macro

```
\def\test#1#2#3{#1#1#2#2#3#3}
```

which is used in "`\test abcde`" within input data will have these parameters:

| | | |
|---:|:---:|:---|
| #1 | ⟵ | a |
| #2 | ⟵ | b |
| #3 | ⟵ | c |

The macro call and the following text correspond to an input of "aabbccde". The
symbols "de" are not used by the macro, but are processed as simple input by TEX.

If we define an additional macro

```
\def\abc{Alphabet}
```

which is just an abbreviation, the combined use

```
\test\abc abc
```

will make the following parameter association:

| | | |
|---:|:---:|:---|
| #1 | ⟵ | \abc |
| #2 | ⟵ | a |
| #3 | ⟵ | b |

Later on the macro \abc will be expanded from the macro text

> \abc \abc aabb

via \abc ⟵ Alphabet to the final input

> AlphabetAlphabetaabbc

(The letter "c" is not a result of the macro expansion but the unused residue of the initial input \test\abc abc.)

If you want to associate more than a simple symbol or a simple command with a parameter, you have to use braces to group the input.
The text

> \test a{bcde}{fg}hij

associates the parameters in the following way:

$$
\begin{array}{ccc}
\#1 & \longleftarrow & a \\
\#2 & \longleftarrow & bcde \\
\#3 & \longleftarrow & fg
\end{array}
$$

The symbols "hij" are the following normal input and are not used by the macro \test. Notice that the grouping braces are *not* inserted into the parameter text, they are only used for delimiting the parameter text.

There is a simple way to separate the parameters by defining symbols (text) that separate them. In the definition

> \def\TEST #1 #2 #3 {#1#1#2#2#3#3}

each parameter is separated from the next one by a blank space. To get a result equivalent to the last example (generated by \test a{bcde}{fg}hij) the input is simply

> \TEST a bcde fg hij

The macro parameters are associated in the same way as in the last example. Any text can be used to separate parameters, not only spaces. By

> \def\restbold#1.{{\bf#1.}}

the following text up to the next "." will be substituted for "#1", but without the ".". The macro will print it in boldface. There is an important fact concerning groups: the separating text has to be put outside grouping braces to be recognized.
The use in

> \restbold A simple text {should ...} follow. But

will result in a substitution for the first parameter of

$$
\#1 \longleftarrow \text{A simple text should ... follow}
$$

The separating text (".") is not contained in the parameter information.
The following application is also possible:

> \def\mytest #1ABC#2.#3${...}

The first parameter will get all information up to the first occurence of "ABC", the second will consist of the following text up to the period ("."), and the last parameter will gather the text up to the next "$" sign.

## 7.3 Macros within Macros

Within the body of a macro you may define a new macro. Whether you can use this newly defined macro after evaluation of the outer macro depends on the grouping. A common use is to define auxiliary macros local to the outer macro.

If you define a macro within another macro you have to pay attention to the use of "#". Inner macro definitions need an additional preceding "#" to distinguish their parameter names from the parameter names of the outer macro.

```
\def\MyMatrix#1{{\def\vector##1{#1_##1,\ldots,#1_n}
              $$\pmatrix{
                \vector1\cr
                \vector2\cr
                \vector3\cr
                \vector4\cr}$$}}
```

This macro uses a submacro `\vector#1{...}`. A call of the outer macro "`\MyMatrix a`" gives

$$\begin{pmatrix} a_1,\ldots,a_n \\ a_2,\ldots,a_n \\ a_3,\ldots,a_n \\ a_4,\ldots,a_n \end{pmatrix}$$

and "`\MyMatrix{\sin\alpha}`" gives

$$\begin{pmatrix} \sin\alpha_1,\ldots,\sin\alpha_n \\ \sin\alpha_2,\ldots,\sin\alpha_n \\ \sin\alpha_3,\ldots,\sin\alpha_n \\ \sin\alpha_4,\ldots,\sin\alpha_n \end{pmatrix}$$

After TeX has finished its work on `\MyMatrix`, the definition of `\vector` is lost, as the macro opens and closes a group and makes its `\vector` macro local. By prefixing any definition with "`\global`" it will be retained after all surrounding groups are closed.

```
{{{{\global\def\ABC{abcdefghijklmnopqrstuvwxyz}}}}
```

`\ABC` is known to TeX after evaluation of the groups.
Similarly,

```
\def\initABC{{\global\def\ABC{ABCDEFGHIJKLMNOPQRSTUVWXYZ}}}
```

will make the macro `\ABC` known after the call `\initABC`.

If the *current* meaning of a macro must be saved, or a macro is to be renamed, the command `\let` will help. By

```
\let\INITABC=\initABC
\def\initABC{{\global\def\ABC{abcdefghijklmnopqrstuvwxyz}}}
```

you will get two commands. The renamed old version `\INITABC` and a new command `\initABC`. "`\let`" *copies* the current definition of a macro to another.

## 7.4 Macro Expansion

When TEX reads the commands of the definition part of a macro, it stores them within its program memory. If you define too many macros, TEX will give an error message. The commands are only stored, not interpreted. There is not even a test whether the commands mentioned actually exist. When the macro is used, the information stored in it is interpreted. As a consequence, all commands contained in the macro are used with their *current* meaning.

```
\def\title{\bigskip\centerline{\bf \titletext}\bigskip}
```

defines \title to generate something like a headline of a chapter. The current meaning of "titletext" will be referenced. Later on you can set "\def\titletext{Computer Architecture}" to redefine the meaning. This will be used in the application of \title. Notice that the meaning of \titletext also depends on grouping by "{" and "}". So you can locally redefine inner parts of foreign macros. This may sometimes cause problems when you unintentionally redefine standard macros of plain TEX. A good candidate to do this — as practice shows — is the command "\big". (People often use it to define a font as "\big", which will destroy "\bigl", "\bigm", and "\bigr", too.)

However, there is a variant of \def, the command \edef "expanded definition", which allows you to fix the meaning of a macro at definition time. All macros and commands used in the defining text are expanded immediately. As a consequence, there can be *no* undefined macro in the text.

```
\def\information{OLD}
\edef\etest{\information}
\def\test{\information}
\def\information{NEW}
```

Afterwards, calls will give the following results:

$$\begin{array}{rcl}
\text{\\information} & \longrightarrow & \text{NEW} \\
\text{\\test} & \longrightarrow & \text{NEW} \\
\text{\\etest} & \longrightarrow & \text{OLD}
\end{array}$$

Sometimes a macro definition will contain a single command that is to remain unexpanded (should be interpreted later). One good reason for this would be that the macro is not yet defined. The command "\noexpand" will help. It suppresses the interpretation/expansion of the following command. This is demonstrated by the slightly modified example:

```
\def\information{OLD}
\edef\etest{\information---\noexpand\information}
\def\information{NEW}
```

This will give

$$\begin{array}{rcl}
\text{\\information} & \longrightarrow & \text{NEW} \\
\text{\\etest} & \longrightarrow & \text{OLD—NEW}
\end{array}$$

Where the instruction "\noexpand" precedes a command, the expansion of the following command is suppressed. Only the command name will be stored in the macro definition, just as \def does.

\edef may be preceded by "\global" like \def. The effect will be the same, definition of a macro ignoring any surrounding groups. The two commands "\global\edef" and "\global\def"may be replaced by "\xdef" and "\gdef", respectively.

There are two further attributes a macro may receive:

\outer  If a macro definition is preceded by \outer, TEX will allow its use only at an outer level. This means any reference within other macros or within a box will cause an error message. A typical example is the command "\bye". There are good reasons for TEX not to stop in the middle of a box or a macro body. "\+" has the same attribute.

\long  TEX will normally not allow a macro parameter to cross paragraph limits and give an error message "runaway arguments". As the building of groups by "{" and "}" can often cause errors, this will keep TEX from interpreting the rest of a document as a parameter. But if you want to allow paragraphs to be used as parameters, you have to say "\long\def ...".

## 7.5 Conditions

Up to now, macro use has been an altogether static affair: every use of a macro generated the same result. But often desired different results are needed, depending on outer conditions. Headlines, e.g., should often consist of different text depending on page numbers, especially on whether they are even or odd. TEX has a lot of conditional commands, which all have the following syntax

$$\texttt{\textbackslash if}<condition><true\text{-}part>\texttt{\textbackslash else}<false\text{-}part>\texttt{\textbackslash fi}$$

If the condition holds, only the elements of the true part will be inserted into the input stream, otherwise the elements of the false part are processed (if present). Notice: the macros of the true part or false part will be expanded only if they belong to the selected part. There are the following possible conditions. The sequence "\if<condition>" is just one single TEX command. Two basic types have to be considered: comparisons (of sizes) and tests (of specific conditions).

### Comparisons of numbers and lengths

The following conditions test whether the left number or dimension is equal to, greater than or less than the right one.

| | |
|---|---|
| \ifnum $number_1$ = $number_2$ | \ifdim $dimension_1$ = $dimension_2$ |
| \ifnum $number_1$ > $number_2$ | \ifdim $dimension_1$ > $dimension_2$ |
| \ifnum $number_1$ < $number_2$ | \ifdim $dimension_1$ < $dimension_2$ |

Examples:

```
\ifnum\pageno=1        ... \else  ... \fi
\ifnum 17>\count0      ... \else  ... \fi
\ifdim\leftskip>\hsize ... \else  ... \fi
\ifdim\ht0>1cm         ... \else  ... \fi
```

This may be used in the following application, in which the footline (with the page number) should be suppressed for the first page:

```
\footline={\ifnum\pageno=1\hss\else\hss\folio\hss\fi}
```

### Tests

The second group of \if instructions consists of tests for specific conditions and comparisons (especially for the identity of objects). Some of these commands are rarely used.

| | |
|---|---|
| \ifodd | tests whether the following number is *odd*. |
| \if | tests whether the next two symbols are equal. For this test, following macros are expanded. |
| \ifcat | checks whether the category codes of the two following tokens agree. |
| \ifx | examines — without full expansion — if the next two commands will expand to the same sequence. This is very useful for checking whether two macros are defined identically. (See the example below.) |

To get different headlines for even and odd numbered pages, \ifodd will be used to determine the kind of the current page. The following example generates headlines with odd page numbers flush right and even page numbers flush left:

```
\footline={\rm\ifodd\pageno\hss\folio\else\folio\hss\fi}
```

Alternating headlines are generated by, e.g.,

```
\def\lefttitle{\it\hfill Author \hfill}
\def\righttitle{\it\hfill My Title \hfill}
\headline={\rm\ifodd\righttitle\else\lefttitle\fi}
```

Pages with odd page numbers will get a centered *"My Title"* as headline, other pages a centered *"Author"*.

A useful application is a test within a macro whether a specific parameter is empty, i.e., no information is given for it. This is done by comparison with an empty macro "\empty". (This definiotion of \empty is superfluous, plain TeX already contains it.) For the comparison, a new macro is defined — here \test, which can be compared with \empty.

```
\def\empty{}              % already exists in plain TeX
\def\myMacro#1#2#3
    {\def\test{#1}        % macro that contains #1
     \ifx\test\empty  ... % commands when #1 is unspecified
       \else          ... % commands when #1 is specified
     \fi}
```

A call as "\myMacro{}{ABC}{DEF}" builds "\def\test{}", which is identical to the test macro "\empty", but "\myMacro{one}{two}{three}" defines \test as \def\test{one}. The comparison by \ifx will fail and the else part will be used.

### Check of mode

The following \if instructions test if TEX is currently in a specific working mode, e.g., a macro can check whether it is called within a formula or within text.

\ifvmode                      tests for *vertical mode* (between paragraphs) or *internal vertical mode* (inside a \vbox).

\ifhmode                      tests for *horizontal mode* (within a paragraph) or *restricted horizontal mode* (inside an \hbox).

\ifmmode                      tests for *mathematical mode.*

\ifinner                      test for *internal vertical mode* or *restricted horizontal mode* inside a \vbox or \hbox.

Some examples: a new command "\stars" is to generate three stars like "⋆⋆⋆" independently of text or mathematical mode. The simple command "\star" is only allowed in formulae, so the following definition gives the intended result:

```
\def\stars{\ifmmode
          {\star}{\star}{\star}%
       \else
          ${\star}{\star}{\star}$%
       \fi}
```

The command \centerline (and rightline, \leftline) does not work correctly within paragraphs. A definition

```
\def\Centerline{\ifhmode
                \ifinner
                \else
                    \par
                \fi
             \fi
             \centerline}
```

helps. If \Centerline is called within a paragraph, the paragraph is finished before the centered text is built.

### Tests of box registers

Further \if tests are available in combination with box registers. (These registers are set by the command \setbox. The detailed description follows in Chapter 8.)

| | |
|---|---|
| \ifhbox | tests whether the box with the given number contains an \hbox. |
| \ifvbox | tests whether the box with the given number contains a \vbox. |
| \ifvoid | tests whether the given box is empty. |

This may be demonstrated by some examples. After

```
\setbox0=\hbox{To be or not to be}   % definition
\setbox1=\vbox{\hrule\vskip1cm\hrule} %
\setbox2=\hbox{}                      %
\box3                                 % output of box3
                                      % (empty afterwards)
```

the command \ifhbox1 gives "*false*". Summing up, the results are

| | $n = 0$ | $n = 1$ | $n = 2$ | $n = 3$ |
|---|---|---|---|---|
| \ifhbox $n$ | true | false | true | false |
| \ifvbox $n$ | false | true | false | false |
| \ifvoid $n$ | false | false | false | true |

## 7.6 Defining Your Own If Commands

Three TeX commands support the construction/definition of your own *if* commands, which are used like ordinary if instructions. The first two are \iftrue and \iffalse, they always give *true* and *false*, respectively. This seems a curious way to build a new condition at first sight, but the idea is to define a macro that expands either into \iftrue or into \iffalse. This is well-supported by the \newif command: after a declaration "\newif\ifdebug" three new commands (built by \newif) are available:

| | |
|---|---|
| \ifdebug | for interrogation |
| \debugtrue | defines \ifdebug to \iftrue, use of \ifdebug will select the true branch from now on. |
| \debugfalse | defines \ifdebug to \iffalse, use of \ifdebug will result in *false* from here. |

The generating command \newif presets the value of the new if command to *false*. In a quite devious manner it checks whether the following command really starts with the sequence "\if".

The commands generated by \newif are used in the same syntax "\if... ... \else ... \fi" or "\if... ... \fi" as the ordinary if statements. This gives the possibility of producing a well structured input that is readable (and understandable) later on.

## 7.7 Tricks with Macros for Advanced Users

> The following macros are intended for a sophisti-
> cated use of TeX only. This subsection may be omit-
> ted on first reading.

TeX's macro environment is very powerful; there are even more commands that determine when a command will be interpreted by changing the expansion sequence.

\afterassignment causes the following command not to be interpreted but to be
stored. Its interpretation is delayed until after the next assignment.
This may be demonstrated by a command which prints all vowels
of a word in a different typeface and underlines them.

```
\def\xyz{\bf\underbar}
\def\vowels#1{\dovowels#1\endlist}
\def\endlist{\endlist}
\def\dovowels{\afterassignment\dobf\let\next= }
\def\dobf{%
    \ifx\next\endlist\let\next\relax
    \else
        \if\next a{\xyz a}%
        \else\if\next e{\xyz e}%
            \else\if\next i{\xyz i}%
                \else\if\next o{\xyz o}%
                    \else\if\next u{\xyz u}%
                        \else\next
                        \fi
                    \fi
                \fi
            \fi
        \fi
        \let\next\dovowels
    \fi\next}
```

Example: \vowels{fundamental} gives "f<u>u</u>nd<u>a</u>m<u>e</u>nt<u>a</u>l".
The interpretation is a little bit complex. We need a *criterion* to
stop when the end of all letters is found. This is done by a macro
\def\endlist{\endlist}. (This macro should never be called in
text, as it would lead to an endless loop.) The command \ifx
checks whether \next and \endlist agree.
After \vowels{fundamental} the commands \dovowels funda-
mental\endlist are generated. \dovowels is the routine that
checks the next token (character or \endlist).
This is performed by storing the command \dobf, delayed until the next assignment in "\afterassignment\dobf", and doing
an assignment "\let\next=". The token "\next" gets the value
of "f" the first time, "u" the second time, up to "\endlist",
each time "\dovowels" is called. After the assignment, "\dobf"

is called automatically. Within "\dobf" the value of "\next" is tested for "a", "e", "i", "o", or "u" by a series of \if commands. At the start of \dobf a check for the end of the list (\endlist) is performed, in this case "\next" gets the value "\relax"(this is TEX's "continue" or "do nothing"), otherwise the macro \dovowels is assigned to \next. As \next is the very last statement of \dobf, dovowels is re-called if there is more to do, otherwise the reentering of \dovowels is skipped.

The second example shall demonstrate s t r e t c h i n g of words. There is the same problem as in the previous example: determining the end of the parameter information. A command "\stretchword{stretchtext}" should give s t r e t c h t e x t. To avoid complexity, accents (and other imbedded commands) are not allowed.

```
\def\stretchword#1{\stretchrest#1\endlist}
\def\endlist{\endlist}
\def\stretchrest{\afterassignment\stretchsymbol
                \let\next= }
\def\stretchsymbol{\ifx\next\endlist
                      \let\next\relax
                      \kern-0.25em
                   \else
                      \next \kern0.25em
                      \let\next\stretchrest
                   \fi
                   \next}
```

This demonstrates the same technique of loop construction. The steps are as follows:
(1) \stretchword{stretchtext}
(2) \stretchrest stretchtext \endlist
(3) \afterassignment\stretchsymbol
     \let\next=stretchtext\endlist
(4) "\stretchsymbol" is stored.
     Remaining input in input buffer:
     \let\next=stretchtext\endlist
(5) "\next=s"
(6) Stored commands are fetched back.
     Input buffer: \stretchsymbol tretchtext\endlist
(7) \stretchsymbol is executed.
     In the end, "\stretchrest" is called.
(8) Input buffer: \stretchrest tretchtext \endlist
     This is the same form as (3). The loop is closed.
A slight change to
\def\stretchword#1{\kern0.25em\stretchrest#1\endlist}
and the deletion of "\kern-0.25em" will give extra space before and after the text that is to be stretched.

\expandafter       changes the sequence TeX commands are *expanded* in. Expansion
                   means that the defining text for macros is inserted into the input
                   buffer. \expandafter causes the next command but one to be
                   expanded first. This will be demonstrated:

```
\def\nextbf#1{{\bf #1}}
\def\mytext{That is an example sentence!}
```

\nextbf prints the information of its parameter in bold typeface.
\mytext is only an abbreviation.

Example: \expandafter\nextbf\mytext
                gives

**T**hat is an example sentence!

but \nextbf\mytext
                gives
**That is an example sentence!**

\futurelet         this command inspects commands from the input buffer to see
                   what future input to expect. It is used in the syntactical form

\futurelet\\*next*\\*test*\\*future*

\\*next* gets the value of \\*future* by an implicit "\let\\*next*=\\*future*",
but \\*future* will stay in the input. Then \\*test* is called and can check
the contents of \\*next*, i.e. the contents of \\*future* without reading
\\*future*.

This means

\futurelet\\*next*\\*test*\\*future*

acts like

\let\\*next*\\*future*\\*test*\\*future*

Note: by the assignment to "\next", the *contents* of "\future"
e.g., the definition if it is a macro, are copied.

An application of "\futurelet" is demonstrated by a macro with
optional paramaters: The command \myop will have "parameters"
which are preceded by "_" or "^" as usual in mathematical mode.
But "_" and "^" may be absent:

"\myop", "\myop_{..}", "\myop^{..}", and "\myop_{..}^{..}",

or "\myop^{..}_{..}" are valid calls.

```
\def\myop{\def\myopUP{\infty}
          \def\myopDOWN{\infty}
          \futurelet\next\myopGO}
\let\sb=_  % standard in plain TeX
\let\sp=^  %
\def\myopGO{\ifx\next\sb\let\next\doDOWN
           \else
               \ifx\next\sp\let\next\doUP
               \else\let\next\UPandDOWN
               \fi
          \fi\next}
\def\doDOWN_#1{\def\myopDOWN{#1}\futurelet\next\myopGO}
\def\doUP^#1{\def\myopUP{#1}\futurelet\next\myopGO}
\def\UPandDOWN{%
      {\vphantom{\big\Vert}%
        _{\myopDOWN}\big\Vert
        ^{\myopUP}}}
```

$$ \myop $$                 *gives*    $\infty\big\Vert^{\infty}_{\infty}$

$$ \myop_\alpha $$          *gives*    $\alpha\big\Vert^{\infty}$

$$ \myop^\beta $$           *gives*    $\infty\big\Vert^{\beta}$

$$ \myop_{aa}^{bb} $$       *gives*    $aa\big\Vert^{bb}$

## A Qualifier for Optional Macro Parameters

The following complex example demonstrates TeX's capabilities to change — from the user's point of view — the syntactical form of the standard definition commands.

A command \optional will be constructed that may precede a \def instruction and change its interpretation. Its use is similar to \long or \global which may also be used in combination with the \def command.*
The resulting form of use for a new command "\test" looks like

   \optional\def\test[*preset value*]#2...{...}

The result is a command \test that can be used as if defined by

   \def\test[#1]#2...{...}

but the information for the first parameter is predefined. A possible application is a variant of \footnote in

   \optional\def\FootNote[$^\ast$]{\footnote{#1}}

that generates a new command \FootNote to be used as \FootNote{footnote text} or, e.g., \FootNote[$^1$]{footnote text}. In the first use, the predefined label

---

* The necessary macros are shown on the following two pages.

━━━━━━━━━━━━━━━━━━━━━━━━━━━━━  macros  ━━━━━━━━━━━━━━━━━━━━━━

- ```
  \catcode`\@=11                        % for hiding some commands
  \def\optional#1#2[#3]{%
     \escapechar=-1
  ```

- ```
     \if\def#1%
  ```

- ```
        \edef#2{\futurelet\noexpand\next
        \csname\string#2@@body\endcsname}%
  ```

- ```
        \expandafter\edef\csname\string#2@@body\endcsname{%
           \noexpand\if[\noexpand\next
              \def\noexpand\next
                 {\csname\string#2@@do\endcsname}%
           \noexpand\else
              \def\noexpand\next{%
                 \expandafter\noexpand
                    \csname\string#2@@do\endcsname
                       [\expandafter\noexpand
                          \csname\string#2@@default\endcsname]}%
           \noexpand\fi
           \noexpand\next}%
  ```

- ```
        \expandafter\noexpand\expandafter
              \def\csname\string#2@@default\endcsname{#3}%
  ```

- ```
        \edef\optional@continue{\expandafter\noexpand
           \expandafter\def\csname\string#2@@do\endcsname[####1]}%
  ```

- ```
        \escapechar="5C\relax
  ```

- ```
        \let\next=\optional@continue
  ```

- ```
     \else
        \escapechar="5C
        \errmessage{invalid use of \string\optional,
                       missing \string\def}%
        \let\next=\relax
  ```

- ```
     \fi
     \next}%
  \catcode`\@=12
  ```

━━━━━━━━━━━━━━━━━━ explanations ━━━━━━━━━━━━━━━━━━

- By this coding trick the character "@" is available as an ordinary letter. The first parameter of \optional will be "\def", the second contains the name of the new macro, e.g., "\test", and lastly, for "#3" the preset value is gathered.

- First we check if \optional is followed by the required "\def".

- Then the new command "\test" — the user interface — is defined that accepts the next token via \futurelet. It starts the "body" routine to check if it is equal to "[". It looks like \edef\test{\futurelet\next\test@@body}

- The testing routine \test@@body will be of the form
  ```
  \def\test@@body{\if[\next
                      \def\next{\test@@do}
                  \else
                      \def\next{\test@@do[\test@@default]}
                  \fi
                  \next}
  ```
  This is done by the \edef construction. Nearly every command has to be preceded by \noexpand to inhibit expansion with the exception of \csname\string...\endcsname sequences. These are needed to get the combined names.

- The command \test@@default with the preset value for "#1" must be defined.

- The command \test@@do that contains the original macro definition part of \test will be created: as these data are still in the input buffer the commands \def\test@@do[#1] are stored within a new command \optional@continue that will be used as the last command of \optional and gathers the macro definition.

- The value of \escapechar is restored.

- The last command to be generated by \optional is preset.

- These commands are used if a command other than \def follows \optional. An error message is generated.

- Finishing the macro \optional and restoring \catcode of "@".

"$\ast$" is used; in the second call the default is overwritten by the specified value of "$1$". The example definition

```
\optional\def\test[ABCD]#2{First: #1, second: #2.}
```

gives for

$\test{1234}$ the parameter values $\begin{array}{rcl} \texttt{\#1} & \longleftarrow & \text{ABCD} \\ \texttt{\#2} & \longleftarrow & 1234 \end{array}$

and the result "First: ABCD, second: 1234"

$\test[1]{2}$ the value $\begin{array}{rcl} \texttt{\#1} & \longleftarrow & 1 \\ \texttt{\#2} & \longleftarrow & 2 \end{array}$

and the result "First: 1, second: 2"

The construction of \optional is quite complicated. It is done in several steps. Depending on the name of the macro that should be defined by \optional\def some further hidden macros are generated. This is carried out by the same technique plain TeX uses, redefinition of the category code of "@". Assuming the new macro should be called "\test" the following internal macros that are dependent on the name "\test" are defined:

\test@@default This internal newly defined macro contains the information of the preset value of the first parameter.

\test@@body    After a use of \test it checks if a "[" symbol follows to indicate overriding the default. If this happens it issues a \test@@do command; otherwise a command sequence
```
\test@@do[\test@default]
```
is generated.

\test@@do      is equivalent to a definition of
```
\def\test[#1]#2{First: #1, second: #2.}
```
It contains the defining commands of the target macro \test. It is called by \test@@body.

Some commands need further explanation:

\string        gives the name of the following command as a simple string. It may be used to print TeX commands, e.g., \string\bigskip prints
                           "bigskip
               with preceding double quotes for the escape character. This is just the character for the \escapechar code in the roman font. If you use the correct font (typewriter) you will even get a backslash, e.g., \tt\string\bigskip gives
                           \bigskip.

\escapechar    The internal register \escapechar sets the code of the character that represents the escape character, usually the backslash, while printing. If it is set to −1, the printout of the escape character is suppressed.

\csname
\endcsname     \csname and \endcsname surround any text — without escape characters — and build a new TeX command that will be preceded by

an inserted escape (backslash). By this method any character can be used for a T<sub>E</sub>X command.

\errmessage   gives the parameter text as an error message to the user. If error stop mode is active the user is asked for additional input.

### Loops

T<sub>E</sub>X offers a method to construct loops similar to those of programming languages. Its use has to follow the syntactical form

```
\loop $\alpha$ \if... $\beta$ \repeat
```

For $\alpha$ and $\beta$ any instructions are possible. They don't even need to be present. For "\if..." any of the preceding \if instructions may be inserted.

First the instructions for $\alpha$ are interpreted, then the if clause is checked. If the result is false, all instructions up to \repeat are skipped and otherwise the instructions for $\beta$ are done. When \repeat is read the loop restarts with the instructions for $\alpha$.

In the following example this is demonstrated:

```
\def\TRIANGLE#1{{\def\bull{}%
            \count1=0
            \loop
                \edef\bull{$\bullet$\bull}
            \ifnum\count1<#1
                \advance\count1 by 1
                \centerline{\bull}
                \vskip-7.7pt
            \repeat
            \vskip 7.7pt\relax}}
```

The call \TRIANGLE{10} gives the following diagram:

Another example demonstrates the possibility to number the lines of a paragraph. Some commands, e.g., \vsplit, are described in detail in the following chapter. So further explanations are omitted.

```
\long\def\NumberParagraph#1{%
   {\setbox1=\vbox{\advance\hsize by -20pt#1}%
    \vfuzz=10pt                    % suppress overfull warnings
    \splittopskip=0pt              % no skip at top of box 1
    \count1=0                      % initialize line count
    \par\noindent                  % start a new paragraph
    \def\rebox{%
       \advance\count1 by 1\relax
       \hbox to 20pt{\strut\hfil\number\count1\hfil}%
       \nobreak
       \setbox2=\vsplit 1 to 6.1pt
       \vbox{\unvbox2\unskip}%
       \hskip 0pt plus 0pt\relax}%
    \loop
       \rebox                      % do one line
       \ifdim \ht1>0pt             % test if more lines
    \repeat
    \par}}
```

This is demonstrated with some lines of text.

```
\NumberParagraph{\noindent
   In the sense in which architecture is an art,
   typography is an art. That is, both come under
   the head of ''making or doing intentionally with
   skill.'' Every work of architecture, every work of
   typography, depends for its success upon the clear
   conveyance of intentions, in words and otherwise,
   from one human mind to others: from the man who
   is supposed to know how the finished thing should
   look and function.   \hfill Beatrice Warde}
```

This gives

1  In the sense in which architecture is an art, typography is an art. That is, both
2  come under the head of "making or doing intentionally with skill." Every work
3  of architecture, every work of typography, depends for its success upon the clear
4  conveyance of intentions, in words and otherwise, from one human mind to others:
5  from the man who is supposed to know how the finished thing should look and
6  function.                                                      Beatrice Warde

This is done by gathering the information of the whole paragraph in box register
1. The line breaking is done with \hsize reduced by 20 pt, i.e. the standard value
of \parindent. A loop splits lines one by one from box register 1, building a new
paragraph in which every line is preceded by the current line number. This works quite
well if there is no mathematical display style formula or \vadjust inserted.

This example anticipates some applications that are possible after a discussion of
how TeX works with boxes. That is the first topic of our next chapter.

# 8 How TEX Works

## 8.1 Boxes

The units of work in TEX's operation are rectangular "boxes". Starting with the atom of all things, the letter, it is considered a box with a specific height and width and also a depth. The "depth" refers to the size of descenders, the parts of some letters, e.g., "g, j, y", that extend below the baseline. This may be compared to the metal letters that have been used for typesetting since Gutenberg. A line of text has been adjusted vertically along the baseline. The sentence "This is a typical text line." is treated by TEX as a sequence of individual elements:

This is a typical text line.

The shape of a letter is unknown to TEX. Only the dimensions of the bounding box give TEX the numbers it can work on. (If a typeface consists of slanted characters, TEX will also know the slant factor.) The example sentence is interpreted as:

Neglecting hyphenation, the input of a paragraph then consists of a series of words. In graphical representation:

TEX combines the individual elements into larger ones, step by step until whole pages are generated. To get a good layout, TEX will *move* elements, e.g., to justify lines within paragraphs the space between words is expanded or compressed. This results in a horizontal movement of words.

## 8.2 TEX's Internal Modes

The current state of TEX's work can be classified as follows. Each state (or mode) determines how elements will be arranged.

- **vertical mode** and **internal vertical mode**
  Elements (boxes) are put one below the other. The elements will be moved up and down for adjustments if dynamic skip is present, e.g., "\vfill".

The *internal vertical mode* is entered by a \vbox command. All information *in* the \vbox is arranged vertically. The collected information is not broken into pages. Some commands like "\end" or "\eject" are not allowed in internal vertical mode, i.e., in a \vbox.

The normal *vertical mode* describes the state of operations when TₑX gathers information, e.g., the lines of a paragraph, \hrule or \medskip . . . , that is broken into pages. This is the initial mode when the TₑX program starts and requests input.

- **horizontal mode**

  In horizontal mode TₑX generates paragraphs. The elements of the paragraph text are gathered and broken into paragraph lines. The lines are adjusted to the value of \hsize. If this is not possible, an error message is given. Horizontal mode is *entered* by the input of ordinary text or other "horizontal material", if your previous current mode was one of the vertical modes.

  Horizontal material consists of \noindent, \hskip, \indent, \vrule, \quad, or \hfill, but especially of normal text including spaces. To suppress horizontal mode spaces within macros, "%" signs are often used to comment out the line ends of the input data.

- **restricted horizontal mode**

  In this mode the elements are put side by side without line breaking. This mode is achieved by \hbox{...}. Between the braces, elements are horizontally arranged.

You can easily change from one mode to another. By encapsulating text in \vbox and \hbox commands modes are changed. After a box is closed the outer mode is active again.

## 8.3 Box Manœuvres

The commands \vbox and \hbox determine how information is arranged *in* the box. A common mistake is to assume that a \vbox as a whole would be set below the preceding information and an \hbox beside it. Instead, this is determined by the outer mode.

\hbox and \vbox automatically open and, at the end, close a new group. All local changes within the box are lost when the box is completed. After a box is finished, TₑX uses the box as *one* piece, an individual element, just a *box*. How this box is used depends on the outer mode.

If several boxes are horizontally arranged the boxes are vertically aligned at the baselines of the boxes. If such a box is built by a \vbox command, the baseline of the last contained box is used as the baseline of the \vbox. After building a \vbox or \hbox such a box is treated as a single element, a box. The following example demonstrates several modes: starting from horizontal mode, building paragraphs, in \par It follows... some information is typeset inside a \vbox.

```
\par A v-box follows
    \vbox{\hbox{enclosed a first h-box}%
        \hbox{in addition, a second h-box}}
    and further text. \par
```

This gives the output:

enclosed a first h-box
A v-box follows in addition, a second h-box and further text.

or, as "box description":

Besides \vbox, there is a variant \vtop. The difference to \vbox is the chosen baseline. \vtop takes the baseline of the first contained box element as the baseline of the resulting box. The last example with \vtop looks like:

```
\par A v-box follows
     \vtop{\hbox{enclosed a first h-box}%
     \hbox{in addition, a second h-box}}and further text. \par
```

This gives

A v-box follows enclosed a first h-box     and further text.
         in addition, a second h-box

The following example demonstrates a mode switch from the internal vertical mode to *horizontal mode*. The switch is caused by \noindent.
The new setting \hsize=0.5\hsize gives paragraphs lines of half the line length.

```
\par It follows a v-box
     \vbox{\hsize=0.50\hsize
          \noindent
          This is a typical text line.
          This is a typical text line.
          This is a typical text line.}
          and further text.\par
```

gives

          This is a typical text line. This is a typical
It follows a v-box text line. This is a typical text line.      and further text.

In the previous examples, boxes have been vertically adjusted to the baseline of the first or last box. It is even possible to center a box by \vcenter. This is only allowed in *mathematical mode*. But this gives no problem, as is demonstrated by:

```
\par A v-box follows
     $\vcenter{\vbox{\hbox{enclosed a first h-box}%
          \hbox{in addition, a second h-box}}}$ and further text.
```

which gives

              enclosed a first h-box
A v-box follows               and further text.
              in addition, a second h-box

## 8.4 Box Registers

In practice, box information is often collected and its use is delayed until the desired position is reached. The TEX program offers 256 box registers numbered 0 to 255. Some are already in use by plain TEX. Conventionally registers 0 to 9 are free for scratch use, but some plain TEX macros also use them. It is preferable to assign the number of a free box register to a name. This reservation and assignment is done by \newbox. After "\newbox\mybox" the newly defined command "\mybox" refers to the reserved number of the box.

The assignment of contents to a box register is done by \setbox. Any kind of box, \hbox, \vbox, \vtop can be used. \vcenter has to be encapsulated by another box before assigning it to a box register.

```
\setbox0=\hbox{test data}
\setbox1=\vbox{\hbox{one}%
               \hbox{two}%
               \hbox{three}}
\newbox\mybox
\setbox\mybox=\hbox{Text for my box!}
```

This stores the information in a box register, as \hbox or as \vbox.

Note: grouping has to be considered with \setbox. After a surrounding group has been closed, the box registers that have been changed are restored to their previous values.

A \global command that precedes the \setbox instruction causes the value to be modified for all scopes. After

```
\setbox0=\hbox{previous data}
{\global\setbox0=\hbox{All done!}}
```

the contents of box register 0 are "\hbox{All done!}".

It has to be remembered that the use of the contents of a box register is independent from building this box. It is not important whether this box was built by a \hbox or \vbox command.

## 8.5 Box Usage

Only storing information in boxes is quite pointless. Several methods are available to refer to the contents of a box:

- Referencing a *copy* of a box, the contents are retained.
- Referencing a box for *output*, the contents are used once and the box register is empty afterwards.
- Referencing a box with *unstructuring*, the outer box structure is removed and the \vbox or \hbox decomposes into its elements.
  In this case, however, it must be specified whether a \vbox or an \hbox is to be unstructured.

By combining these possibilities, you get the following commands:

*for output:*

\box  *n*              The command "\box*n*" yields the contents of the specified box register. Afterwards the box register is empty. The input

```
\setbox0=\hbox{H\aa amburgef\"onstiv}
\box0
```

is equivalent to "\hbox{H\aa amburgef\"onstiv}". Whether the contents of the box register is built by an \hbox or a \vbox command is of no consequence.

*for copy*

\copy  *n*           The command "\copy*n*" gives the contents of the specified box register without emptying the box register. The input

```
\setbox0=\hbox{Letter}
\copy0
```

gives the same result as "\hbox{Letter}". The structure of the contents is again not considered.

*for output and copy with unstructuring:*

\unhbox  *n*     This command yields the contents of a box register, but removes the outer \hbox. The box register is empty afterwards.

```
\setbox0=\hbox{digit}
\setbox1=\hbox{\hbox{one }\hbox{two}}
\unhbox0  % like 'digit'
\unhbox1  % like '\hbox{one }\hbox{two}'
```

The \unhbox commands give an output equivalent to "digit" and "\hbox{one }\hbox{two}". If you try to use \unhbox with a box register that contains a \vbox, an error occurs.

\unvbox  *n*     This works like \unhbox, but the box register has to contain a \vbox or \vtop. The box register is empty afterwards.

It is *not* possible to insert the inner contents of a \vbox into an \hbox via \unvbox. The material is classified as "vertical", TeX will output an error message "missing } inserted" and close the current \hbox. The same error will be generated if you type " ... \hbox{\medskip ... "; this is just not material for an \hbox.

The use of \vbox without unstructuring gives no problems.

If you want to get the single elements of a \vbox see \vsplit with "loops" in Section 7.7.

\unhcopy  *n*   works like "\unhbox *n*", but the contents of box register *n* are retained.

\unvcopy  *n*   corresponds to \unhcopy, but works only with boxes constructed by \vbox or \vtop.

## 8.6 Box Dimensions

The contents of a box register hold defined dimensions. For each box, TEX knows three sizes: the width of the box (\wd), the height (\ht), and the depth (\dp). Height and depth are measured from the baseline. Symbols without descenders have a depth of zero, symbols with descenders, e.g, "y", a depth greater than zero.

The *natural width* of a box is determined by its contents. Additionally, you can specify externally the desired width of a box. With commands like

"\hbox to 2 cm{...}" and "\vbox to 2cm{...}"

you define the size of a box exactly. Normally such a box contains *dynamic* material, e.g., \hfil, \hfill, \hss for \hbox defined registers and \vfil, \vfill, \vss for \vbox registers. TEX will give an error message "Underfull ..." or "Overfull ..." if the external size doesn't fit the enclosed material.

On the other hand you can specify an incremental size that is added to the natural width of a box. By

```
\hbox spread 1cm {...}
\vbox spread 1cm {...}
```

the boxes are enlarged by 1 cm. Dynamic skip has to be present to fill up the extra space.

The dimensions of box registers that are set by \setbox may be referenced or even changed. For each register there are three associated registers:

| width | height (above baseline) | depth (below baseline) |
|---|---|---|
| \wd0 | \ht0 | \dp0 |
| \wd1 | \ht1 | \dp1 |
| after "\newbox\mybox": | | |
| \wd\mybox | \ht\mybox | \dp\mybox |

So it is very easy to get at the dimensions of a given text:

```
\setbox0=\hbox{\it Ludwig van Beethoven}
```

Afterwards "\wd0" contains the exact width of the text that would be used when typing "\it Ludwig van Beethoven". This dimension may be referred to as in "\parindent=\wd0" or "\hskip\wd0".

Fixed size boxes can be used to generate forms whose elements are boxes that are put beside and above each other.

This is demonstrated by a simple form whose height is 30 % of that of a normal page. It is divided into two even-sized columns. The right column is divided horizontally into two elements. The left main column receives a centered text, the two elements at the right get ordinary paragraph text and the upper one is set with diminished line length.

```
\def\MyForm#1#2#3{\par\hrule\noindent
    \vbox to 0.3\vsize                  % left main box
        {\hsize=0.5\hsize                % :
        \vfill                           % :
        \hbox to \hsize                  % :
            {\hfill#1\hfill}             % :
        \vfill}                          % :
    \vbox to 0.3\vsize                  % right main box
        {\hsize=0.5\hsize                % :
        \hbox                            % :  upper right
            {\vbox to 0.15\vsize         % :  :
                {\narrower               % :  :
                    \par\noindent#2\vfill}}  % :  :
        \hbox                            % :  lower right
            {\vbox to 0.15\vsize         % :  :
                {\par\noindent#3\vfill}}     % :  :
        }                                % :  :
    \hrule}
```

The outer dimensions of the form are

By calling

```
\MyForm{\bf t i t l e}%
    {\it This information is for people on top of it all.
        This information is for people on top of it all.
        This information is for people on top of it all.
        This information is for people on top of it all.}
    {\bf This is a lower line. This is a lower line.
        This is a lower line. This is a lower line.}
```

you get

> *This information is for people on top of it all. This information is for people on top of it all. This information is for people on top of it all. This information is for people on top of it all.*

t i t l e

**This is a lower line. This is a lower line. This is a lower line. This is a lower line.**

## 8.7 Frames

With our knowledge of the \hbox and \vbox commands, macros for frames can be built.

Starting with a macro "\frame":

```
\def\frame#1#2{
    \vbox{\hrule
        \hbox
            {\vrule
            \hskip#1
            \vbox{\vskip#1{}
                #2
                \vskip#1}
            \hskip#1
            \vrule}
        \hrule}}
%
% #1 is the distance to the
%    framing line
% #2 is the information to
%    frame
```

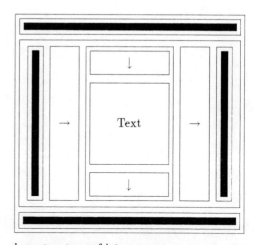

box structure of \frame

The macro \frame generates the structure of boxes that is shown in the above diagram. \hrule and \vrule commands are marked by thick rules, \hskip and \vskip by "→" and "↓". The box structure itself is described by framed boxes in the diagram.

The command \frame on the outer level builds a large \vbox. This \vbox consists of a \hrule at the top, an intermediate \hbox, and a \hrule at the bottom. The middle \hbox is built from 5 elements, (1) a \vrule, (2) some skip (\hskip), (3) an inner \vbox, (4) some skip again (\hskip), and (5) a final \vrule. The inner box (\vbox) is structured from top to bottom by \vskip, the parameter information ("#2"), and a further \vskip.

After these long and involved descriptions some examples:

```
$$ \frame{0.5cm}{\hsize=0.7\hsize % short lines
      \noindent\bf To read means to obtain meaning from words
                    and legibility is that quality which enables
                    words to be read easily, quickly, and accurately.
      \smallskip
      \hfill \it John Charles Tarr} $$ % $$ for centering
```

gives

> **To read means to obtain meaning from words and legibility is that quality which enables words to be read easily, quickly, and accurately.**
>
> *John Charles Tarr*

Multiple frames are also possible:

```
$$\frame{0.1cm}%
   {\frame{0.5cm}{\hsize=0.7\hsize % short lines
      \noindent\bf To read means to obtain meaning from words
                    and legibility is that quality which enables
                    words to be read easily, quickly, and accurately.
      \smallskip
      \hfill \it John Charles Tarr}}$$
```

gives

> **To read means to obtain meaning from words and legibility is that quality which enables words to be read easily, quickly, and accurately.**
>
> *John Charles Tarr*

The framed information is put into a \vbox. As \hsize=0.7\hsize is given, line breaking is done — in horizontal mode — with a value of 70 % of the old line length. By "\noindent" internal vertical mode is left and horizontal mode is entered. The command \smallskip finishes the current paragraph and reenters internal vertical mode. By \hfill horizontal mode , building a paragraph, is again entered; this gives a single paragraph line, whose text is typeset flush right.

This can also be accomplished by "\rightline{\it John Charles Tarr}".

It is easy to modify \frame with an additional parameter that specifies the thickness of the rules.

```
\def\Frame#1#2#3{                    %
    \vbox{\hrule height#2            %  #1 is the distance
        \hbox{\vrule width#2         %
            \hskip#1                 %  #2 is the thickness
            \vbox{\vskip#1{}         %
                #3                   %  #3 is the information
                \vskip#1}            %
            \hskip#1
            \vrule width#2}
        \hrule height#2}}
```

A multiple use of "\Frame":

```
$$\Frame{0.1cm}{1.5pt}%
    {\Frame{0.5cm}{0.4pt}{\hsize=0.7\hsize % short lines
    \noindent\bf To read means to obtain meaning from words
                and legibility is that quality which enables
                words to be read easily, quickly, and accurately.
    \smallskip
    \hfill \it John Charles Tarr}}$$
```

yields

**To read means to obtain meaning from words and legibility is that quality which enables words to be read easily, quickly, and accurately.**

*John Charles Tarr*

Note: frames are a very intense optical element. They should not be used too heavily. On the other hand, rules within tables are recommended for structuring the information.

## 8.8 Blocks and Shadows

The preceding macros for framing an object may be modified to get "shadowing" and "blocking" effects. The base macros for both tasks generate a vertical rule to the right of the object and a horizontal rule below the object. These rules may be shortened on the top and left-hand sides to get the desired optical effect. Furthermore the thickness of the generated rules is a parameter.

```
\def\BaseBlock#1#2#3#4#5{%           %  #1 offset of vertical rule
    \vbox{\setbox0=\hbox{#5}%          %  #2 thickness of vertical rule
        \offinterlineskip             %  #3 offset of horizontal rule
        \hbox{\copy0                   %  #4 thickness of horizontal rule
            \dimen0=\ht0              %  #5 information
            \advance\dimen0 by -#1
            \vrule height \dimen0 width#2}%
        \hbox{\hskip#3\dimen0=\wd0
            \advance\dimen0 by -#3
            \advance\dimen0 by #2
            \vrule height #4 width \dimen0}%
    }}%
```

The information of parameter #5 is put into a scratch box to get the size of it for computing the rule lengths. The result is a "\vbox" with the following box structure:

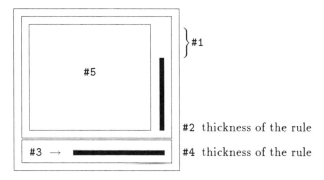

The generated \BaseBlock macro may be used very simply to get a shadowing effect by applying it as follows:

```
\def\Shadow#1{\BaseBlock{4pt}{2pt}{4pt}{6pt}{#1}}
```

The given parameters generate 4 pt and 6 pt rules. The vertical and horizontal offsets are equal. As the \BaseBlock doesn't generate a surrounding frame it will usually be combined with \frame. Applied to the preceding example text as

```
$$\Shadow{\frame{0.5cm}{\hsize=0.7\hsize
    \noindent\bf To read means to obtain meaning from words
        ...
    \hfill \it John Charles Tarr}}$$
```

it will generate the output

> **To read means to obtain meaning from words and legibility is that quality which enables words to be read easily, quickly, and accurately.**
>
> *John Charles Tarr*

In contrast to the example for generation of shadows in Section 6.6 the rules are built in one piece. In that example \halign was used; this one will divide the vertical rules into several pieces.

To get a "block" effect, a set of very thin rules is put to the right of the information and below the information with increasing offset. This is done by a loop construction. The rules are generated with a thickness of 0.4 pt and an offset of 0.4 pt. This is the default thickness of rules. \LoopBlock adds to the information of the first parameter "#2" times additional thin rules. Grouping by \begingroup and \endgroup will restrict any register changes to the \LoopBlock macro. For this purpose, \begingroup and \endgroup are equivalent to braces.

```
\def\LoopBlock#1#2{%
\begingroup
  \dimen2=0.4pt     % offset increment
  \def\doblock{%
   \expandafter\setbox\expandafter2\BaseBlock
       {\count1\dimen2}{0.4pt}{\count1\dimen2}{0.4pt}{\box2}}%
  \setbox2=\vbox{#1}%  starting information
  \count1=0
  \loop
     \advance\count1 by 1
     \doblock
     \ifnum\count1<#2
  \repeat
  \box2
\endgroup}
```

After encapsulating this in the macro:

```
\def\Block#1{\LoopBlock{#1}{10}}
```

The input

```
$$\Block{\frame{0.5cm}{\hsize=0.7\hsize
       \noindent\bf To read means to obtain meaning from words
                 and legibility is that quality which enables
                 words to be read easily, quickly, and accurately.
             \smallskip
             \hfill \it John Charles Tarr}}$$
```

now produces the output

**To read means to obtain meaning from words and legibility is that quality which enables words to be read easily, quickly, and accurately.**

*John Charles Tarr*

## 8.9 Dynamic Skip

The skip commands for horizontal and vertical space

| horizontal space | vertical space |
|---|---|
| \quad | \smallskip |
| \qquad | \medskip |
|  | \bigskip |
| \hskip *dimension* | \vskip *dimension* |

generate space of a *fixed* size. In the following some commands are described that generate dynamic space. This may stretch or even shrink, depending on the command. It is used for alignment and justification like centering, setting flush left or flush right, or flush top or flush bottom.

| horizontal | vertical | function |
|---|---|---|
| \hfil | \vfil | stretchable space |
| \hfill | \vfill | stretchable space, stronger than \hfil or \vfil |
| \hss | \vss | stretchable and shrinkable space |

Example:

```
\frame{0.2cm}{\hbox to 6cm{\hfil A}}          % to the right
\frame{0.2cm}{\hbox to 6cm{B \hfil}}          % to the left
\frame{0.2cm}{\hbox to 6cm{\hfil C \hfil}}    % centered
\frame{0.2cm}{\hbox to 6cm{\hfil D \hfil\hfil}} % partitioned (1:2)
\frame{0.2cm}{\hbox to 6.4cm{\hfil E \hfill}}   % to the left !
```

gives                                            marked by arrows:

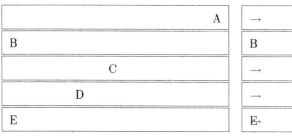

Besides these there are "\hfilneg" and "\vfilneg" that cancel a preceding "\hfil" or "\vfil". There is no "\hfillneg" or "\vfillneg".

*Overlapping*

The commands \hss and \vss that generate shrinkable space allow overprinting. The two standard macros of plain TeX, \rlap and \llap, use these. They are defined by

```
\def\llap#1{\hbox to 0pt{\hss#1}}
\def\rlap#1{\hbox to 0pt{#1\hss}}
```

\rlap prints the information given as a parameter to the right without moving the current position, \llap prints to the left without changing the position.

"1\llap{/}2" gives "⁄2", and "1\rlap{/}2" gives "1⁄".

Similar to setting flush left and right horizontally, the corresponding effect within a \vbox may be achieved with \vfil and \vfill.

```
\def\testbox#1{\frame{0.2cm}{\hbox{#1}}}
\frame{0.4cm}{\hbox{
            \vbox to 4cm{\vfil\testbox A}
    \vrule\ \vbox to 4cm{\testbox B\vfil}
    \vrule\ \vbox to 4cm{\vfil \testbox C \vfil}
    \vrule\ \vbox to 4cm{\vfil \testbox D \vfil\vfil}
    \vrule\ \vbox to 4cm{\vfil \testbox E \vfill}}}
```

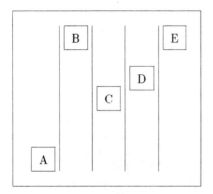  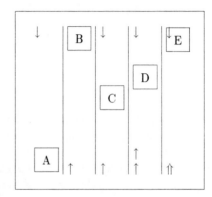

## 8.10 Box Movements

Until now information has been moved *inside* a box. It is also possible to move a complete box when it is used. The movement of such a box can only be done *orthogonally* to the current setting direction, which depends on the mode, i.e., up and down during horizontal modes, to the left and right during vertical modes. In an \hbox or within a paragraph the commands "\raise" and "\lower" are applicable:

```
\par The following word is put \raise3pt\hbox{high}
     but the next \lower3pt\hbox{low}!
```

gives:

The following word is put ^high but the next _low!

The commands use the syntactical form

\raise *dimension box-specification*

\lower *dimension box-specification*

An input "\raise3pt\hbox{...}" acts identically to "\lower-3pt\hbox{...}".

During vertical mode the commands "\moveleft" and "\moveright" can be used. Their syntax is the same as with \raise or \lower.

Example:

```
$$\vbox{\hbox{line 1}
       \hbox{line 2}
       \moveleft  10pt \hbox{line 3}
       \moveright 10pt \hbox{line 4}
       \hbox{line 5}}$$
```

generates

line 1

line 2

line 3

    line 4

line 5

The $$\vbox{...}$$ surrounding commands center the whole output.

In practice information is relatively often set beside the logical text area of a box. The *logical size* of a box, which TEX uses to put boxes beside and above one another, and where the information is really printed, are two different matters.

A quite handy example is demonstrated by the following macro that generates a marginal note. By \note, an arrow is typeset right beside the current line in the margin area. (This is done in the current line.) Here we find positioning outside the logical limits of boxes.  ⇐

Before starting, remember the command "\vadjust". The information specified in "\vadjust{...}" as parameter is considered to be vertical material, i.e. internal vertical mode is active. The given information is *inserted* behind the current line where the \vadjust command has been issued. If you look closely you will detect an extra

vertical skip that has been generated by a "\vadjust{\medskip}". The macro for the "\note" command is defined by

```
\def\note{\vadjust{\vbox to 0pt
    {\vss
     \hbox to \hsize{\hskip\hsize
                     \quad
                     $\Leftarrow$\hss}
     \vskip3.5pt}}}
```

It is a proper technique to move "empty" boxes, i.e. boxes with logical size zero. Such a box may be put anywhere without affecting the current position. But take care that the correct dimensions, width, or height and depth of a box, are set to zero, otherwise there will be some unexpected moving.

Note: if boxes are arranged vertically the standard registers controlling line spacing are still in use:

| | |
|---|---|
| \baselineskip | defines the standard distance between the baseline of two consecutive boxes. |
| \lineskiplimit | sets the lower limit for the distance between two boxes that are put above one another. If the distance is smaller than this limit, the value of \lineskip will be used to separate boxes vertically. (It is preset to 0 pt.) |
| \lineskip | defines the minimal skip between boxes that is used if boxes are too close. (It is preset to 1 pt.) |

If boxes should exactly touch each other, either the value (\lineskip) has to be modified or — preferably – one of the predefined macros to handle this problem should be used:

| | |
|---|---|
| \offinterlineskip | inhibits control by \lineskiplimit and \lineskip. |
| \nointerlineskip | cancels the effect of \lineskiplimit and \lineskip *once*. Afterwards the standard mechanism takes effect. |

*control of baselines*

As mentioned before, \vbox and \vtop boxes are vertically adjusted to their baseline when used in horizontal mode. (\vbox uses the baseline of its last inner box, \vtop uses the baseline of its first (top) box.) When macros are defined, the baseline of boxes is often unknown as it depends on the parameter information. Maybe an enlarged typeface is chosen with enlarged depth values. By "\hrule height 0pt" an additional rule may be inserted. This gives a calculatable baseline for adjusting the boxes. As it is specified with "height 0pt", it is invisible and doesn't change vertical positions.

But often a \strut command is needed to force an appropriate height and depth for a box that agrees with the standard dimensions of text lines. By "\strut" the minimal height is set to 8.5 pt and the minimal depth to 3.5 pt. If a box is followed by a horizontal rule (\hrule), this may touch the preceding information if this doesn't contain any element with descenders, e.g., "y". This is the standard application of \strut. (Additionally extra skip, e.g., \smallskip, should be considered to get an optically pleasing result.)

## 8.11 Partial Output of Boxes

The command "\vsplit" allows you to get only a *part* of a \vbox. It has the syntactical form:

> \vsplit *box number* to *dimension*

The upper part of a \vbox is split off with the specified size. The same mechanisms as during pagebreaking are used to get an optimal breakpoint. The unused part remains in the source box. This quite easily allows the construction of macros for double column typesetting. At the start, all the information is gathered in a single box.

Example:

```
\setbox0=\vbox{\hsize=0.4\hsize
              \it
              \obeylines
              2 onions
              5 tablespoons vegetable oil
              40 g all-purpose flour
              $\it 1/4$ l beef gravy
              $\it 1/8$ l sour cream
              salt
              pepper
              1 teaspoon lemon juice
              2 gherkins
              100 g mushrooms
              500 g fillet of beef}
```

Box register 0 contains the text line by line. Especially \ht0 contains the height of the box. After some arithmetic operations

```
\dimen1=0.5\ht0
\advance\dimen1 by 0.5\baselineskip
```

the desired size for splitting is obtained. The addition of 0.5 \baselineskip forces a possible extra odd line to the left side column. After

```
\splittopskip=0pt
\setbox1=\vsplit 0 to \dimen1
```

the upper half of box register 0 has been moved to register 1. Boxes 0 and 1 can be combined without problems. The internal register "\splittopskip" has been set to 0 pt to omit extra vertical space at the beginning of the box. This skip is equivalent to the "\topskip" used for page breaking that determines the distance between the first line's baseline and the beginning of the text area.

The combination of the two halves is done by using \vtop. An additional baseline as first box is generated by "\hrule height 0pt".

```
\hbox to \hsize{\hfil\vtop{\hrule height 0pt
                \box1}%
          \hfil\vtop{\hrule height 0pt
                \box0}%
          \hfil}
```

gives in doublecolumn format "Bœuf Stroganoff":

| | |
|---|---|
| *2 onions* | *pepper* |
| *5 tablespoons vegetable oil* | *1 teaspoon lemon juice* |
| *40 g all-purpose flour* | *2 gherkins* |
| *1/4 l beef gravy* | *100 g mushrooms* |
| *1/8 l sour cream* | *500 g fillet of beef* |
| *salt* | |

Note: as \vsplit works like ordinary page breaking, you may get log messages such as "Overfull vbox...". These may be suppressed by assignment of a larger value to \vfuzz.

    Another example of the use of \vsplit is demonstrated on page 122.

## 8.12 Count and Dimension Registers

Besides the box registers, TₑX offers some other kinds of register that have been used in part. All registers are numbered from 0 to 255. The first ten (0...9) are free for scratch use within macros by convention. They are also used by plain TₑX macros. For special purposes a register may be reserved and named by the associated \new... command.

\count0...    register for positive and negative integer numbers.
          By convention, \count0 contains the current page number that may be referred to by \pageno.

\dimen0 ...    dimension register for the storing of lengths. These act in the same way as the previously mentioned registers \ht, \dp, \wd that are associated with box registers.
          Lengths can be stored using different units of measure like pt, cm, etc.

\skip0 ...    are registers that contain lengths — similar to \dimen —, but these may additionally accept "plus" and "minus" parts for dynamic skip, e.g., "1cm plus 2mm minus 3mm".

\muskip0 ...    are skip registers for use in mathematical mode. Only the unit "mu" may be used. In practice \muskip registers are rarely used.

| reservation | assignment / change | ouput / test |
|---|---|---|
| \newcount\mycount | \count1=17<br>\mycount=4<br>\mycount=\count2<br>\advance\mycount by 1 | \number\count1<br>\number\mycount<br>\ifnum\mycount>1 ... |
| \newdimen\mydimen | \dimen1=17cm<br>\mydimen=4cm<br>\advance\mydimen by 1pt<br>\mydimen=0.5\mydimen | \hbox to \dimen1 ...<br>\vbox to \mydimen ...<br>\ifdim\dimen1 > 1cm<br>\ifdim\mydimen < 1 pt |
| \newskip\myskip | \skip1=5cm<br>\skip1=5cm minus 1cm<br>\myskip=1pt plus 1pt<br>\skip1=2\myskip<br>\advance\myskip by 1pt | \vskip\skip1<br>\hskip\skip1<br>\vskip\myskip |
| \newmuskip\mymuskip | \muskip1=5mu<br>\mymuskip=5mu minus 1mu | \mskip\muskip1<br>\mskip\mymuskip |

## 8.13 Token Registers

Furthermore, there are 256 *token registers* available that may be used similarly to macro definitions. They are denoted by \toks0 to \toks255. A token register contains a set of TeX commands. Token registers have implicitly been used by "\headline" and "\footline" that are predefined by plain TeX. Conventionally the first ten registers are free for scratch use, reservation and assignment of a name is done by \newtoks.

| *reservation* | *assignment* | *output* |
|---|---|---|
| | \toks0={abc} | \the\toks0 |
| | \headline={\hss\folio\hss} | \the\headline |
| | \toks1=\toks0 | \the\toks1 |
| \newtoks\ToksOne | \ToksOne={\vfil} | \the\ToksOne |
| \newtoks\ToksTwo | \ToksTwo=\ToksOne | \the\ToksTwo |

Token registers may be used more intuitively if operations like assignments, e.g., in \headline, or \footline, are performed. Assignment instructions are fairly represented by the syntactical form, e.g., "\CurrentNames={Adam and Eve}".

The information is stored without expansion of any commands. During the assignment care is taken of grouping braces.

The contents of a token register are referred to by a preceding "\the". This sometimes causes irritations if it is mistakenly forgotten. The following text will be interpreted as text to be assigned.

As token registers are rarely used they are demonstrated below with some short examples. After definition of registers by

> \newtoks\ToksOne    \newtoks\ToksTwo    \newtoks\ToksThree

the registers are modified with application of the macros from the following page:

| | |
|---|---|
| \toks1={one} | \toks4=\FirstOf{\toks1} |
| \toks2={two} | \toks5=\RestOf{\toks2} |
| \toks3={{one}{two}} | \toks7=\FirstOf{\toks3} |
| \ToksOne={\number1} | \toks8=\RestOf\ToksOne |
| \ToksTwo=\toks2 | \toks9=\Union(\toks1,\toks2) |
| \ToksThree=\toks3 | \MoveRest(\toks9 to\toks0) |

This results in

| | | | | | |
|---|---|---|---|---|---|
| \the\toks1 | $\longrightarrow$ | one | \the\toks4 | $\longrightarrow$ | o |
| \the\toks2 | $\longrightarrow$ | two | \the\toks5 | $\longrightarrow$ | wo |
| \the\toks3 | $\longrightarrow$ | {one}{two} | \the\toks7 | $\longrightarrow$ | one |
| \the\ToksOne | $\longrightarrow$ | \number1 | \the\toks8 | $\longrightarrow$ | 1 |
| \the\ToksTwo | $\longrightarrow$ | two | \the\toks9 | $\longrightarrow$ | onetwo |
| \the\ToksThree | $\longrightarrow$ | {one}{two} | \the\toks0 | $\longrightarrow$ | netwo |

```
%  1. joining of two token registers
%
%         results in " #1={ <contents of #2> <contents of #3>} "
%
\def\JoinToks#1=(#2+#3){#1=\expandafter\expandafter\expandafter
                       {\expandafter\the\expandafter#2\the#3}}
%===============================================================
%
%  2. similar without target specification
%        results in " { <contents of #1> <contents of #2> } "
%
\def\Union(#1,#2){\expandafter\expandafter\expandafter
                  {\expandafter\the\expandafter#1\the#2}}
%
\def\UpToHere{\relax}%
\def\IgnoreRest#1#2\UpToHere{#1}                   % helper macro
\def\IgnoreFirst#1#2\relax\UpToHere{#2}            % helper macro
%===============================================================
%  3. gives the first element of the token register #1
%
\def\First#1{\expandafter\IgnoreRest\the#1{}\UpToHere}
%===============================================================
%  4. gives the first element of token the register #1 with
%        surrounding braces " { ... } "
%
\def\FirstOf#1{\expandafter\expandafter\expandafter
              {\expandafter\IgnoreRest\the#1{}\UpToHere}}
%===============================================================
%  5.   assigns the first element of the token register #1 to
%        to token register #2
%
\def\MoveFirst(#1to#2){#2=\FirstOf{#1}}
%===============================================================
%  6.   puts all but the first element of the token register #1
%
\def\Rest#1{\expandafter\IgnoreFirst\the#1\relax\UpToHere}
%===============================================================
%  7.   as in (6), with surrounding braces " { ... }"
%
\def\RestOf#1{\expandafter\expandafter\expandafter
             {\expandafter\IgnoreFirst\the#1\relax\UpToHere}}
%===============================================================
%  8.   as in (5), with all elements but the first
%
\def\MoveRest(#1to#2){#2=\RestOf{#1}}
```

# 9 Variations on Typesetting Mathematical Formulae

## 9.1 Spacing within Formulae

The following parameters describe global mechanisms for controlling mathematical typesetting. They should only be changed if that is absolutely necessary. They are reproduced here only for the sake of completeness and to demonstrate the possibilities of the TeX program. The same is true for the other sections of this chapter.

One of the controlling parameters is the distance of a formula from its surrounding text: "\mathsurround". This is the space inserted between text and formula. The parameter controls the generation of additional space. It is preset to zero. The command "\mathsurround=1pt", e.g., sets the distance to 1 pt.

\thinmuskip, \medmuskip, and \thickmuskip are the internal variables for *small, medium,* or *large* distance between formula elements.

TeX controls the distance between the constituents of a formula by inspecting the functions of the formula elements. The following different types of elements exist:

| function | commands | examples of predefined members |
|---|---|---|
| ordinary symbols | \mathord | $ABC \ldots xyz \ldots 012 \ldots \alpha\beta \ldots$ |
| (large) operators | \mathop | $\sum \int \prod \cdots$ |
| binary operators | \mathbin | $+ - * \ldots$ |
| relations | \mathrel | $> = < \ldots$ |
| opening 'brackets' | \mathopen | $( [ \{ \ldots$ |
| closing 'brackets' | \mathclose | $) ] \} \ldots$ |
| punctuation | \mathpunct | $. , \ldots$ |
| subformula | \mathinner | |

The instructions in the "commands" column give explicit typesetting attributes to an expression by changing its function. \mathop{\Gamma} generates a mathematical symbol with the function "large operator" and the associated behaviour.

Hidden in a macro

```
\def\OpGamma{\mathop{\Gamma}}
```

you get an operator which looks like an ordinary "$\Gamma$". A command

```
\def\plus{\mathbin{\hbox{\it plus}}}
```

defines a new binary operator "\plus", which acts like a standard operator, e.g., "+".
By `$17\plus4=21$` the text "17 *plus* 4 = 21" is typeset in a convenient mode.

The importance of a meaningful use of mathematical commands with the correct
function for their elements is demonstrated: "<" and ">" are relations, "\left<" and
"\right>" generate opening and closing delimiters, and \mid is a relation, while \vert
is an ordinary symbol.

The second line shows a better result for correct input:

```
$       < x \vert y        > = \sum_i x_i y_i$
$\left< x \mid y \right> = \sum_i x_i y_i$
```
$< x|y > = \sum_i x_i y_i$

$\langle x \mid y \rangle = \sum_i x_i y_i$

A further example shows the colon ":" and its varying uses. ":" is defined as a relation,
but may be used with the name "\colon" for punctuation and with "\mathbin:" as a
binary operator.

```
$$ G \mathbin: H = G - H  $$ % binary operator
$$ G        :   H = G - H  $$ %     compared to normal
$$ f \colon  M \to N  $$ % punctuation
$$ f       :    M \to N  $$ %     compared to normal
```

gives

$$G : H = G - H$$

$$G : H = G - H$$

$$f\!:\! M \to N$$

$$f : M \to N$$

The difference between the first and second lines is small, but a close look shows
that in the second line ":" and "=" are treated equally (with the same spacing to the
left and right).

The space between formula elements is represented by the values of \thinmuskip,
\medmuskip, and \thickmuskip. The following table describes which values are used.
If no space is inserted the table entries contain a rule "—", entries enclosed by brackets
"[ ]" are treated as zero in scriptstyle and scriptscriptstyle (for subscripts etc.).

Changes of the values are demonstrated by the following formula, which is typeset
tightly, normally, and loosely.
The input

```
$$\int {dx \over x^3 \sqrt{\left(x^2+a^2\right)^3} }=
       - {1 \over 2 a^2x^2 \sqrt{x^2+a^2} }$$
```

with different values for interformulae spacing:

| *right* / *left* | ordinary symbols | operators | binary operators | relations |
|---|---|---|---|---|
| ordinary symbols | — | \thinmuskip | [\medmuskip] | [\thickmuskip] |
| operators | \thinmuskip | \thinmuskip | — | [\thickmuskip] |
| binary operators | [\medmuskip] | [\medmuskip] | — | — |
| relations | [\thickmuskip] | [\thickmuskip] | — | — |
| opening 'brackets' | — | — | — | — |
| closing 'brackets' | — | \thinmuskip | [\thickmuskip] | [\thickmuskip] |
| punctuation | [\thinmuskip] | [\thinmuskip] | [\thickmuskip] | [\thickmuskip] |
| subformula | [\thinmuskip] | \thinmuskip | [\thickmuskip] | [\thickmuskip] |

| *right* / *left* | opening 'brackets' | closing 'brackets' | punctuation | subformula |
|---|---|---|---|---|
| ordinary symbols | — | — | — | [\thinmuskip] |
| operators | — | — | — | [\thinmuskip] |
| binary operators | [\medmuskip] | — | — | \medmuskip |
| relations | [\thickmuskip] | — | — | [\thickmuskip] |
| opening 'brackets' | — | — | — | — |
| closing 'brackets' | — | — | — | [\thinmuskip] |
| punctuation | [\thinmuskip] | [\thinmuskip] | [\thinmuskip] | [\thinmuskip] |
| subformula | [\thinmuskip] | — | [\thinmuskip] | [\thinmuskip] |

spacing between formula elements

| output with | \thinmuskip<br>\medmuskip<br>\thickmuskip |
|:---:|:---:|
| $$\int \frac{dx}{x^3 \sqrt{(x^2+a^2)^3}} = -\frac{1}{2a^2 x^2 \sqrt{x^2+a^2}}$$ | 0.5 times the standard value |
| $$\int \frac{dx}{x^3 \sqrt{(x^2+a^2)^3}} = -\frac{1}{2a^2 x^2 \sqrt{x^2+a^2}}$$ | normal |
| $$\int \frac{dx}{x^3 \sqrt{(x^2+a^2)^3}} = -\frac{1}{2a^2 x^2 \sqrt{x^2+a^2}}$$ | 2.0 times the standard value |
| $$\int \frac{dx}{x^3 \sqrt{(x^2+a^2)^3}} = -\frac{1}{2a^2 x^2 \sqrt{x^2+a^2}}$$ | 3.0 times the standard value |

## 9.2 Defining Your Own Mathematical Symbols

Sometimes an author wishes to use mathematical symbols which he builds up from other elements of the TeX typefaces. The following example demonstrates this:

```
\def\squarebox#1{\mathop{\mkern0.5\thinmuskip
                 \vbox{\hrule
                       \hbox{\vrule
                             \hskip#1
                             \vrule height#1 width 0pt
                             \vrule}%
                       \hrule}%
                 \mkern0.5\thinmuskip}}
```

defines a macro \squarebox, which generates a square of explicit size. The result is used as a "large operator".
With the input

```
$$\squarebox{7pt}_{i=1}^n\Gamma_i = B$$
```

you get

$$\squarebox{7pt}_{i=1}^n \Gamma_i = B$$

There is a disadvantage: if such an operator can be used in display or textstyle formulae different sizes are needed. Even an application with superscripts and subscripts of first and second order should generate a different result, automatically. The command "\mathchoice" helps: it generates a version for each variant of formula setting:

```
\def\Squarebox{\mathchoice{\squarebox{8pt}}%        displaystyle
                         {\squarebox{6pt}}%        textstyle
                         {\squarebox{4pt}}%        scriptstyle
                         {\squarebox{3pt}}}%       scriptscriptstyle
```

The input

```
$$                      \Squarebox_{i=1}^n \Gamma_i=B$$
$$\textstyle            \Squarebox_{i=1}^n \Gamma_i=B$$
$$\scriptstyle          \Squarebox_{i=1}^n \Gamma_i=B$$
$$\scriptscriptstyle \Squarebox_{i=1}^n \Gamma_i=B$$
```

produces the desired result

$$\square_{i=1}^n \Gamma_i = B$$

$$\square_{i=1}^n \Gamma_i = B$$

$$\square_{i=1}^n \Gamma_i = B$$

$$\square_{i=1}^n \Gamma_i = B$$

The same basic macro by "\def\op{\mathbin{\squarebox{5pt}}}" is used to define a binary operator (here in a simple variant without \mathchoice).

```
$$\def\op{\mathbin{\squarebox{3.5pt}}}
    f_1 \op f_2 \op f_3 \op \ldots \op f_n = \Squarebox_{i=1}^n f_i $$
```

yields

$$f_1 \square f_2 \square f_3 \square \ldots \square f_n = \square_{i=1}^n f_i$$

The following example demonstrates an application of a single symbol of a scaled typeface:

```
\font\bigmath=cmsy10 scaled \magstep4  % for the big symbol
\def\Star{\mathop{\vphantom{\sum}%
                  \lower2.5pt\hbox{\bigmath\char3}}}
$$\Star_{i=1}^n \Gamma_i=C$$
```

generates

$$\underset{i=1}{\overset{n}{\ast}} \Gamma_i = C$$

If it is used in textstyle, as in $\Star_{i=1}^n \Gamma_i=C$, you get the result

$$\ast_{i=1}^n \Gamma_i = C.$$

## 9.3 Changes of Layout

The layout of mathematical formulae is quite standardized. Some changes are common in the context of display style formulae. Publishers sometimes want to get formulae flush left and not centered. There are some plain TEX macros that have to be changed to get the desired result.

Two TEX commands, "\everymath" and "\everydisplay" will be discussed before we start explaining the layout changes. The parameter of each of these macros consists of a sequence of commands that are stored and automatically executed in a textstyle formula (for \everymath) just after the starting "$" and in a display style formula (for \everydisplay) just after the starting "$$".† The following commands change the mathematical layout for displayed formulae:

```
\newdimen\mathindent          % amount to indent
\mathindent=\parindent        % preset (= paragraph indentation)
\def\eqno{$\hfill$}
\def\leqno{$\hfill$}
\long\def\leftdisplay#1$${\line{\hskip\mathindent
                               $\displaystyle#1$\hfil}$$}
\everydisplay{\leftdisplay}
\catcode'\@=11     % Temporarily '@' is a letter
                   % Internal TeX commands are used.
\def\eqalignno#1{%
        \displ@y \tabskip=0pt
        \advance\displaywidth by -\mathindent
        \vbox{%
           \halign to \displaywidth{%
              \hfil$\displaystyle{##}$\tabskip=0pt
           &$\displaystyle{{}##}$\hfil\tabskip=\centering
           &\llap{$##$}\tabskip=0pt\crcr#1\crcr}}}
\def\leqalignno{\eqalignno}
\catcode'\@=12     % '@' is the same as before
```

To change some of the plain TEX macros a good knowledge of how they work is needed. Here the changes are described in short:
After "\everydisplay{\leftdisplay}" the command "\leftdisplay" is inserted just after the starting "$$" *automatically*. The only parameter of \leftdisplay is delimited by "$$". The whole formula will become the parameter of \leftdisplay. The formula will be typeset normally, but aligned within the output line on the left-hand side.

Some internal macros \eqno, \leqno, \eqalignno, and \leqalignno must also be changed to fit the new conditions, \eqalignno in particular has to be modified, because

---

† There are a few other \every... commands that store command sequences for later automatic execution:
\everypar for commands at the start of each paragraph
\everyhbox for commands at the start of each \hbox
\everyvbox for commands at the start of each \vbox

there is some internal use of \halign. Instructions for numbering on the left-hand side are changed to get the numbers on the right.

Some examples demonstrate the new layout. The input

```
$$ A + B = C $$
$$ A + B = C \eqno (2) $$
$$ A + B = C \leqno (3) $$
$$ \eqalign{ A + B &= C \cr
              C   &= A + B \cr}$$
$$ \eqalignno{ A + B &= C      & (6) \cr
                B &= C - A &        \cr
                A &= C - B & (8) \cr}$$
$$ \det A= \left\vert \matrix { a & b & c \cr
                                 b & c & a \cr
                                 c & a & b \cr}
          \right\vert \leqno (X) $$
```

gives the following output, where \mathindent — the new formula indentation — is preset to the current value of \parindent.

$$A + B = C$$

$$A + B = C \qquad\qquad (2)$$

$$A + B = C \qquad\qquad (3)$$

$$\begin{aligned} A + B &= C \\ C &= A + B \end{aligned}$$

$$\begin{aligned} A + B &= C & (6) \\ B &= C - A \\ A &= C - B & (8) \end{aligned}$$

$$\det A = \begin{vmatrix} a & b & c \\ b & c & a \\ c & a & b \end{vmatrix} \qquad\qquad (X)$$

## 9.4 Simulation of Superscripts and Subscripts

Subscripts are introduced by "_" and superscripts by "^". Using the same convention for private macros poses no difficulties. You can simply define

```
\def\myop_#1^#2{...}
```

But this defines both parameters as mandatory. Otherwise TeX will give an error message "Use of \myop doesn't match its definition". An example which circumvents this restriction is given in Section 7.7. It produces results like this:

| | | | |
|---|---|---|---|
| `$$ \myop` | `$$` | *gives* | $\infty\big\|^{\infty}$ |
| `$$ \myop_\alpha` | `$$` | *gives* | $\alpha\big\|^{\infty}$ |
| `$$ \myop^\beta` | `$$` | *gives* | $\infty\big\|^{\beta}$ |
| `$$ \myop_{aa}^{bb}` | `$$` | *gives* | $aa\big\|^{bb}$ |

## 9.5 AMS Fonts

Many installations provide the additional typefaces of the American Mathematical Society with a lot of mathematical symbols. The commands are usually defined by reading the definition file with "\input mssymb". This makes the following characters available, which are *not* TeX standard. They are only summarized:

### "Blackboard" symbols

| | | | |
|---|---|---|---|
| `\Bbb A` | 𝔸 | `\Bbb N` | ℕ |
| `\Bbb B` | 𝔹 | `\Bbb O` | 𝕆 |
| `\Bbb C` | ℂ | `\Bbb P` | ℙ |
| `\Bbb D` | 𝔻 | `\Bbb Q` | ℚ |
| `\Bbb E` | 𝔼 | `\Bbb R` | ℝ |
| `\Bbb F` | 𝔽 | `\Bbb S` | 𝕊 |
| `\Bbb G` | 𝔾 | `\Bbb T` | 𝕋 |
| `\Bbb H` | ℍ | `\Bbb U` | 𝕌 |
| `\Bbb I` | 𝕀 | `\Bbb V` | 𝕍 |
| `\Bbb J` | 𝕁 | `\Bbb W` | 𝕎 |
| `\Bbb K` | 𝕂 | `\Bbb X` | 𝕏 |
| `\Bbb L` | 𝕃 | `\Bbb Y` | 𝕐 |
| `\Bbb M` | 𝕄 | `\Bbb Z` | ℤ |

## Ordinary Characters

| | | | | |
|---|---|---|---|---|
| \square | □ | \nexists | ∄ |
| \blacksquare | ■ | \mho | ℧ |
| \lozenge | ◊ | \thorn | ð |
| \blacklozenge | ◆ | \beth | ℶ |
| \backprime | ‵ | \gimel | ℷ |
| \bigstar | ★ | \daleth | ℸ |
| \blacktriangledown | ▼ | \digamma | ϝ |
| \blacktriangle | ▲ | \varkappa | ϰ |
| \triangledown | ▽ | \hslash | ℏ |
| \angle | ∠ | \hbar | ℏ |
| \measuredangle | ∡ | \yen | ¥ |
| \sphericalangle | ∢ | \checkmark | ✓ |
| \circledS | Ⓢ | \circledR | Ⓡ |
| \complement | ∁ | \maltese | ✠ |
| \varnothing | ∅ | | |

## Binary Operators

| | | | | |
|---|---|---|---|---|
| \boxdot | ⊡ | \curlyvee | ⋎ |
| \boxplus | ⊞ | \leftthreetimes | ⋋ |
| \boxtimes | ⊠ | \rightthreetimes | ⋌ |
| \centerdot | · | \dotplus | ∔ |
| \boxminus | ⊟ | \intercal | ⊺ |
| \veebar | ⊻ | \circledcirc | ⊚ |
| \barwedge | ⊼ | \circledast | ⊛ |
| \doublebarwedge | ⩞ | \circleddash | ⊝ |
| \Cup | ⋓ | \divideontimes | ⋇ |
| *or* \doublecup | ⋓ | \ltimes | ⋉ |
| \Cap | ⋒ | \rtimes | ⋊ |
| *or* \doublecap | ⋒ | \smallsetminus | ∖ |
| \curlywedge | ⋏ | | |

## Relations

| | | | |
|---|---|---|---|
| \circlearrowright | ↻ | \downharpoonright | ⇂ |
| \circlearrowleft | ↺ | \upharpoonleft | ↿ |
| \rightleftharpoons | ⇌ | \downharpoonleft | ⇃ |
| \leftrightharpoons | ⇋ | \rightarrowtail | ↣ |
| \Vdash | ⊩ | \leftarrowtail | ↢ |
| \Vvdash | ⊪ | \leftrightarrows | ⇆ |
| \vDash | ⊨ | \rightleftarrows | ⇄ |
| \twoheadrightarrow | ↠ | \Lsh | ↰ |
| \twoheadleftarrow | ↞ | \Rsh | ↱ |
| \leftleftarrows | ⇇ | \rightsquigarrow | ⇝ |
| \rightrightarrows | ⇉ | \leftrightsquigarrow | ↭ |
| \upuparrows | ⇈ | \looparrowleft | ↫ |
| \downdownarrows | ⇊ | \looparrowright | ↬ |
| \upharpoonright | ↾ | \circeq | ≗ |
| or \restriction | ↾ | | |
| \succsim | ≿ | \trianglerighteq | ⊵ |
| \gtrsim | ≳ | \trianglelefteq | ⊴ |
| \gtrapprox | ⪆ | \between | ≬ |
| \multimap | ⊸ | \blacktriangleright | ▶ |
| \therefore | ∴ | \blacktriangleleft | ◀ |
| \because | ∵ | \eqcirc | ≖ |
| \doteqdot | ≑ | \lesseqgtr | ⋚ |
| or \Doteq | ≑ | \gtreqless | ⋛ |
| \triangleq | ≜ | \lesseqqgtr | ⪋ |
| \precsim | ≾ | \gtreqqless | ⪌ |
| \lesssim | ≲ | \Rrightarrow | ⇛ |
| \lessapprox | ⪅ | \Lleftarrow | ⇚ |
| \eqslantless | ⪕ | \varpropto | ∝ |
| \eqslantgtr | ⪖ | \smallsmile | ⌣ |
| \curlyeqprec | ⋞ | \smallfrown | ⌢ |
| \curlyeqsucc | ⋟ | \Subset | ⋐ |
| \preccurlyeq | ≼ | \Supset | ⋑ |
| \leqq | ≦ | \subseteqq | ⫅ |
| \leqslant | ⩽ | \supseteqq | ⫆ |
| \lessgtr | ≶ | \bumpeq | ≏ |
| \risingdotseq | ≓ | \Bumpeq | ≎ |
| \fallingdotseq | ≒ | \lll | ⋘ |
| \succcurlyeq | ≽ | or \llless | ⋘ |
| \geqq | ≧ | \ggg | ⋙ |
| \geqslant | ⩾ | or \gggtr | ⋙ |
| \gtrless | ≷ | \pitchfork | ⋔ |
| \sqsubset | ⊏ | \backsim | ∽ |
| \sqsupset | ⊐ | \backsimeq | ⋍ |

| | | | |
|---|---|---|---|
| \lvertneqq | | \succnapprox | |
| \gvertneqq | | \lnapprox | |
| \nleq | | \gnapprox | |
| \ngeq | | \nsim | |
| \nless | | \napprox | |
| \ngtr | | \nsubseteqq | |
| \nprec | | \nsupseteqq | |
| \nsucc | | \subsetneqq | |
| \lneqq | | \supsetneqq | |
| \gneqq | | \subsetneq | |
| \nleqslant | | \supsetneq | |
| \ngeqslant | | \nsubseteq | |
| \lneq | | \nsupseteq | |
| \gneq | | \nparallel | |
| \npreceq | | \nmid | |
| \nsucceq | | \nshortmid | |
| \precnsim | | \nshortparallel | |
| \succnsim | | \nvdash | |
| \lnsim | | \nVdash | |
| \gnsim | | \nvDash | |
| \nleqq | | \nVDash | |
| \ngeqq | | \ntrianglerighteq | |
| \precneqq | | \ntrianglelefteq | |
| \succneqq | | \ntriangleleft | |
| \precnapprox | | \ntriangleright | |
| | | | |
| \nleftarrow | | \nRightarrow | |
| \nrightarrow | | \nLeftrightarrow | |
| \nLeftarrow | | \nleftrightarrow | |
| | | | |
| \lessdot | | \approxeq | |
| \gtrdot | | \succapprox | |
| \shortmid | | \precapprox | |
| \shortparallel | | \curvearrowleft | |
| \thicksim | | \curvearrowright | |
| \thickapprox | | \backepsilon | |

## Openings

| | |
|---|---|
| \ulcorner | |
| \llcorner | |

## Closings

| | |
|---|---|
| \urcorner | |
| \lrcorner | |

# 10 Error Messages

## 10.1 What To Do When Errors Occur

No TEX input is perfect from the beginning; in nearly all cases errors and therefore error messages will occur.

There are a few simple correction possibilities available when entering into a dialogue with the TEX program. An existing input file, however, cannot be changed during the TEX run.

When an error occurs, an error message is generated. If the user enters a "?" the different possibilities for action are displayed. An input of "H" gives a more detailed explanation of the error.

```
Type <return> to proceed, S to scroll future error messages,
R to run without stopping, Q to run quietly,
I to insert something,
E to edit your file,
1 or ... or 9 to ignore the next 1 to 9 tokens of input,
H for help, X to quit.
```

The most important actions are the following:

*(return)* An empty input *(return)* just continues the TEX run until the next interruption — end of input or next error.

X E An input of X or E cancels the program run *immediately*.

S An input of S continues the TEX run without stopping for new errors, the error messages are shown on the display, however.

R Q With these inputs, error messages are only written to the logfile from now on. There are no more terminal inputs in any case, not even for missing files. If "Q" was input no further output is sent to the terminal.

The other commands provide limited means of getting around the error. Usually, this is very difficult. The best way to make a new attempt is to edit the input file.

## 10.2 Common Errors and Their Causes

The following examples contain the most common error messages. Some errors rarely occur except as *after-effect errors*. They can sometimes be quite irritating.

```
Undefined control sequence
The control sequence at the end of the top line
of your error message was never \def'ed. If you have
misspelled it (e.g., '\hobx'), type 'I' and the correct
spelling (e.g., 'I\hbox'). Otherwise just continue,
and I'll forget about whatever was undefined.
```

Typically a non-existing command has been used. Sometimes a blank space at the end of a command has been omitted, as in the word "hors d'\oeuvre". The intended command "\oe" has not been recognized, and the command "\oeuvre" does not exist. This typing mistake can be fixed by inputting "I\oe uvre".

```
Missing { inserted
A left brace was mandatory here, so I've put one in.
```

TeX has inserted an opening brace that was missing — at least in TeX's view. The bracket structure of the input is damaged. This will usually lead to further errors.

```
I've run across a '}' that doesn't seem to match anything.
For example, '\def\a#1{...}' and '\a}' would produce
this error. If you simply proceed now, the '\par' that
I've just inserted will cause me to report a runaway
argument that might be the root of the problem. But if
your '}' was spurious, just type '2' and it will go away.
```

A closing brace is interpreted as an end symbol, but there is no corresponding opening brace.

```
Missing number, treated as zero
```

TeX expects a number at this point, and the input doesn't contain any. The input "\pageno=\par", e.g., leads to this message.

```
Use of ... doesn't match its definition
If you say, e.g., '\def\a1{...}', then you must always
put '1' after '\a', since control sequence names are
made up of letters only. The macro here has not been
followed by the required stuff, so I'm ignoring it.
```

A macro has been found that can only be used within a certain textual context. The call to this macro must be corrected.

```
Missing   ... inserted
```

TEX has tried to correct the input by inserting some element.
`Missing } inserted`, e.g., can occur easily in the following situation: for the input
"`\hbox{\smallskip ...}`" TEX has to close the `\hbox` immediately.

```
Dimensions can be in units of em, ex, in, pt, pc,
cm, mm, dd, cc, bp, or sp; but yours is a new one!
I'll assume that you meant to say pt, for printers' points.
```

A wrong unit of dimension has been found, e.g., `\vskip 3mc` instead of `\vskip 3cm`.
TEX has replaced this with "`pt`". This usually leads to a faulty layout.

```
Paragraph ended before ... was complete
```

The typical error here is that a macro call is incomplete, because the closing brace is
missing. TEX finds a paragraph end before the call was completed.

```
Parameters must be numbered consecutively
```

The definition of a macro is incorrect: the parameters are not numbered in ascending
order, e.g., `\def\mmm#1#3#2{ ...` instead of `\def\mmm#1#2#3{ ....`

```
File ended within ...
```

The cause is nearly always a missing brace for a procedure call. This is very common
in complex mathematical formulae. The name of the incomplete procedure is shown.

```
I can't find file ...
```

The *file* for an "`\input`" command does not exist.

```
not loadable: Metric (TFM) file not found
```

The typeface that is referenced in a `\font` command does not exist. This is either a
typing mistake, or the corresponding file is missing.

```
not loadable: Bad metric (TFM) file
```

and

```
I wasn't able to read the size data for this font,
so I will ignore the font specification.
[Wizards can fix TFM files using TFtoPL/PLtoTF.]
You might try inserting a different font spec;
e.g., type 'I\font<same font id>=<substitute font name>'.
```

A defective metric file was found. The TEX program suggests substituting a different
font definition.

```
not loaded: Not enough room left
```

TeX has not found enough memory to load the metric information for this additional font. You can use "\tracingstats=1" to get an analysis of memory use at the end of the TeX run.

```
Missing character: There is no ... in font ...
```

When a font could not be found or was not loaded (see above), this error message is generated for each attempt to set a character from the font. This error can also occur when special fonts are used that do not have all characters defined. If such a non-existing character is referenced, this message will appear.

```
Underfull \hbox (badness ... ) has occurred ...
Overfull \hbox (badness ... ) has occurred ...
Underfull \vbox (badness ... ) has occurred ...
Overfull \vbox (badness ... ) has occurred ...
```

These are the most common error messages of all. In most cases a line is too short or too long, because the TeX program could not find a place to break a line in a paragraph. This is the typical cause of Overfull \hbox ... The start of the corresponding line is shown.

The problem for a \vbox is in most cases that \eject has been used without providing enough dynamic skip to fill the page. This is easily corrected by writing \vfill\eject.

When explicit \vbox and \hbox commands are involved, where these have been given with explicit dimensions, it is mostly necessary to insert a \vfill or \hfill.

The typical elements leading to an "Overfull \hbox..." are overlong lines. The following message is "... pt too wide". All messages that specify a length of less than 1 pt can be safely ignored. These lengths are barely discernible in the final output. The limit for showing occurrences of an overfull box can be increased by the command "\hfuzz=1pt", so that the messages are suppressed.

The standard cause during the breaking of a paragraph is incomplete hyphenation. The TeX program shows the last words of the overfull line, including the suggested hyphenation positions. In this way corrections can be performed without the need to produce real output on any device.

```
Missing # inserted in alignment preamble
There should be exactly one # between &'s, when an
\halign or \valign is being set up. In this case you had
none, so I've put one in; maybe that will work.
```

The use of an \halign command is incorrect: the error is in the template line.

```
Only one # is allowed per tab
There should be exactly one # between &'s, when an
\halign or \valign is being set up. In this case you had
more than one, so I'm ignoring all but the first.
```

In the template line of an \halign two # were found with no intervening &. This character is probably missing.

```
I've inserted something that you may have forgotten.
(See the <inserted text> above.)
```

TeX has inserted some additional material. Careful !
In most cases a "$" has been inserted, because the TeX program has found a command that is only allowed in mathematical mode. The following input will usually be severely misinterpreted.

```
You've closed more groups than you opened.
Such booboos are generally harmless, so keep going.
```

There was one more closing brace "}" found than there were opening braces encountered. This should be corrected to keep the files tidy.

```
Extra }, or forgotten {
```

There was one more closing brace "}" found than there were opening braces encountered. This should be corrected to keep the files tidy.

```
I've deleted a group-closing symbol because it seems to be
spurious, as in '$x}$'. But perhaps the } is legitimate and
you forgot something else, as in '\hbox{$x}'. In such cases
the way to recover is to insert both the forgotten and the
deleted material, e.g., by typing 'I$}'.
```

A closing brace was found in a syntactically incorrect place.

```
Please use ... for accents in math mode
I'm changing \accent to \mathaccent here; wish me luck.
(Accents are not the same in formulas as they are in text.)
```

This is, in almost all cases, an after-effect: TeX has inserted a $ sign, because the program believed the information to belong to mathematical mode. The symbols ^ and _, e.g., are *only* allowed in mathematical mode as subscript or superscript symbols. Similarly handled are some symbols that are considered mathematical operators. This forced mathematics afterwards usually runs on into plain text input containing, e.g., accents.

## 10.3 Logging Parameters

Some commands are responsible for determining how much information the log corresponding to the input will contain. For error analysis, a more complete log is often desired. The most important parameters influencing the logging are:

| | |
|---|---|
| `\tracingonline=1` | This command sends all test output to the terminal too. Otherwise these are written to the logfile only. |
| `\tracingcommands=1` | Each *executed* command is logged. |
| `\tracingcommands=2` | All commands are logged, even if they are skipped because they are in the non-selected part of an `\if`.... |
| `\tracingmacros=1` | For each macro call, the values of the parameters are logged. |

After the input

```
\tracingmacros=1
\def\value#1#2{{\bf #1} $\to$ {\bf #2}}
\value{1\$}{2 DM}
```

the logfile contains

```
\value #1#2->{\bf #1} $\to $ {\bf #2}
#1<-1\$
#2<-2 DM
\bf ->\fam \bffam \tenbf
\bf ->\fam \bffam \tenbf
```

Note: the command "`\bf`" is a macro itself, as the example shows.

| | |
|---|---|
| `\tracingall` | *All* logging options are activated. The information generated is very extensive. |
| `\tracingstats=1` | At the end of the TeX run, statistical information about TeX's memory use is printed. This helps to find out how much space is available for additional fonts or macros. |
| `\tracingstats=2` | A partial statistical output is done at the end of each page. |

Example statistical output (the maximum values are implementation-dependent):

```
Here is how much of TeX's memory you used:
193 strings   out of 8196
 1431 string characters out of 28137
 18143 words of memory out of 65001
 1039 multiletter control sequences out of 7000
15847 words of font info for 54 fonts ,
        out of 40000 for 150
0 hyphenation exceptions  out of 307
 12i,16n,8p,201b,91s stack positions
        out of 400i,40n,60p,1000b,1200s
```

# 11 Output Routines

## 11.1 Use of Output Routines

The ordinary user who does not change the layout of the pages will not think about output routines. Only if the structure of a page that consists of headline, text area, footline, and possibly insertions by "\topinsert" or "\footnote" is to be modified, do output routines have to be modified. Often a slight change of the standard output routine will give the desired effect.

The output routine is defined by plain TeX as a macro that is called automatically when a page is "filled", i.e. when enough material has been gathered to fill up to "\vsize". This will invoke the output routine. Within the output routine, the page may be effectively printed to the dvi file by "\shipout". Before the page is printed the information is combined with headlines, footlines and insertions. TeX does this by passing the following information in predefined registers to the output routine:

\box255          contains the text of the text area that is broken into pages of height "\vsize". The content of "\box255" is a "\vbox". It only contains the information of the text area excluding footnotes or insertions, e.g., by "\topinsert".

\outputpenalty   is a numeric register that contains the penalty of the page break position. This value may be checked, e.g., by

                         \ifnum\outputpenalty>10 ...
                 In truth the output routine is also invoked if a
                         \penalty $\leq -10000$
                 that has more than 10000 positive units, is encountered. This gives a method to force the invocation of the output routine. In fact "\eject" is defined by
                         \def\eject{\par\penalty-10000 }
                 This provides a means to transfer additional information to the output routine by specifying values such as "-10001, -10002 ...". These values may be checked and may control extra functions.

\insertpenalties contains the number of insertions that are still stored in insertion registers, e.g., by "\insert" or "\topinsert".

\deadcycles          counts the number of consecutive calls of the output routine when
                     this does not give a call of "\shipout". If the value of the register
                     \deadcycles exceeds the limit in "\maxdeadcycles", an error oc-
                     curs. \maxdeadcycles is an internal register that is preset to 25.
                     It may be changed if needed.

## 11.2 The Standard Output Routine

This section discusses the standard output routine of plain TₑX that gives the normal
text page. It is defined by

```
\output={\plainoutput}

\def\plainoutput{
        \shipout\vbox {\makeheadline    % 1. combine information
                       \pagebody        %     and print page
                       \makefootline}   %
        \advancepageno                  % 2. page counting
        \ifnum\outputpenalty>-20000     % 3. special commands at
          \else\dosupereject\fi}        %     program end
```

The register "\output" stores the command for the output routine. The function is
similar to the registers \headline and \footline. Here, it only contains the name of
the macro "\plainoutput" that effectivly does the task.

This is done in three main steps:

1. Building and printing the page

```
\shipout\vbox {\makeheadline
               \pagebody
               \makefootline}
```

   The command "\shipout" prints the information of the following box — as a
   single page — into the dvi file. The box consists of three elements:
   a) "\makeheadline" generates the headline (empty by default).
   b) "\pagebody" builds the information of the text area.
   c) "\makefootline" adds the footline below the text.
2. In "\advancepageno" the page number is changed.
3. The last step tests if the current call to the output routine was caused by a
   program end. Then the value ($\outputpenalty \leq -20000$) will force the printing
   of insertions still stored.

*1.a) generating the headline*

The macro "\makeheadline" generates a logical empty \vbox with the height 0 pt. In
this \vbox a skip backwards is set for positioning the headline above the following text
area.

```
\def\makeheadline{\vbox to 0pt
               {\vskip -22.5pt
                \line{\vbox to 8.5pt{}\the\headline}
                \vss}
               \nointerlineskip}
```

The curious value of "\vskip -22.5pt" is based on the standard dimensions of lines with a cumulated size of 12 pt that is divided in 8.5 pt above and 3.5 pt below the baseline. Furthermore, the baseline of the first text line in the text area is typeset with \topskip=10pt distance to the top of the text area. Some arithmetic calculations show that the baseline of the headline and the baseline of the text area have a distance of 24 pt. The command "\nointerlineskip" suppresses any additional vertical space between the box generated by the headline and the text area.

If enlarged typefaces are used, distances may be modified. A simple change like turning "\vskip -22.5 pt" into "\vskip -34.5pt" doubles the space between head-line and text.

*1.b) building the text area*

The macro "\pagebody" generates the text area. It calls a submacro "\pagecontents" to do the work.

```
\def\pagebody{\vbox to \vsize{\boxmaxdepth=\maxdepth
                            \pagecontents}}
```

At the beginning, the maximum depth of the page is limited to "\maxdepth" which is preset to 4 pt by plain TEX.

```
\def\pagecontents{\ifvoid\topins\else\unvbox\topins\fi
                  \dimen0=\dp255
                  \unvbox255
                  \ifvoid\footins
                  \else
                    \vskip\skip\footins
                    \footnoterule
                    \unvbox\footins
                  \fi
                  \ifraggedbottom\kern-\dimen0\vfil\fi}
```

This looks quite complicated, as several objects are being handled. First there is a check

```
\ifvoid\topins\else\unvbox\topins\fi
```

to see if any insertions for the top of the text area are present. These would have been generated by "\topinsert". The output is done by "\unvbox\topins". The next command "\dimen0=\dp255" saves the depth of the box containing the information for the ordinary text area for later use. By "\unvbox255" the text area is contributed to the page. This empties "\box255". Finally, footnotes will be added:

```
\ifvoid\footins        % any footnotes ?
    \else
      \vskip\skip\footins  %   some white space
      \footnoterule        %   add dividing rule
      \unvbox\footins      %   output the footnote
\fi
```

This starts with a check whether footnotes are present by "\ifvoid\footins". If there are some footnotes pending, a small vertical space is typeset above the footnotes by the commands "\vskip\skip\footins", the separating rule for footnotes is generated by "\footnoterule" and then the footnote information stored in "\box\footins" is added by "\unvbox\footins".

If the pages are to be typeset with "ragged" bottoms a correction of the box length follows.

This finishes the text area.

*1.c) footline*

The macro "\makefootline" ,which is defined by

```
\def\makefootline{\baselineskip=24pt
                \line{\the\footline}}
```

generates the footlines of pages. Just as with the headline, the footlines are generated with the distance of a normal line height to the text area. But here another method is chosen. The value for line distances "\baselineskip" is doubled locally. This produces a distance of 24 pt between the baseline of the footline and the last line of the text area.

*2. page counting*

The output routine is the place to change the page numbers. By convention, page numbers are decremented if they are less than zero otherwise they are incremented by 1 as expected.

```
\def\advancepageno{
        \ifnum\pageno < 0 \global\advance\pageno by -1
        \else               \global\advance\pageno by  1 \fi}
```

*3. specials at program end*
By the commands

```
\ifnum\outputpenalty>-20000\else
      \dosupereject\fi
```

an extra invocation of the output routine is forced to ship out retained insertions. "\dosupereject" may generate an additional page.

```
\def\dosupereject{
        \ifnum\insertpenalties>0
          \vbox to -\topskip{\line{}\vss}
          \vfill\supereject\fi}
```

This is done by generating a penalty in "\supereject" that is defined by the commands "\par\penalty-20000". It forces a call to the output routine.

## 11.3 Variations of the Output Routine

The most simple use of an output routine is the application of a \shipout command. It needs as a parameter a box that is printed as a single page. Maybe \box0 contains a constructed box that should be printed without surrounding headline and footline. The single command "\shipout\box0" will generate the page.

The definition of the plain TEX output routines is strongly structured into a set of macros. This allows dedicated modification of the plain TEX output routine. Remember the page is built by the commands

```
\shipout\vbox{\makeheadline
        \pagebody
        \makefootline}
```

| \makeheadline |
|---|
| \pagebody |
| \makefootline |

It is quite easy to modify "\makeheadline". Positioning backwards within the *token* register \headline is usually more complicated.
Example:

```
\def\makeheadline{%
    \vbox{\hrule
        \line{%
            \vrule\quad
            $\vcenter{%
                \vbox{\it\medskip
                        \hbox{Buck \& Duck}
                        \hbox{Software}
                        \medskip}}$
            \quad\vrule
            \hfil\tenrm\the\headline\hfil
            \vrule\quad
            $\vcenter{%
                \vbox{\bf\hbox{BuDu --- Page \folio}}}$
            \quad\vrule}%
        \hrule}
    \nointerlineskip}
```

"\headline" will contain the simple page titles.
After \headline={Prime Numbers} the page titles are generated as

| *Buck & Duck* *Software* | Prime Numbers | **BuDu — Page 155** |
|---|---|---|

As this headline is larger than the ordinary headline, the size of the text area should be modified.

*multi-column printing*

Remember that page breaks will be adjusted to "\vsize" and line breaks according to "\hsize" during the course of building paragraphs. As the two columns of a double-column output should not touch each other, additional space between the columns is needed. This will give an effective width of the text area greater than $2 \times$ \hsize.

The output routine will be called when a column is filled. What will be done is rather simple: a finished left column will not be printed, but stored away; a right column will be printed combined with its saved left counterpart.

The macros needed are like the following. First, some registers are defined:

```
\newdimen\FullWidth          \newif\ifright
\FullWidth = \hsize          \newbox\LeftColumn
\hsize=0.45 \hsize
```

This defines the column width to be 45 % of the normal width "\hsize" of the text area. By "\newif\ifright", a new \if command is defined to determine whether a right or left column follows. Similar to the standard output routine, there are definitions such as

```
\def\DoubleColumn{%
   \ifright
      \shipout\vbox{\longheadline
                    \hbox to \FullWidth
                         {\box\LeftColumn
                          \hfil
                          \leftline{\pagebody}}
                          \longfootline}
      \global\rightfalse
      \advancepageno
   \else
      \global\setbox\LeftColumn=
               \leftline{\pagebody}
      \global\righttrue
   \fi
   \ifnum\outputpenalty>-20000\else
        \dosupereject \fi}
\output={\DoubleColumn}
```

The commands \longheadline and \longfootline are missing. They have to be defined along the lines of \makeheadline and \makefootline. The command \line that is used within \makeheadline and \makefootline is defined by

```
\def\line#1{\hbox to \hsize{#1}}
```

It has to be substituted by an "\hbox to \FullWidth". This will finish a normal layout.

The preceding macros give a simplified solution of the problem. Footnotes and insertions are handled for each column but they are only stored, not printed. Furthermore, the text has to end with a right column, so the end of input should contain the command

```
\ifright\hbox{}\vfill\eject\fi
```

The next missing feature are balanced columns. The last page of a double column text should not contain a long and a short column, but two even-sized columns. This is a little bit complicated: the two columns are stored into a new \vbox by "\unvbox". This box must be divided into two new colums by a "\vsplit" command. This method is described in Section 8.11.

## 11.4 Page Marks

There are some commands to mark positions with specific text that may be referenced while in the output routine. This is quite useful for section titles. When the page is finished, the current section title can be referred to and used, e.g., within the headline.

---

| *Didone* | 157 | *Mécane* |
|---|---|---|

their previous oval forms have become circles. Hairlines and main strokes differ extremely. The axis of bowls is vertical.

*Old Face, Old Style* — Its shows a smooth transition from the stems to the serifs. The serifs get rounded edges. The cross stem of the 'e' is horizontally arranged.  *Garalde*

*Sans Serif* — These typefaces have no serifs. Sometimes they are called "Grotesque". Crossbars and stems are optically of the same thickness.  *Lineale*

*Egyptian Group, Slab Serif* — All elements have the same optical stroke thickness.  *Mécane*

---

The current section titles are used in the headline on the left and right sides. A simple operation to put them into a macro will not help, as the information will change too often within the current page. The text has to contain \mark commands to store the information that is requested later. The command "\mark{..information..}" is used in the preceding example in

```
...
\mark{Didone}
\mark{Garalde}
\mark{Lineale}
\mark{M\'ecane}
...
```

The commands are given at the beginning of each section. The output routine will refer to the information by

\botmark    is the last text which is stored by \mark on the current page.

\firstmark    gives the text of the first \mark command on the current page. If there is none, the text of the last preceding \mark command will be referenced.

\topmark    gives the text of the \mark that is valid at the top of the current page. This is the \botmark of the preceding page.

The results of the commands will be demonstrated by the following table:

| page | \mark commands | result of \topmark | result of \firstmark | result of \botmark |
|------|----------------|--------------------|----------------------|--------------------|
| 1 | — | *empty* | *empty* | *empty* |
| 2 | \mark{A} | *empty* | A | A |
| 3 | — | A | A | A |
| 4 | \mark{B} + \mark{C} | A | B | C |
| 5 | \mark{D} | C | D | D |
| 6 | — | D | D | D |

The headline of the preceding example is defined by

```
\headline={\rlap{\centerline{\tenrm\folio}}% page number
          \tenit \topmark \hss \botmark}
\footline={\hss}
```

The commands "\rlap{\centerline{\tenrm\folio}}" center the line number with respect to the full line width without including the size of the text on the left and on the right.

```
\line{\tenit\topmark\hss{\tenrm\folio}\hss\botmark}
```

A further remark:

For documents similar to an encyclopaedia or a dictionary there are different layouts possible to put \topmark or \firstmark text into the headline. The headline may contain the current paragraph title or the name of the first new paragraph.

# 12 Example Applications

This chapter demonstrates some complex applications of TeX. Included are a lot of macro definitions that do the work. Macros of different packages cannot always be combined with those of other examples.

## 12.1 Histogram

A simple graphical application is implemented by use of \vrule and \hrule commands to show histograms. The following example defines a \diagram macro.

*Macro parameters of* \diagram

#1 unit of measure, e.g., "cm", or "pt", or a register that is defined by "\newdimen"
#2 width of the diagram (in units of #1)
#3 height of the diagram (in units of #1)
#4 title that is typeset at the top (with centering)
#5 title that is typeset below the table (with centering)
#6 information

The information for #6 may contain the following additional commands:

\bBlock{ *height* }{ *subtitle* } generates a "bold" block. The information of "*subtitle*" will be set centered below the block.

\hBlock{ *height* }{ *subtitle* } typesets a "hatched" block.

\oBlock{ *height* }{ *subtitle* } builds an "outlined" block.

| | |
|---|---|
| \bBlockTop{ *height* } | puts a bold block onto the top of the preceding block. |
| \hBlockTop{ *height* } | ditto, a hatched block is used. |
| \oBlockTop{ *height* } | ditto, an outlined block is used. |
| \NewWidth{ *value* } | redefines the width of the following blocks in units of "#1". The width of each block is preset to 0.3 cm. |

These extra macros are defined locally to "\diagram". After \diagram is finished the inner macros are unknown. It is quite easy to extend the macros by blocks with other optical characteristics. The combination of the elements uses the standard technique of combining elements with zero size.

The elements in the example are horizontally aligned by the insertion of "\hfill".

The macros are:

```
%
% utility macro to build a frame around information
%
\def\BuildFrame#1{\vbox{\hrule
                        \hbox{\vrule\vbox{#1}\vrule}%
                        \hrule}}

\def\diagram#1#2#3#4#5#6{{%
%
%   constants
%
    \dimen1=0.3cm % width of a block (default)
%
%   change the width of a block
%
    \def\NewWidth##1{\dimen1=##1#1\relax}%
%
%  1.  lower title of a block
%
\def\LowerTitle##1{\setbox0=\hbox{##1}%
   \hbox to 0pt{\kern0.5\dimen1%
   \kern-0.5\wd0\vbox to 0pt{\kern0.3cm\box0\vss}\hss}}%
%
%  2.a  build a bold block
%
\def\bBlock##1##2{\LowerTitle{##2}\dimen3=##1#1%
   \vrule width\dimen1 height##1#1}%

%
%  2.b  set a bold block on top of preceding block
%
\def\bBlockTop##1{\kern-\dimen1{%
   \dimen0=##1#1\advance\dimen0 by \dimen3%
   \vrule width\dimen1 height\dimen0 depth-\dimen3}%
   \advance\dimen3 by ##1#1}%
%
%   3.a  typeset an outlined block
%
\def\oBlock##1##2{\LowerTitle{##2}%
   \dimen3=##1#1%
   {\dimen2=\dimen1\advance\dimen2 by-0.1cm
   \vrule height##1#1 width0.05cm
   \vrule height0.05cm width\dimen2  \kern-\dimen2
   \dimen0=-0.05cm \advance\dimen0 by ##1#1\relax
   \vrule height##1#1 width\dimen2 depth-\dimen0
   \vrule height##1#1 width0.05cm}}
```

```
%
%  3.b.  put an outlined block on top
%
\def\oBlockTop##1{\kern-\dimen1{%
  \dimen0=##1#1\advance\dimen0 by \dimen3
  \vrule height\dimen0 width0.05cm depth-\dimen3
  \dimen4=0.05cm\advance\dimen4 by \dimen3
  \kern-0.05cm
  \vrule height\dimen4 width\dimen1 depth-\dimen3
  \dimen0=##1#1\advance\dimen0 by \dimen3
  \kern-0.05cm
  \vrule height\dimen0 width0.05cm depth-\dimen3
  \kern-\dimen1
  \dimen0=##1#1\advance\dimen0 by \dimen3
  \dimen2=\dimen0\advance\dimen2 by-0.05cm
  \vrule height\dimen0 width\dimen1 depth-\dimen2}%
  \advance\dimen3 by ##1#1}%

%
%   4.a  generate a hatched block
%
\def\hBlock##1##2{\LowerTitle{##2}%
   \dimen3=##1#1%
   \hbox to \dimen1{\vrule width0.025cm
     \xleaders
     \hbox{\hskip0.025cm\vrule width0.025cm height##1#1}\hfill}}%

%
%   4.b  build a hatched block on top
%
\def\hBlockTop##1{\kern-\dimen1{%
  \dimen0=##1#1\advance\dimen0 by \dimen3
  \hbox to\dimen1{\vrule width0.025cm height\dimen0 depth-\dimen3
    \xleaders\hbox{\hskip0.025cm
                \vrule width0.025cm height\dimen0 depth-\dimen3}%
        \hfill}}%
  \advance\dimen3 by ##1#1}%

%
%  build the diagram
%
\vbox to #3#1{%
\bigskip
\ifx#4\void\else\hbox to #2#1{\hss#4\hss}\fi
\vfill
\hbox to #2#1{#6\hss}\vskip1cm
\ifx#5\void\else\hbox to #2#1{\hss#5\hss}\vskip1cm\fi
\vss}}}
```

An example use of \diagram:

```
\def\put#1#2{\hbox{\setbox0=\hbox{#2}
                \vtop{\hbox to \wd0{\hfil#1\hfil}\hbox{#2}}}}
\newdimen\mydimen \mydimen=0.3cm
\centerline{\BuildFrame{%
   \diagram{\mydimen}
            {35}
            {18}
            {\bf Output in 1888}
            {\bf in 1000 t}
            {\NewWidth{0.6}
             \hfill \bBlock {9.37} {\put{9.37}{Alpha-Town}}
             \hfill \oBlock {3.00} {\put{3.00}{Beta City}}
             \hfill \hBlock {5.16} {\put{5.16}{Delta Village}}
             \hfill \bBlock {4.04} {\put{4.04}{Etaville}}
             \hfill}}}
\centerline{\BuildFrame{%
   \diagram{cm}
            {12}
            {16}
            {\bf Output in 1888}
            {\bf in 1000 t}
            {\NewWidth{0.6}
             \hfill \bBlock {9.37} {\put{9.37}{Alpha-Town}}
             \hfill \oBlock {3.00} {\put{3.00}{Beta City}}%
                    \hBlockTop{4}
             \hfill \hBlock {5.16} {\put{5.16}{Delta Village}}
             \hfill \bBlock {4.04} {\put{4.04}{Etaville}}
             \hfill}}}
```

yields

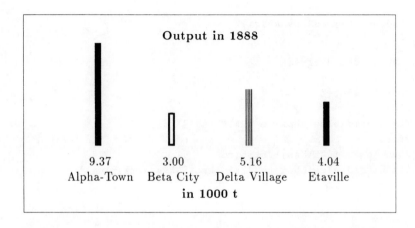

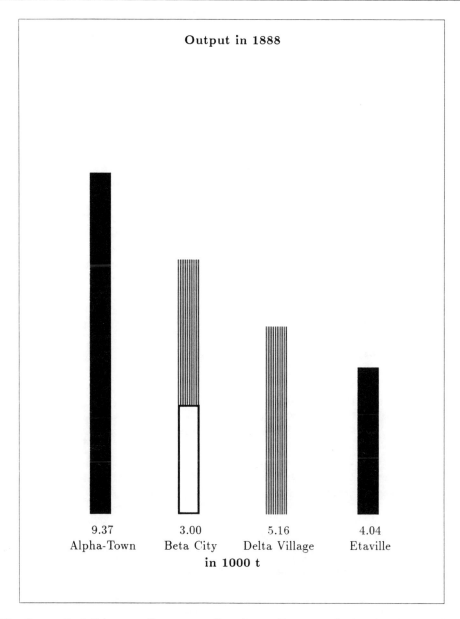

The first call of "\diagram" uses a scaling factor "\mydimen" that has been defined before. The measuring unit corresponds to 0.3 cm.

## 12.2 Building Quotes

Typesetting German text needs different forms of quotes that are not present in the character set offered by TEX. There are "lower quotes" « „ » with the shape of two commas at the beginning of spoken text, and two upper quotes « " » at the end.

Besides these French *guillemets* are also missing. These are « text ». In German the
pointed ends are typeset outwards, in Switzerland » inwards «.

TeX's powerful macro capabilities allow the construction of these symbols.

```
\let\less=<
\let\greater=>
\def\comma{,}
\def\textless{\leavevmode
            \raise1pt\hbox{$\scriptscriptstyle<$}}
\def\textlless{\leavevmode
            \raise1pt\hbox{$\scriptscriptstyle\ll$}}
\def\textgreater{\leavevmode
            \raise1pt\hbox{$\scriptscriptstyle>$}}
\def\textggreater{\leavevmode
            \raise1pt\hbox{$\scriptscriptstyle\gg$}}
%%
\catcode'\,=\active  % ATTENTION !    All applications of
\catcode'\<=\active  %                \ifdim ... < ... etc.
\catcode'\>=\active  %                must precede these macros.
\catcode'\?=\active  %                '<' and '>' will not be
\catcode'\!=\active  %                recognized otherwise.
%%
\def\ignore#1{}
\def?{\char"3F{\kern0pt}}
\def!{\char"21{\kern0pt}}
\def,{\comma\futurelet\next\commatest}
\def\commatest{\ifmmode\else
                \ifx\next,\kern-.11em\fi
            \fi}
\def<{\futurelet\next\lesstest}
\def>{\futurelet\next\greatertest}
\def\lesstest{\ifmmode \less  \let\next=\relax
            \else
                \ifx\next<\textlless \let\next=\ignore
                \else \textless  \let\next=\relax\fi
            \fi\next}
\def\greatertest{\ifmmode \greater  \let\next=\relax
                \else
                \ifx\next>\textggreater \let\next=\ignore
                    \else \textgreater \let\next=\relax\fi
            \fi\next}
```

This is done by checking on each occurrence of a comma or less or greater sign, whether
the following character is of the same sort. If this happens the suitable commands will
be executed and two characters are typeset very tightly.

The cumbersome redefinition of "?" and "!" is caused by ligatures that are generated automatically if the letters ?' and !' are found side by side. These character
pairs will usually generate the Spanish punctuations "¿" and "¡", but they are sensible
combinations in German.

The macro `\def?{\char"3F{}}` simply gives a character of the code table. The command `{\kernOpt}` inhibits the integration of the two symbols into a ligature. The command "`\leavevmode`" forces entry of *horizontal mode*.
The example

```
<< To tex or not to tex? >> asked the king.
>> To tex or not to tex? << asked the queen.
,,A {\tt\string\strut} is missing!'' spoke the princess.
 ,You forgot {\tt\string\offinterlineskip}!'   said the wizard.
```

produces as output

&laquo; To tex or not to tex? &raquo; asked the king.
&raquo; To tex or not to tex? &laquo; asked the queen.
„A \strut is missing!" spoke the princess.
‚You forgot \offinterlineskip!' said the wizard.

A closer look will also show that "<" and ">" did not change their meaning within mathematical formulae.

## 12.3 Lecture Script

The following example will demonstrate a utility to generate lecture scripts that contain the material of foils and additional comments. The macros allow the production of the complete script in diminished size and also the separate generation — enlarged — of the contents of the foils.

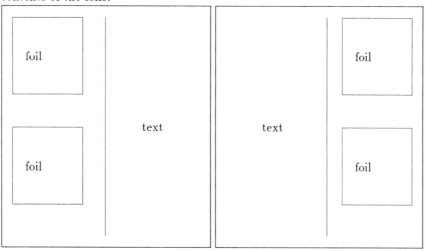

← even page number                                        odd page number →

1 motivation
2 project organization
3 program design
   3.1 modular programming
   3.2 bottom up / top down
   3.3 data structures
4 program coding
   4.1 programming tools
   4.2 structured programming
   4.3 portability
   4.4 programming style
   4.5 defensive programming
5 testing
6 debugging

This lecture will give information on the fundamentals of *good* programming.

List of answers to *good programs* question:

17 × is readable (for man)
12 × is clearly structured
12 × runs
 9 × does the required work
 8 × handles errors of users
 8 × is easy to correct
 8 × runs quickly
 7 × is well documented
 6 × may be extended
 5 × is well adopted to the machine
 5 × needs little memory
 4 × contains comments
 2 × is easy to use
 1 × is portable
 1 × is testable

## Questionnaire

1 What do you think is a *good* programmer?

2 What do you think is a *good* program?

The necessary macros are:

```
\newdimen\papersize          % full paper size
\newdimen\columnsize         % width of a text column
\newdimen\slidehsize         % width of transparency
\newdimen\slidevsize         % height
\newbox\upperbox             % upper slide
\newbox\lowerbox             % lower slide
%
\newif\ifslides              % \slidestrue -> \ifslides := true
                             % \slidesfalse -> \ifslides := false
                             % after " \slidestrue "
                             %         only slides are
                             %         generated
%
\papersize=\hsize
\columnsize=0.5\hsize
%
\slidehsize=\hsize
\advance\slidehsize by - \columnsize
\advance\slidehsize by - 3em             % \qquad
%
\slidevsize=0.4\vsize
%
\hsize=\columnsize
%
\def\makeheadline{\vbox to 0pt
                  {\vskip -22.5pt
                   \hsize=\papersize
                   \line{\vbox to 8.5pt{}\the\headline}%
                   \vss}%
                  \nointerlineskip}
%
\def\makefootline{\baselineskip=24pt
                  \hbox to \papersize{\the\footline}}
\def\fulloutput{\shipout\vbox{\makeheadline
                              \makepagebox
                              \bigskip
                              \bigskip
                              \makefootline}%
                \advancepageno
                \ifnum\outputpenalty>-20000
                    \else\dosupereject\fi}
```

```
%
% builds a frame
%
%  #1 <- distance to frame
%  #2 <- thickness of rules
%  #3 <- information
%
\def\frame#1#2#3{\vbox{\hrule height #2
                      \hbox{\vrule width #2
                            \hskip#1
                            \vbox{\vskip#1{}#3\vskip#1}%
                            \hskip#1
                            \vrule width#2}%
                      \hrule height#2}}
%
% gives a framed box
%
\def\framebox#1{\vbox to 0.5\vsize
                   {\ifvoid#1\vfil\else
                      \frame{0.2cm}{0.4pt}{\box#1}\vfil\fi}}
\def\makepagebox{\hbox to \papersize
                   {\ifodd\pageno
                      \vtop to \vsize{\hrule height 0pt
                                     \boxmaxdepth=\maxdepth
                                     \pagecontents\vfil}%
                      \hfil
                      \vtop to \vsize{\hrule height 0pt
                                     \framebox\upperbox
                                     \nointerlineskip
                                     \framebox\lowerbox}%
                    \else
                      \vtop to \vsize{\hrule height 0pt
                                     \framebox\upperbox
                                     \nointerlineskip
                                     \framebox\lowerbox}%
                      \hfil
                      \vtop to \vsize{\hrule height 0pt
                                     \boxmaxdepth=\maxdepth
                                     \pagecontents}%
                    \fi}}
```

```
\def\slideoutput{\ifvoid\upperbox\else
                 {\count1=1\shipout\vbox{\framebox\upperbox}}\fi
                 \ifvoid\lowerbox\else
                 {\count1=2\shipout\vbox{\framebox\lowerbox}}\fi
                 \advancepageno
                 \setbox0=\vbox{\box255}}
%
\output={\ifslides\slideoutput\else\fulloutput\fi}
%
%    \endslide will be redefined after \beginslide.
%
%    This generates an error message,
%    if \endslide is called first without a \beginslide.
%
\def\endslide{\errmessage{beginslide is missing}}
%
\outer\def\beginslide{
  \ifvoid\upperbox
    \begingroup
    \def\endslide{\vfil\egroup\endgroup}
    \global\setbox\upperbox
        \vbox to \slidevsize\bgroup\hsize=\slidehsize
  \else
    \ifvoid\lowerbox
    \begingroup
    \def\endslide{\vfil\egroup\endgroup}
    \global\setbox\lowerbox
        \vbox to \slidevsize\bgroup\hsize=\slidehsize
    \else
      \vfill\eject
      \begingroup
      \def\endslide{\vfil\egroup\endgroup}
      \global\setbox\upperbox
        \vbox to \slidevsize\bgroup\hsize=\slidehsize
    \fi
  \fi}
```

Some comments on the macros:

1. The new \if command "\ifslides" defines whether the whole text or only slides will be printed. After a command "\slidestrue" *only* the foils are generated. Pages are numbered using \count register 1. The counting will be in steps of "1.1, 1.2, 2.1, 2.2, ...", where "3.2" denotes the the second slide of page 3.
2. The variable \papersize stores the original width of the text area (\hsize); \columnsize holds the width of the text column, while \slidehsize and \slide-vsize contain the dimensions for a single slide.
3. The text for a slide is surrounded by the commands \beginslide and \endslide.

First the upper slide box is generated, then the lower one. When both boxes are filled a page break occurs.

These macros change the output routine. The standard functions given by \headline and \footline remain unchanged. The headlines and footlines are generated with the full text width. Footnotes are only typeset within the text column. The text column is used as usual without modification apart from the line length.

The preceding example is generated by

```
\beginslide
\raggedright
\item{1}motivation
\item{2}project organization
   ...
\itemitem{4.5} defensive programming
\item{5} testing
\item{6} debugging
\endslide
%
\beginslide
\centerline{\bf Questionnaire}
\raggedright
\medskip
\item{1} What do you think is a {\it good} programmer?
   ...
\endslide
%
\noindent
This lecture will give information on the
fundamentals of {\it good} programming.
\bigskip
\bigskip
\noindent List of answers to {\it good programs} question:
\medskip
{\obeylines
\itemitem{17 $\times$}   is readable (for man)
\itemitem{12 $\times$}   is clearly structured
   ...
}
\vfill\eject
```

# 13 Data Organization

## 13.1 Standard Files

When TEX is running it uses some files that have specific contents and are named by convention.

TEX gives each file a name with a specific extension of 3 letters that identifies the contents — if the operating system of your computer allows this. E.g., the extension ".TEX" (MS-DOS, UNIX, ...) or "_TEX" (NOS/VE) is expected at the end of input file names for TEX instructions.

The conventions are

.TEX for input files — also for "\input" — but also for files used with "\write".
   If the extension is missing in the call, it will be appended. The commands

       \input DATA
       \input DATA.TEX

   will read the same file on most systems.

.FMT identifies *format* files.
   The format file is selected at program start. Typical input is "&plain" or "&lplain" (see Section 2.5).
   In a compact form, format files contain macros, hyphenation tables and *font metrics* (sizes of letters). They are read much quicker than if everything has to be loaded from source files.

.LOG for the *log* file. It contains error messages and warnings. All terminal input is also written to the log file.

.DVI identifies the output file with the printing information (device independent file). This file is used by the printer driver to generate the final output.

.TFM identifies font metric files that contain information about specific fonts. It is read when a "\font" command is given.
   The file "CMSSI10.TFM", e.g., holds the information for the typeface "cmssi10" (sans serif italic 10 pt), that is used when "\font\sani=cmssi10" is given.

If the input is given interactively at program start, the job name will be set to "TEXPUT". "TEXPUT.LOG" will contain the log and "TEXPUT.DVI" the printing information. If a file name is specified, the name of this file without extension will be used for the job name.

If the input file is called "TEXDATA.TEX", the log file will be named "TEXDATA.LOG", the file with the print information "TEXDATA.DVI". As mentioned before the separating symbol "." may differ for some operating systems. The same is true for the filenames.

## 13.2 Organization of Input Files

During work on a larger project or for regularly repeated tasks the input data should be prepared in a structured form. The normal arrangement uses the division of data into several input files. Then files are read by the \input command when needed.

### Macro Organization

The most important part of systematic work with TEX is the handling of macros. The division into a fundamental subset, i.e. the private extensions to plain TEX, and several add-on packages is recommended. The extra macros are invoked when needed.

When such packages are prepared you should pay attention to prevent name conflicts between several packages.

Possible macro subsets are private names for typesetting mathematical formulae. Such a subset may contain handy abbreviations for heavily used subformulae, e.g., matrices, integrals, or even short names for greek letters. Other packages may contain private layouts for footnotes, e.g., prepared switches to use diminished font sizes with changed interline skip.

These simple macro packages change only one single aspect of plain TEX's behaviour, like redefinition of \footnote.

The top part of a macro hierarchy contains command sets for generating specific tasks, e.g., the company's telephone directory or — do not neglect this important application — greeting and invitation cards.

Practice has shown that it is quite convenient to collect in one place all instructions that influence layout, e.g., height and width of the text area. Font definitions should also be in one place only, it is especially important to name fonts with regard to their function. It is better to refer to "\footnotefont" than to "\smallroman". The latter name leads to a use in other places. This gives difficulties when changes are required later on. A good compromise is to first define "\font\eightrm=cmr8" and then say "\let\footnotefont=\eightrm". Then you can also use, without loading the font repeatedly, "\let\smallcitationfont=\eightrm".

### Organization of Input Data

The major principle for input data: use small units. It is very clumsy to put a 100 page document into one file. (I hope your favorite editor can load it.) Any change in the second half of the document can only be checked after 50 pages of unmodified code have been processed.

A division of a book input showing the structure of chapters and sections is self-evident. A control file at the top level will contain instructions like

```
              \input macros
\pageno=1     \input chapter1
\pageno=7     \input chapter2
\pageno=13    \input chapter3
     . . .
```

Large chapters can be divided into "CHAP1A.TEX", "CHAP1B.TEX", etc. The file "CHAP-TER1.TEX" can then contain

```
% chapter 1
\input chap1a
\input chap1b
\input chap1c
```

The top level file is easily modified to generate only parts of a document. The command language of your operating system may give aids to integrate this into a command procedure.

## 13.3 INITEX

Nearly all implementations offer a special variant of the TEX program called INITEX. This special program allows the generation of *format* files. INITEX reads all commands, i.e., macro definitions, and the language dependent hyphenation patterns that are later used during generation of paragraph lines.

All commands that are prepared by INITEX may be redefined later. This is quite often demonstrated by the redefining of plain TEX macros in this book.

The output of INITEX, after a "\dump" command, consists of the mentioned *format* file. The advantage of doing this lies in the quick loading of the *format* file by TEX. Macros, fonts, and hyphenation patterns are already read and stored in a — program-wise — convenient way to reread it. The name of the format file may be specified at the start of TEX, see Section 2.5.

The standard macros of plain TEX are usually stored in a file called "PLAIN.TEX". The hyphenation patterns for American English are stored in "HYPHEN.TEX". The patterns are loaded by the command "\patterns{...}" that is only available in INITEX. If "\patterns{...}" is left out TEX will not hyphenate a single word. There are patterns available for several other languages, e.g., French, German, Portuguese, Spanish. The standard TEX program can only use the patterns of *one* language in a format file.

You can pattern your own applications after the structure of "PLAIN.TEX". You could, e.g., load the hyphenation patterns by "\input HYPHEN".

After you have read all commands with INITEX, the last command will be "\dump" and INITEX writes the format file into a file with the name extension ".FMT".

The handy format files cause two slight problems. First, they are not portable between TEX implementations. A PC version format file cannot be used by the TEX implementation of a mainframe. Portable macros are only macros in source text (with comments please).

Second, macros need program memory. Maybe a lot of program memory is wasted by unused macros. Then it is better to read only the macros that are necessary for the current input.

## 13.4 Access to Text Files

The normal output of a TEX run is written to the dvi file to be shown on the screen or printed by a driver later on. Some information is also written to the log file: errors and warnings.

Apart from these, reading from and writing to text files is also possible.
A short description:

| *input* | *output* | *function* |
|---|---|---|
| \newread \name | \newwrite \name | get a free file number |
| \openin n = file name | \openout n = file name | open file |
| \read n to \destination | \write n { . . . } | read / write |
| \closein n | \closeout n | close file |
| \ifeof n | | check for end of file |

Before the first read or write, a file has to be associated with a file (access) number between 0 and 15. This is done by "\openin" and "\openout". All further "\read" and "\write" commands use this number. If a number is used without a previous \openin or \openout, or which is out of range, the output will be written to the log file and to the terminal. (If a negative number is used, printing to the terminal will be suppressed.)

Examples:

```
\write -1 {test position 4}
\write 66 {after critical part}
```

prints "after critical part" to the log file and to the terminal, the text "test position 4" is only written to the log file. The association of file name and file number can be done directly. However, it is better to request a free number by \newread or \newwrite, which assigns it to a symbolic name. Instead of

```
\openin 7 = DATA
\read 7 to \MyDataLine
\openout 12 = OUTFILE
\write 12 {I am on page \folio}
```

it is better to write

```
\newread\DataFile    \newwrite\OutputFile
\openin\DataFile=DATA
\read\DataFile to \MyDataLine
\openout\OutputFile= OUTFILE
\write\OutputFile{I am on page \folio}
```

The symbolic name is also more intuitive.

## 13.5 Input from Text Files

After \newread\DataFile a free file number is reserved. The input file has to be opened. By \openin TEX knows which file should be used. By

    \openin\DataFile=MYDATA

the file number \DataFile will point to "MYDATA.TEX". The extension ".TEX" is appended following the same rules as when the "\input" command is used. If "\openin" is omitted, the input is requested from the terminal.

The input itself is requested by

    \read\DataFile to \DataLine

One line of the file "MYDATA.TEX" is read to "\DataLine". This has the same function as a definition of \DataLine as a macro without parameter. If "MYDATA.TEX" contains

    Bodoni, Giambatista
    Did\^ot, Firmin
    Fournier, Pierre Simon

three times "\read\DataFile to \DataLine" is equivalent to

    \def\DataLine{Bodoni, Giambatista }
    \dof\DataLine{Did\^ot, Firmin }
    \def\DataLine{Fournier, Pierre Simon }

This explains why care is taken to group by braces during \read operations. If a line contains a non-matched open brace, several lines will be read for "definition" until the matching brace is found.

Note: the line ends of the input files cause a trailing blank to be stored in \DataLine.

With "\ifeof\DataFile" you can check whether the end of "MYDATA.TEX" is reached.

If \read is given for an unopened file input is requested from the terminal. If the file number is $\geq 0$, the name of the target macro, here \DataLine, is written as a request:

    \DataLine=

When a read with a negative number is given, e.g., "\read -1 to \DataLine", input is requested from the terminal, but the question text will be suppressed.

If the same file number should be used for several files one after the other, the current file has to be closed by "\closein\DataFile". Then a new "\openin\DataFile" with a new file name may follow.

## 13.6 Output to Text Files

To read text files by \read is quite simple compared to \write operations. The most important fact shall be mentioned at the very beginning:

> **Any write operation \openout, \write, or \closeout, is not executed immediately, but delayed until the page is "printed" on which these commands appear. "Printing" means \shipout during the output routine.**

This seems curious at first glance, but there are good reasons: during the output routine the interesting registers like page count are well-defined. This may be used for building a keyword register.

On the other hand, any write command may be preceded by "\immediate", this will force immediate execution of the following \openout, \write, or \closeout command.

Note that the delayed standard operation will expand macros during the output routine. This will give unwanted results if the contents of the macro have been changed in between.

It is recommended to open files during macro definitions right at the start. For example,

```
\newwrite\IndexFile
\newwrite\ContentsFile
\immediate\openout\IndexFile=INDEX.TEX
\immediate\openout\ContentsFile=CONTENTS.TEX
```

opens two files for index and contents files. Entries to a keyword register may be generated by \write commands like:

```
\write\IndexFile{Error \folio}
\write\IndexFile{Convergence \folio}
```

The output file INDEX.TEX will contain the following information

```
Error 17
Convergence 18
```

To use the index file later on, calls to macros may also be written to the output file. A sort run should cause no problems, as the output is done line by line. The command "\string" generates the name of the following instruction, so that it can be written to the output file. By "\string\Object" the text "\Object" will be built.

```
\write\IndexFile{\string\Object:Error \string\Page \folio}
\write\IndexFile{\string\Object:Convergence \string\Page \folio}
```

It is easy to build a macro to do the work:

```
\def\Index#1{\write\IndexFile{\string\Object:#1
                      \string\Page \folio}}
```

This is called by \Index{Error} and \Index{Convergence}. The output file will contain the following information:

```
\Object:Error \Page17
\Object:Convergence \Page18
```

After sorting, this file may be read directly by \input to generate a keyword index. Suitable macros \Object and \Page have to be provided, of course. As the \Index macro has been defined without "\immediate", the "\write" operations will occur during the output routine.

It is more difficult if only *part* of the information should be expanded immediately and the other part during the output routine (to get the correct page numbers). This may be needed when the current value of a running number or any other macro contents that change quite often are referenced.

This is demonstrated in the following example. The changing elements of a \write are

a) the current number of an equation (referenced with the current value at the time of the call).

b) some text of a title stored within a macro, this is also referenced at the time of the call.

c) the current page number, which is only known during the output routine.

This problem can be solved by a macro that gathers the current values by \edef and stores them within the parameter information of the write command. The parts that should only be expanded in the output routine are preceded by \noexpand (for \edef). Here it is the page number \folio.

```
% prerequisites:
%      \newcount\FormulaNo
%      \newwrite\IndexFile
%      \openout\IndexFile= ???
%      \def\FormulaTitle{ ... }
\def\Reference{%
        \edef\WriteIndex{%
            \write\IndexFile{\string\FormulaNo:\number\FormulaNo
                             \string\FormulaTitle: \FormulaTitle
                             \string\Page: \noexpand\folio}}%
        \WriteIndex}
```

The use looks like

```
\advance\FormulaNo by 1
\def\FormulaTitle{Extensions}
        . . .
\Reference
\advance\FormulaNo by 1
\def\FormulaTitle{Diophantine Equation}
        . . .
\Reference
```

A call of \Reference will redefine \WriteIndex with the current contents. For the second call this looks like

```
\write\IndexFile{\string\FormulaNo:1
                 \string\FormulaTitle: Diophantine Equation
                 \string\Page: \folio}
```

and generates the following lines:

```
\FormulaNo:1\FormulaTitle: Extensions\Page: 1
\FormulaNo:2\FormulaTitle: Diophantine Equation\Page: 1
```

### Problems with other macros

Accented letters will be written with the command sequence that generates the accent. A letter like "ä", written as {\accent"7F a}, will cause some irritation if this is the input of a sort run for further processing. Accents may be redefined locally to get an acceptable sorting key. The same is true for specific national characters. The following macros achieve this for umlauts, "ß", and "œ".

```
\def\Umlaut#1{#1e}    % for redefinition of \"
\def\Eszett{ss}       %                          \ss
\def\Diphthongoe{oe} %                           \oe
%
\def\Reference{%
   {\let\"=\Umlaut\let\ss=\Eszett\let\oe=\Diphthongoe
    \xdef\SortTitle{\FormulaTitle}}
     \edef\WriteIndex{%
         \write\IndexFile{\string\FormulaNo:\number\FormulaNo
                          \string\FormulaTitle: \SortTitle
                          \string\Page: \noexpand\folio}}%
       \WriteIndex}
```

An example of this case — a bit far-fetched — would be

```
\def\FormulaTitle{hors d'\oe uvre}
\Reference
```

which yields in the output file

```
\FormulaNo:17\FormulaTitle: hors d'oeuvre\Page: 1
```

Furthermore, if commands should be written to index files without expansion the instruction \noexpand should precede them.

# 14 Appendix

The appendix contains the following elements:

1. A short description of *all* TeX-commands

   Partly, they have references and examples. It is noted whether a command may be used in text or mathematical mode.

   A page number is given in *italic* letters (e.g., '123'), when the reference is to an example.

   Primitives of TeX, built in commands, are marked by an an asterisk (∗).

2. An index of key words.

3. A table of fonts

   The basic fonts of plain TeX are demonstrated with their characteristic font data.

4. A bibliography

## 14.1 Short Description of Plain TeX Commands

| command | description | pp. |
|---|---|---|
| \␣ | forces the output of a space. <br> \S \S yields "§§", but \S\ \S gives "§ §". | 13, *14* |
| # | is the parameter symbol for tables and macros. | 81, 96 |
| \# | text mode: yields — # —. | 5 |
| \$ | text mode: yields — $ —. | 5 |
| $ | starts (and stops) mathematical formulae in text. | 52, *59* |
| $$ | starts (and stops) display style formulae. | 56, *59* |
| % | begins a comment: the rest of the current line will be ignored. | 4 |
| \% | text mode: yields — % —. | 5,6 |
| & | tabbing symbol for \halign and \settabs\+ ... \cr | 77, 81 |

| command | description | pp. |
|---|---|---|
| \& | yields — & —. | |
| ' | text mode: (apostrophe or right quote) yields — ' —. | 6 |
| \' | text mode: *acute accent* \'o yields — ó —. | 14 |
| ' ' | text mode: acts like a double quote — " —. (ligature symbol) | 6 |
| ` | text mode: (accent) — ` — | 6 |
| \` | text mode: *grave accent* \`o yields — ò —. | 14 |
| " | (double quote) yields — " —. | 6 |
| \" | text mode: *umlaut* \"o yields — ö —. | 14, *38* |
| ( | left parenthesis — ( — if used as \left( or \right(, adjusted in size automatically in mathematical mode | 61 |
| ) | right parenthesis — ) — if used as \left) or \right), adjusted in size automatically in mathematical mode | 61 |
| [ | left bracket — [ — if used as \left[ or \right[, adjusted in size automatically in mathematical mode | 61 |
| ] | right bracket — ] — if used as \left] or \right], adjusted in size automatically in mathematical mode | 61 |
| { | Left grouping brace: it starts a new group (block) or marks the beginning of a macro parameter. The command \bgroup is equivalent with starting a new group. | 4, 5, 54 |
| } | Right grouping brace: it finishes the innermost group (or a macro parameter). A group that is started by { or \bgroup may also be closed by \egroup. | 4, 5, 54 |
| \{ | left brace in mathematical mode "{" (This may be substituted by the command \lbrace.) In combination with \left,\right or \big.. it will be adjusted in size. | 61 |
| \} | right brace in mathematical mode "}" (The command may be substituted by \rbrace) (See also \{) | 61 |
| + | math mode: binary operator in $1 + 1 = 2$ | |
| \+ | start of a tabbing line: (See also \tabalign) Example: \settabs 3 \columns \+one & two & three \cr | 77 |
| − | math mode: binary operator in $1 - 1 = 2$ text mode: hyphen in compound words (e.g., vis-à-vis) | 5 |
| * \- | text mode: marks all possible hyphenating positions in a word. hyphen\-ation permits just one break. | 37 |

| command | description | pp. |
|---|---|---|
| `--` | text mode: 'en-dash',<br>`lines 10--20` yields — lines 10–20 —. | 5 |
| `---` | text mode: em-dash (e.g., she loves — me) | 5 |
| `*` | math mode: binary operator $a * b$ | |
| `\*` | math mode: sets possible hyphenation positions in product formulae<br>`$ (a+b) \* (c+d) \* ... $` yields the symbol "×" as hyphenating symbol (`\times`), if the formula is broken into several lines within a paragraph. | 75 |
| `/` | slash — / — | |
| * `\/` | *italic correction*<br>in text mode, generates a horizontal correction to the following text, if this is not typeset in italic.<br>Example: (Note the skip between — *t* n —)<br>`{\it italic foot} note` → *italic foot* note<br>`{\it italic foot\/} note` → *italic foot* note | |
| `|` | math mode: ordinary symbol — │ —<br>(equivalent with `\vert`, but `\mid` acts as a relation)<br>(In combination with `\left,\right` or `\big..` its size will be adjusted.) | 61, *66* |
| `\|` | math mode: ordinary symbol — ‖ —<br>(equivalent with `\Vert`, but `\parallel` acts as a relation)<br>(In combination with `\left,\right` or `\big..` its size will be adjusted.) | 61, *63* |
| `\` | *escape, backslash* starts a lot of T<sub>E</sub>X commands | |
| `<` | math mode: relation    `$1<2$` yields $1 < 2$ | |
| `=` | math mode: relation    `$0=1-1$` yields $0 = 1 - 1$ | |
| `>` | math mode: relation    `$2>1$` yields $2 > 1$ | |
| `\>` | math mode: medium mathematical space<br>(with the amount of `\medmuskip`) | 64, 133 |
| `\,` | math mode: thin mathematical space<br>(with the amount of `\thinmuskip`) | 64, 133 |
| `.` | period (punctuation mark)<br>At punctuation symbols there is extra horizontal space, this may be suppressed by use of '`\frenchspacing`'. | 6 |
| `;` | semicolon (punctuation mark) | |
| `\;` | math mode: thick mathematical space<br>(with the amount of `\thickmuskip`) | 64, 133 |
| `?` | question mark (punctuation mark) | |
| `?`` | punctuation (question mark, accent) *ligature* — ¿ — | |
| `!` | exclamation mark (punctuation mark) | |

| command | description | pp. |
|---|---|---|

**! '** — punctuation (exclamation mark, accent) *ligature* — ¡ —

**\!** — math mode: negative thin mathematical space *(back-skip)* with the amount of -\thinmuskip
$\int\int_a^b f(x) = \int\!\!\int_a^b f(x)$
yields $\int \int_a^b f(x) = \int\int_a^b f(x)$                          64, 133

**_** — *underscore* math mode: starts subscripts (index) and anything that is typeset 'below'
$x_{ij}$ yields $x_{ij}$
substitute with the same effect: \sb (subscript)                         51

**\_** — in text mode, produces — _ —.
(This is done by a \hrule command with width 0.3 em!, the character 95 of typewriter fonts is often preferable.)          5

**^** — *circumflex* math mode: starts superscripts (exponents) and anything that is typeset 'above',
$x^2$ produces $x^2$
substitute with the same effect: \sp (superscript)                       51

**^^** — starts a substitution for ASCII characters with ordinal 0 to 31 and 127, ^^ may be read as *control*
^^M represents *control M*, which is just a *CR* = *return*.

**~** — *tilde* generates a space and inhibits the line break in this position (protected space).
Example: Dr.~N.~O.~Body — it is defined by
\catcode'\~=\active \def~{\penalty10000\ }

**\~** — text mode: (tilde) \~ o yields — õ —.                            14

**@** — *at sign (commercial at)* normal text symbol (Within plain TeX macros often used as letter symbol with category code 11; this results in "hidden" commands.)

**\aa** — text mode: yields — å—.                                        14

**\AA** — text mode: yields — Å—.                                        14

**\* \above** — math mode: fraction with explicit thickness of the fraction line                                                                  58
$$ a \above 2pt b $$ produces $\frac{a}{b}$
(See also \atop,\over)

**\* \abovedisplayshortskip** — extra spacing above a mathematical display style formula: if the last line of the preceding paragraph is very short and produces no optical conflict with the formula.
preset value: \abovedisplayshortskip=0pt plus 3pt

| command | description | pp. |
|---|---|---|

\* **\abovedisplayskip**

     contains the value for spacing above a display style formula.
(See also \abovedisplayshortskip)
preset value:
\abovedisplayskip=12 pt plus 3pt minus 9pt

\* **\abovewithdelims**                                                 63

     math mode: fraction with explicit thickness of the fraction line and explicitly given delimiter symbols

     $$ a \abovewithdelims<> 2pt b $$ produces $\left\langle \frac{a}{b} \right\rangle$

\* **\accent**      text mode: TEX primitive command to build accents in      *38*
text mode. For example \" is defined by
\def\"#1{{\accent"7F #1}}
(The position "7F of computer modern fonts usually contains umlaut dots, see font tables below. It is even possible to change the font between accenter and accentee: \tenrm\accent"7F\tenbf a sets a bold "a" with roman umlaut dots.)

     **\active**      name of the \catcode value of *active* characters. These      *164*
are symbols, which can be used as (re-)definable one symbol commands.
Example: ~ (tilde) is an active character, generated by \chardef\active=13
                 \catcode'\~=\active
with definiton: \def~{\penalty10000\ }
(See also \catcode)

     **\acute**      math mode: mathematical accent      55
$\acute x$ yields $\acute{x}$.

\* **\adjdemerits**      Additional demerits which are accumulated in the course of paragraph building when two consecutive lines are visually incompatible. In these cases, one line is built with very much space for justification and the other one with very little.
preset value: \adjdemerits=10000

\* **\advance**      general purpose command to add some quantities      18, *32*,
Example:      *112*,
\advance\baselineskip by -1pt      *123,129*,
\advance\leftskip by 1cm      *177*
\advance\count7 by -3
\advance\pageno by 2
(See also \multiply, \divide)

| command | description | pp. |
|---|---|---|
| \advancepageno | command of the output routine to update the page number. If the page number is less than zero, it will be decremented by 1 otherwise incremented by 1.<br>(This macro corresponds with \folio and is only called by \plainoutput.) | 154 |
| \ae | text mode: scandinavian lower case æ dipthong | 14 |
| \AE | text mode: scandinavian upper case Æ dipthong | 14 |
| * \afterassignment | All commands that follow as a parameter are stored and their interpretation is delayed *until* the *next assignment* has been done. Several \afterassignment commands are possible, the stored commands are interpreted in the same order in which they are preserved.<br>Example:<br>\def\doit{\afterassignment\doitmore\dimen1=}<br>defines a routine \doit with a pseudo parameter of a length syntax. (The value is assigned to \dimen1 and can be used within the continuation macro \doitmore.) | 103, *105* |
| * \aftergroup | The next *token* — in contrast to \afterassignment — will be stored and its interpretation starts after closing the current group. Several \aftergroup commands are possible, the stored commands are interpreted in the order in which they are preserved. | |
| \aleph | math mode: produces the ordinary symbol — ℵ —. | 73 |
| \allocationnumber | internal counter for plain TeX's \new.. commands \newcount, \newdimen ...<br>May not be changed externally! | |
| \allowbreak | math mode: determines extra positions for line breaking of formulae within paragraphs in *text style*. | 75 |
| \alpha | math mode: greek letter — $\alpha$ — | 52 |
| \amalg | math mode: binary operator — $\amalg$ — | 71 |
| \angle | math mode: ordinary symbol — $\angle$ — | 73 |
| \approx | math mode: relation — $\approx$ — | 72 |
| \arccos | math mode: large operator — arccos — | 64 |
| \arcsin | math mode: large operator — arcsin — | 64 |
| \arctan | math mode: large operator — arctan — | 64 |
| \arg | math mode: large operator — arg — | 64 |
| \arrowvert | math mode: delimiter symbol, which may only be used in combination with \left, \right or \big..<br>$\big\arrowvert$ produces │ | 61 |

| command | description | pp. |
|---|---|---|
| \Arrowvert | math mode: delimiter symbol, which may only be used combined with \left, \right or \big.. $\big\Arrowvert$ yields $\|$ | 61 |
| \ast | math mode: binary operator $a\ast b$ yields — $a * b$ —. | 71 |
| \asymp | math mode: relation — $\asymp$ — | 72 |
| at | key word within \font commands Example: \font\bigrm=cmr10 at 12pt | 43 |
| * \atop | math mode: generates a fraction without fraction line Example: $$ x \atop x+1 $$ yields $x \atop x+1$ (See also \above,\over) | 58 |
| * \atopwithdelims | | 63 |
| | math mode: builds a fraction without fraction line but with explicitly given surrounding delimiters Example: $ n \atopwithdelims<> k$ yields $\left\langle n \atop k \right\rangle$ | |
| \b | text mode: *underbar* accent \b o yields — o̲ —. | 14 |
| \backslash | math mode: ordinary symbol $ M\backslash N $ yields — $M\backslash N$ —. (See also binary operator \setminus) | 73 |
| \bar | math mode: accent $\bar x$ yields — $\bar x$ —. | 55 |
| * \baselineskip | normal distance between baselines within paragraphs preset value: \baselineskip=12pt A line has a height of 8.5pt for ascenders and a depth of 3.5pt for descenders. Varying the value of the register \baselineskip produces different line spacing. | 18ff |
| * \batchmode | switches to *batchmode:* if an error occurs, there is no interruption and no question for extra input. All error messages are written into the log file only. | |
| * \begingroup | starts a new group, similar to '{' and '\bgroup'. In contrast *this* group has to be closed by a corresponding '\endgroup' command, otherwise an error will occur. | 23 |
| * \belowdisplayshortskip | | |
| | math mode: determines the vertical space below a display style formula, if the following paragraph line does not overlap the formula part. preset value: \belowdisplayshortskip=7pt plus 3pt minus 4pt | |
| * \belowdisplayskip | | |
| | math mode: standard empty space below a formula in *display-style* preset value: \belowdisplayskip=12pt plus 3 pt minus 9pt | |
| \beta | math mode: greek letter — $\beta$ — | 52 |

| command | description | pp. |
|---|---|---|
| \bf | **boldface,** switches to the boldface font family (Distinguish between the switch to a font and a family switch, which is important in mathematical mode!) | 42 |
| \bffam | internal number of the **boldface** font family (Do not change!) | |
| \bgroup | acts like a '{' — It starts a new group. The group may be closed with '}' or '\egroup'. This command is important for macros, which will start a group but not close it: After \def\test{\bgroup} a call of \test acts like '{', and \def\test{\hbox\bgroup} will open an hbox like an '\hbox{' command. But there are differences between \def\test\bgroup and \def\test{. Furthermore, start and stop of a macro parameter (e.g., \leftline{ABC}) are *not* substitutable with \bgroup and \egroup.) | |
| \big | math mode: enlarges the following delimiter a bit. The result is regarded as an ordinary symbol. Example: $(a+b) \big\vert (c+d)$ produces $(a+b)\vert(c+d)$ (\big can easily be redefined by mistake, e.g., as a font name.) | 62 |
| \Big | math mode: enlarges the following delimiter. \Big is about 1.5 × \big. The result is an ordinary symbol. | 62 |
| \bigbreak | text mode: determines a good position for page breaking and produces the same space as \bigskip. It corresponds with the commands \smallbreak, \medbreak like $1:2:4$. | 32 |
| \bigcap | math mode: large operator — $\bigcap$ — | 59 |
| \bigcirc | math mode: binary operator — $\bigcirc$ — | 71 |
| \bigcup | math mode: large operator — $\bigcup$ — | 59 |
| \bigg | math mode: enlarges the following delimiter up to 2 × \big. The result is typeset as an ordinary symbol. | 62 |
| \Bigg | math mode: enlarges the following delimiter up to 2.5 × \big. (This is the largest variant of the '\big..' series.) The result is typeset as an ordinary symbol. | 62 |
| \biggl | math mode: enlarges the following delimiter up to 2 × \bigl. The result is typeset as a left opening. *"big left"* | 62 |
| \Biggl | math mode: enlarges the following delimiter up to 2,5 × \bigl. The result is typeset as a left opening. *"big left"* | 62 |

| command | description | pp. |
|---|---|---|
| \biggm | math mode: enlarges the following delimiter up to 2 × \bigm. The result is typeset as a relation. *"big middle"* | 62 |
| \Biggm | math mode: enlarges the following delimiter up to 2,5 × \bigm. The result is typeset as a relation. *"big middle"* | 62 |
| \biggr | math mode: enlarges the following delimiter up to 2 × \bigr. The result is typeset as a right closing. *"big right"* | 62 |
| \Biggr | math mode: enlarges the following delimiter up to 2,5 × \bigr. The result is typeset as a right closing. *"big right"* | 62 |
| \bigl | math mode: enlarges the following delimiter a little. The result is typeset as a left opening. *"big left"* | 62 |
| \Bigl | math mode: enlarges the following delimiter up to 1.5 × \bigl. The result is typeset as a left opening. *"big left"* | 62 |
| \bigm | math mode: enlarges the following delimiter a little. The result is typeset as a relation. *"big middle"* | 62 |
| \Bigm | math mode: enlarges the following delimiter up to 1.5 × \bigr. The result is typeset as a relation. *"big middle"* | 62 |
| \bigodot | math mode: large operator — $\odot$ — | 59 |
| \bigoplus | math mode: large operator — $\oplus$ — | 59 |
| \bigotimes | math mode: large operator — $\otimes$ — | 59 |
| \bigr | math mode: enlarges the following delimiter a little. The result is typeset as a right closing. *"big right"* | 62 |
| \Bigr | math mode: enlarges the following delimiter up to 1.5 × \bigr. The result is typeset as a right closing. *"big right"* | 62 |
| \bigskip | text mode: generates vertical space with the size of the register \bigskipamount. One \bigskip corresponds to 2 × \medskip or 4 × \smallskip. In plain TEX a \bigskip is simply equivalent to an empty line. \bigskip is defined by \def\bigskip{\vskip\bigskipamount} | 15 |
| \bigskipamount | text mode: register, which contains the skip value for \bigskip. preset value: \bigskipamount=12pt plus 4pt minus 4pt (See also \medskipamount, \smallskipamount) | |
| \bigsqcup | math mode: large operator — $\bigsqcup$ — | 59 |
| \bigtriangledown | math mode: binary operator — $\bigtriangledown$ — | 71 |
| \bigtriangleup | math mode: binary operator — $\triangle$ — | 71 |
| \biguplus | math mode: large operator — $\biguplus$ — | 59 |
| \bigvee | math mode: large operator — $\bigvee$ — | 59 |
| \bigwedge | math mode: large operator — $\bigwedge$ — | 59 |

| command | description | pp. |
|---|---|---|

**\* \binoppenalty**  math mode: is the penalty for a break of a text style formula into two lines of a paragraph after a binary operator. (See also \relpenalty).
preset value: \binoppenalty=700

**\bmod**  math mode: operator 'mod' used as binary operator      59
Example: (See also \pmod)
$ 17 \bmod 7 = 3$ produces — 17 mod 7 = 3 —

**\bordermatrix**  math mode: variant of \pmatrix — generates a matrix,      65
where the parentheses do not surround the first column
and the first line. These may be used for labeling.
$\bordermatrix{a&b&c\cr d&e&f\cr g&h&i\cr}$

$$\begin{matrix} & a & b & c \\ d & \begin{pmatrix} e & f \\ g \quad\; h & i \end{pmatrix} \end{matrix}$$

**\bot**  math mode: ordinary symbol — $\bot$ —      73
(See also \top — $\top$ —)

**\* \botmark**  reference to the information which is stored by \mark.      157ff
This produces the *last* \mark-text of the *current* page.
\botmark may be used within \headline or \footline,
i.e. within the *output routine*.
(See also \firstmark,\topmark,\mark)

**\bowtie**  math mode: relation — $\bowtie$ —      72

**\* \box**  is a reference to a box register $(0 \ldots 255)$. It produces      116
the contents of the specified box. After execution of the
command the box will be empty.
\setbox0=\hbox{abc}
\box0 is then equivalent to \hbox{abc}.

**\* \boxmaxdepth**  maximum *(depth)* of a box. Usually it contains the value
of \maxdimen, so that boxes can be built with arbitrary
depth.
(Within the output routine \boxmaxdepth is varied to
build the footnotes at the bottom of the page.)

**bp**  unit of measure: *big point*      12
$72 \, \mathrm{bp} = 1 \, \mathrm{inch} = 2.54 \, \mathrm{cm}$

**\brace**  math mode: generates 'binomial expression' with curly      58
braces
$ n \brace k+1$ produces $\left\{ {n \atop k+1} \right\}$
defined by
\def\brace{\atopwithdelims\{\}}

**\braceld**  math mode: end piece of a curly brace *(brace left/down)*
— ⟋ —

**\bracelu**  math mode: end piece of a curly brace *(brace left/up)*
— ⟍ —

| command | description | pp. |
|---|---|---|
| \bracerd | math mode: end piece of a curly brace *(brace right/down)* — ﹂ — | |
| \braceru | math mode: end piece of a curly brace *(brace right/up)* — ﹁ — | |
| \bracevert | math mode: thick vertical rule, built from a part of a large parenthesis: It may only be used in combination with \big.. or \left, \right. $\big\bracevert$ produces — \| — | |
| \brack | math mode: 'binomial expression' with brackets. $ n \brack k+1 $ yields $\left[{n \atop k+1}\right]$ defined by \def\brack{\atopwithdelims[]} | 58 |
| \break | text mode: forces a line break, if used within a paragraph, otherwise a page break. defined by \def\break{\penalty-10000 } This means: a break scores 10,000 units of reward. (See also \nobreak) | 31 |
| \breve | math mode: mathematical accent $\breve x$ yields — $\breve{x}$ — | 55 |
| * \brokenpenalty | penalty for a page break, where the last line of the previous page contains a hyphenation. preset value: \brokenpenalty=100 | |
| \buildrel | math mode: By \buildrel *text above* \over *relation* you can build annotated relations. Example: $\buildrel \alpha\beta \over \longrightarrow$ yields $\buildrel \alpha\beta \over \longrightarrow$. | 73 |
| \bullet | math mode: binary operator — • — | 71 |
| by | is an optional keyword in combination with \advance ... by ... \multiply ... by ... \divide   ... by ... | *18, 130* |
| \bye | finishes a TeX run, defined by \outer\def\bye{\par\vfill\supereject\end} All stored insertions like \topinsert and footnotes are printed. In contrast to a simple \end the last page is filled with vertical space. | |
| \c | text mode: *cedille* \c o yields — ọ —. | 14 |
| \cal | math mode: produces calligraphic capital letters: $\mathcal{ABCDEFGHIJKLMNOPQRSTUVWXYZ}$. use $\cal A$ ... $\cal Z$ | 73 |
| \cap | math mode: binary operator — ∩ — | 71 |

| command | description | pp. |
|---|---|---|

\cases — math mode: matrix-like construction with a curly brace on the left side. This is usually used for definitions. The first column is typeset in mathematical mode, the second column in text mode automatically.   —   68

`$f(x)=\cases{x&for $x>0$\cr -x&otherwise\cr}$`

$$f(x) = \begin{cases} x & \text{for } x > 0 \\ -x & \text{otherwise} \end{cases}$$

* \catcode — This internal TEX command defines the interpretation of each character that TEX reads. There are 16 category codes which determine all character functions. The following table shows the standard representation.   —   *23, 108, 138, 164*

```
 0  \catcode'\\=0      escape symbol
 1  \catcode'\{=1      left brace — begin group
 2  \catcode'\}=2      right brace — end group
 3  \catcode'\$=3      math shift
 4  \catcode'\&=4      alignment tab
 5  \catcode'\^^M=5    end of input line
 6  \catcode'\#=6      macro parameter character
 7  \catcode'\^=7      math. superscript
 8  \catcode'\_=8      math. subscript
 9  \catcode'\^^@=9    a character to be ignored
10  \catcode'\ =10     space
11  are letters (A...Z, a...z)
12  are other characters
13  are active characters (e.g., ~ tilde)
14  \catcode'\%=14     start of comment
15  are invalid characters (e.g, ^^?)
```

Example: plain TEX redefines '@' to a letter symbol by \catcode'\@=11 before using it within hidden macro names. Afterwards it receives its normal value (12).

cc — unit of measure: *cicero*   —   12
$1 \, cc = 12 \, dd = 0.451 \, cm$

\cdot — math mode: binary operator — · —   —   71

\cdotp — math mode: punctuation — · —

\cdots — math mode: subformula — ··· —   —   66, *69*
in `$a_1\cdot a_2\cdot\;\cdots\;\cdot a_n$`
used as $a_1 \cdot a_2 \cdot \cdots \cdot a_n$

\centering — internal dimension, used within macros for typesetting mathematical formulae by \eqalignno ...
preset value:
\centering=0pt plus 1000pt minus 1000pt

| command | description | pp. |
|---|---|---|
| \centerline | text mode: \centerline{ ..text.. } centers the information given as a parameter within a line. This command may only be used in vertical mode, i.e. not within a paragraph.<br>defined by<br>\def\line{\hbox to \hsize}<br>\def\centerline#1{\line{\hss#1\hss}}<br>(See also \leftline, \rightline) | 7, 16, 32, 40, 158 |
| * \char | text mode: generates a single character from the current font. \char is followed by the code number of the character in the range $0 \ldots 127$. (There are fonts with a possible code set of $0 \ldots 255$.) The code number may be given in decimal, octal or hexadecimal form.<br>The character 'A' is then represented by \char65 or \char'81 or \char"41.<br>As the sequence '\ generates the code of the following character (See also \catcode) it is even possible to write \char'\A, but 'A' is probably easier. | |
| * \chardef | defines a command name for a single character.<br>\chardef\%="25 is equivalent to<br>\def\%{\char"25 }<br>Instead of \% a '\percent' or similar may also be used. | 23 |
| \check | math mode: mathematical accent<br>$\check x$ yields — $\check{x}$ —. | 55 |
| \chi | math mode: greek letter — $\chi$ — | 52 |
| \choose | math mode: binomial coefficients<br>$ n \choose k $ produces $\binom{n}{k}$. | 58 |
| \circ | math mode: binary operator — $\circ$ —<br>$ a \circ b \circ c$ produces $a \circ b \circ c$. | 71 |
| * \cleaders | *centered leaders*<br>\cleaders <*object*> <*skip*><br>The contents of <*object*>, this may be an \hbox, \vbox, \vrule or \hrule, will be repeated as often as the following <*skip*> part determines. <*skip*> may be a \hskip <*dimension*> or \vskip <*dimension*>, but also \hfill or \vfill. If a dynamic skip (\hfill, \vfill) is used, this construct must be contained in an outer box with explicit width. If the series of boxes does not fill out the <*skip*> exactly, it will be centered.<br>(See also \leaders, \xleaders) | |
| \cleartabs | text mode: this command may be used between \+ and \cr in tabbing lines. From the current position all further defined tabbing positions (to the right) are deleted. If a '&' follows, it defines a new tabbing position at the current position. | 81 |

| command | description | pp. |
|---|---|---|
| * \closein | closes an additional input file. It has a parameter $0\ldots15$, which is the number of an open file. A file is opened by \openin and input is done by \read. (See also \newread) | 174, 175 |
| * \closeout | closes an additional output file. It has a parameter $0\ldots15$, which is the number of an open file. A file is opened by \openout and output is done by \write. (See also \newwrite) | 174, 176 |
| * \clubpenalty | penalty for a broken page, with a single line of a paragraph remaining on the bottom of the preceding page. preset value: \clubpenalty=150 | |
| \clubsuit | math mode: ordinary symbol — ♣ — (See also \diamondsuit, \heartsuit, \spadesuit) | 73 |
| cm | unit of measure: centimeter $1\,\mathrm{cm} = 28.54\,\mathrm{pt}$ | 12 |
| cmbx | is the internal font name (file name) *bold extended text fonts*, used in combination with design size (e.g., cmbx5 ... cmbx10, cmbx12). | 19, 43, 44 |
| cmex | is the internal font name (file name) for the large (extended) symbols of mathematical typesetting, used in combination with design size (e.g., cmex10). | 44 |
| cmmi | is the internal font name (file name) for the font with the *italic* characters in mathematical mode *(math italic)*, used in combination with design size (e.g., cmmi5 ... cmmi10, cmmi12). | 44 |
| cmr | is the internal font name (file name) *computer modern roman* for the standard typeface, used in combination with design size (e.g., cmr5 ... cmr10, cmr12, cmr17). | 19, 37, 44 |
| cmsl | is the internal font name (file name) *slanted* for the slanted font used in combination with design size (e.g., cmsl8 ... cmsl10, cmsl12). | 44 |
| cmsy | is the internal font name (file name) for the normal symbols of mathematical type setting, used in combination with design size (e.g., cmsy5 ... cmsy10). | 44 |
| cmti | is the internal font name (file name) *text italic* for the usual *italic* font, used in combination with design size (e.g., cmti7 ... cmti10, cmti12). | 44 |
| cmtt | is the internal font name (file name) *typewriter type*, used in combination with design size (e.g., cmtt8 ... cmtt10, cmtt12). (In this font all characters have the same width.) | 44 |

| command | description | pp. |
|---|---|---|
| \colon | math mode:<br>colon used as punctuation — : —. | 134 |
| \columns | text mode: keyword used with the \settabs command<br>Example: \settabs 5 \columns divides the line into<br>5 equal sized columns for use by \+ .. & .. \cr<br>instructions. | 77 |
| \cong | math mode: relation — $\cong$ — | 72 |
| \coprod | math mode: large operator — $\coprod$ — | 59 |
| * \copy | copies the contents of a box register; the old contents<br>remain. The command is followed by a number of a box<br>register 0 . . . 255.<br>\setbox0=\hbox{abracadabra }\copy0\copy0<br>produces — abracadabra abracadabra — | 117,<br>*123* |
| \copyright | symbol — © — | |
| \cos | math mode: large operator — cos — | 64 |
| \cosh | math mode: large operator — cosh — | 64 |
| \cot | math mode: large operator — cot — | 64 |
| \coth | math mode: large operator — coth — | 64 |
| * \count | references one of 256 *integer* counter registers (0 . . . 255).<br>\count0 is predefined as the current page number, i.e.,<br>\pageno, the registers 1 to 9 are free.<br>By performing, e.g., \count1=17, you can perform an<br>assignment, \number\count1 prints the number. \ad-<br>vance, \multiply and \divide change it.<br>By \newcount\num you can define a *free* register with a<br>symbolic name, which can be changed by \num=333 and<br>printed by \number\num. \romannumeral\num prints as<br>"cccxxxiii". | *112*,<br>130 |
| * \countdef | defines a symbolic name for a count register. Plain TeX<br>defines \countdef\pageno=0 to get the name \pageno<br>for the register 0, which contains the page numbering<br>by convention. To get a new and free count register use<br>\newcount.<br>(See also \count) | |
| * \cr | determines the end of an alignment line ( \+ ... & ...<br>\cr) in \halign or \matrix, \eqalign ... | 77ff |
| * \crcr | generates a \cr if no \cr (or \noalign) is following.<br>With the help of this command, macros can be con-<br>structed, which are independent of a forgotten "\cr" in<br>their macro calls. It is like an emergency brake. | |
| \csc | math mode: large operator — csc — | 64 |

| command | description | pp. |
|---|---|---|
| * \csname | may only be used in the combined pair of<br>\csname ... \endcsname<br>The text between the two commands builds the name<br>of a TEX command, which is executed. (All characters<br>but no commands are possible.)<br>Example:<br>\def\duo#1#2{\csname#1#2\endcsname}<br>\duo{small}{skip} yields \smallskip | 110,<br>*108* |
| \cup | math mode: binary operator — $\cup$ — | 71 |
| \d | text mode: *dot under* accent \d o yields — ọ —. | 14 |
| \dag | math mode: ordinary symbol — † — | 73 |
| \dagger | math mode: binary operator — † — | 71 |
| \dashv | math mode: relation — ⊣ —<br>(See also \vdash — ⊢ —) | 72 |
| * \day | internal register, preset with the current day; output<br>by \the\day or \number\day. It may be changed by<br>assignment \day=31 or even \advance or \multiply.<br>(See also \month, \year, \time) | |
| dd | unit of measure: *didôt point*<br>1157 dd = 1238 pt | 12 |
| \ddag | math mode: ordinary symbol — ‡ — | 73 |
| \ddagger | math mode: binary operator — ‡ — | 71 |
| \ddot | math mode: (*double dot*) mathematical accent<br>$\ddot x$ yields — $\ddot{x}$ — | 66 |
| \ddots | math mode: (*diagonal dots*) subformula — $\ddots$ —<br>(See also \ldots, \vdots, \cdots) | |
| * \deadcycles | internal register, which the *output routine* uses to avoid<br>endless loops. It counts consecutive invocations of the<br>output routine which do no \shipout command. The<br>corresponding register \maxdeadcycles contains an up-<br>per limit which forces an error.<br>(See also \maxdeadcycles) | |
| * \def | starts the definition of a macro — Example:<br>\def\DoubleBigskip{\bigskip \bigskip}<br>or a macro with parameters:<br>\def\term#1{#1_1,#1_2,#1_3\ldots#1_n}<br>used by $\vec\gamma=(\term\gamma)$:<br>$$\vec{\gamma} = (\gamma_1, \gamma_2, \gamma_3 \ldots \gamma_n)$$ | 95ff |

| command | description | pp. |
|---|---|---|

* `\defaulthyphenchar`

determines the character that is used in line breaking for the hyphenation of words (usually "-"). It initializes the font specific `\hyphenchar` value when the `\font` command is executed. You can overwrite this value. After

`\hyphenchar\tenrm='\=`

a "=" sign will be used within the font `\tenrm`.

* `\defaultskewchar`

determines the character that is used to position accents in mathematical mode. Other accents are typeset with respect to this symbol. It initializes the font specific `\skewchar` value when the `\font` command is executed.

`\deg`    math mode: large operator — deg —    64

* `\delcode`

math mode: (internal command) defines additional information for input characters. This specifies a small variant for the symbol representation in *text style* and a large variant for *display style*.
Plain TEX specifies this for ( ) [ ] < > \ / |.
This information is used when such a character follows a `\loft`, `\right` or `\abovewithdelims`, `\atopwithdelims` or `\overwithdelims`. The input is hexadecimal. It will be demonstrated for a '[' sign.
`\delcode'[="05B302`
The input consists of two parts: '0 5B' and '3 02'. The first digit of each group is the family number: 0 is roman (cmr), for the text style variant; 3 is math extension (cmex), for the display style variant. The following two digits define the code in the font table.

* `\delimiter`

math mode: (internal command) This generates a specific character in text style variant and display style variant. Additionally, it determines how the character acts within the formula (ordinary, large operator, ... ).
`\def\langle{\delimiter"426830A }` defines `\langle`.
The seven digit number has to be partitioned into

' 4 / 2 68 / 3 0A'

The first digit defines a "left opening", the following two groups are interpreted in the same way as for `\delcode`.
(See also `\mathchar`)

| command | description | pp. |
|---|---|---|

There are eight possible classes:

0   ordinary symbol ($\alpha$)
1   large operator ($\sum$)
2   binary operator ($\star$)
3   relation ($>$)
4   left opening ($\{$)
5   right closing ($\}$)
6   punctuation (.)
7   like 0, with extra function
    The family number will be substituted, if a family
    switch (by \fam) occurred in mathematical mode.

\* `\delimiterfactor`

math mode: *(internal register)* defines how much a surrounding delimiter has to be scaled by \left, \right corresponding to the inner subformula.
preset value: \delimiterfactor=901
That means scaled by at least 90.1 %.

\* `\delimitershortfall`

math mode: *(internal register)* defines the maximum difference between the size of a surrounding delimiter and the size of the inner formula.
preset value: \delimitershortfall=5pt

`\delta`     math mode: greek letter — $\delta$ —    52

`\Delta`     math mode: greek letter — $\Delta$ —    53

`depth`     keyword for the \vrule and \hrule commands for the definition of the depth (below the baseline) of a rule.    39
Example: \vrule height 5cm depth 2cm width0.4pt
(See also height and width)

`\det`     math mode: large operator — det —    64

`\diamond`     math mode: binary operator — $\diamond$ —    71

`\diamondsuit`     math mode: ordinary symbol — $\diamondsuit$ —    73
(See also \clubsuit, \heartsuit, \spadesuit)

`\dim`     math mode: large operator — dim —    64

| command | description | pp. |
|---------|-------------|-----|
| * \dimen | references a dimen register $(0 \ldots 255)$. By \dimen0=5cm a register will be changed, by, e.g., \vskip\dimen0 or \hbox to \dimen0 used. \newdimen\myregister defines a symbolic name myregister for a free register. (0 up to 9 are also free by convention, but are used by plain TEX macros, too.) Afterwards you can write \myregister=5cm or \hbox to \myregister. \dimen registers consist of a simple length, there is no glue defined by 'plus' and 'minus' parts by skip registers. For dynamic parts *skip* or *muskip (math mode registers)* have to be used. | *127*, 130 |
| * \dimendef | defines a symbolic name for a dimen register. After the instruction \dimendef\mydimen=17 you can use it in \hbox to \mydimen. It is preferable to do such definitions by \newdimen\mydimen, the allocation of register 17 is quite obscure. The command \dimendef is used by \newdimen. | |
| * \discretionary | general declaration of a possible hyphenation position The text to be inserted before break, after break and in case of no break has to be given. \discretionary{ *before* }{ *after* }{ *without* } \- is defined as \discretionary{-}{}{}. \def\ck{\discretionary{k-}{k}{ck}} helps with the hyphenation of German words 'ba\ck en' for 'backen' or 'bak-ken'. | 38 |
| * \displayindent | math mode: *internal register* This will be automatically changed in display style formulae to the current value of \hangindent after '$$'. This gurantees that the formula will be centered with regard to the current line length of indented text. | |
| * \displaylimits | math mode: changes the positioning of superscripts and subscripts as in display style formulae. In contrast to \limits which generates changes even in text style formulae, \displaylimits only generates 'displayed limits' if the current mode is display style. This can be used to restore the original version of typesetting limits after a \nolimits or \limits command. | |
| \displaylines | math mode: centers several formulae below each other. \displaylines{$formula_1$\cr $formula_2$\cr ...} | |
| * \displaystyle | math mode: forces *display style* mode within a mathematical formula. The (sub-)formula will be typeset as if it has been enclosed by $$ ... $$. (See also \textstyle, \scriptstyle, \scriptscriptstyle) | *56, 57, 58* |

| command | description | pp. |
|---|---|---|

\* \displaywidowpenalty

    *(internal register)* penalty for a page break that breaks a single line of a paragraph to the next page when this line is followed by a display style formula.
preset value: \displaywidowpenalty=50

\* \displaywidth    math mode: *(internal register)* the current value of the register \displaywidth is adjusted at the beginning of each displayed formula (after \$\$) automatically. It depends on \hangindent and \hsize, among others.

\div    math mode: binary operator — $\div$ —    71

\* \divide    general purpose command to divide quantities
Example:
\divide\vsize by 2
\divide\count0 by 3
(Results are rounded down.)

\do    helper macro for the \dospecials command

\dospecials    internal TeX command. It generates a call to \do with one parameter for all TeX characters that have special functions. These are space and \, {, }, \$, &, %, #, ^, _, ~ and the control sequences ^^K, ^^A.

\dosupereject    internal macro of the standard output routine    154
It forces the shipout of all insertions (footnotes etc.).

\dot    math mode: accent    56
\$\dot x\$ produces — $\dot{x}$ —.

\doteq    math mode: relation    72
\$a \doteq b\$ yields — $a \doteq b$ —.

\dotfill    text mode: fills a box with dots    92
\hbox to 2cm{A\dotfill Z} yields "A . . . . . . . . . Z".

\dots    yields — ... —. It may be used in text mode as well as    6, 66
in mathematical mode.

\* \doublehyphendemerits
    demerits for two consecutive lines of a paragraph that are both hyphenated.
preset value: \doublehyphendemerits=10000

\downarrow    math mode: relation — $\downarrow$ —    72
adjusted by \big.., \left and \right

\Downarrow    math mode: relation — $\Downarrow$ —    72
adjusted by \big.., \left ad \right

\downbracefill    may be used in text mode, especially in tables. It fills a    92
box with a brace.
\hbox to 3cm{\downbracefill} yields

$$\overbrace{\phantom{xxxxxxxxxxxx}}$$

(See also \upbracefill)

| command | description | pp. |
|---|---|---|
| * \dp | sub-register of a box register $(0 \ldots 255)$<br>It refers to the depth of a box register. The depth may be examined and also changed.<br>Example:<br>`\setbox0=`<br>  `\hbox{\vrule height5cm depth3cm width0.4pt}`<br>results in 3 cm for `\dp0`<br>(See also \ht *height* and \wd *width*) | 118 |
| * \dump | TₑX command, which may only be used in INITEX. This is a special version of the TₑX program with the capability to write so-called *format files*. Format files are usually read at the beginning of a TₑX run. | 173 |
| * \edef | defines a new macro similar to \def, but the commands in the macro body are expanded immediately.<br>`\def\a{aa!!} \edef\A{\a\a}` is equivalent to<br>`\def\A{aa!!aa!!}`. (A hint: \noexpand may precede commands in the definition. This will suppress expansion of the following command.) | 99, *108*, 177 |
| \egroup | similar to "}" — \egroup finishes a group, which is opened by \bgroup or a normal '{' sign.<br>(See also \begingroup, \endgroup) | |
| \eject | forces a page break (with invocation of the output routine). Usually, this is only meaningful in combination with \vfill as \vfill\eject. This fills the current page, which at least suppresses some warning messages. | 31, 151 |
| \ell | math mode: ordinary symbol, yields — $\ell$ —. | 73 |
| * \else | is a sub-command, which can only be used in combination with an \if... or \ifcase command. It starts the *else* part of a condition.<br>`\if...  .. \else .. \fi`<br>`\ifcase .. \or .. \or .. \else .. \fi` | 100ff |
| em | unit of measure: font specific width of an "M"<br>This is represented by \fontdimen6 *<font>*.<br>(Example: `\fontdimen6\tenrm`)<br>It is also the width of a \quad: \| \|. | 12 |
| \empty | helper macro with an empty macro body<br>It is defined by `\def\empty{}`<br>It may be used for comparing with possibly empty macro parameters. | 101 |
| \emptyset | math mode: ordinary symbol — $\emptyset$ — | 73 |
| * \end | end command for the TeX program<br>The command \bye is preferable; it fills the last page with a \vfill and forces the shipout of stored footnotes. | 7 |

| command | description | pp. |
|---|---|---|
| * \endcsname | is the second part of the sequence '\csname ..text.. \endcsname'. The included text will be interpreted as a TeX command. (See also \csname) | 110, 108 |
| \endgraf | defined by \let\endgraf=\par This stores the old command for backup and restore purposes. Plain TeX does not use it for anything else. | |
| * \endgroup | closes a group that is started with '\begingroup'. If the group to be closed is not started with \begingroup an error will occur. \begingroup and \endgroup have to be paired. (See also \bgroup, \egroup) | 23 |
| * \endinput | acts as a logical end of an input file. All information after \endinput will not be read. This is an easy method to stop interpretation of a file when debugging. | |
| \endinsert | second part of the insertion commands: \topinsert ... \endinsert \midinsert ... \endinsert \pageinsert ... \endinsert | 35 |
| \endline | defined by \let\endline=\cr This stores the old command for restoring, if \cr has been redefined. (Plain TeX uses this in \bordermatrix.) | |
| * \endlinechar | is the number of the ASCII code that represents the line end. (preset value: 13 (CR=control M)) | |
| \enskip | horizontal skip with the size of 0.5 em (half a \quad) defined by \def\enskip{\hskip.5em\relax} In contrast to \enspace a line break is possible. | 16 |
| \enspace | horizontal skip with the size of 0.5 em (half a \quad) defined by \def\enspace{\kern.5em } There is no line break possible in this position. | 16 |
| \epsilon | math mode: greek letter — $\epsilon$ — (See also \varepsilon — $\varepsilon$ —) | 52 |
| \eqalign | math mode: macro to align multi-line formulae \eqalign{ first part & second part \cr                first part & second part \cr} It aligns the parts at the '&' positions. Example: $$\eqalign{a&=b+c\cr a-b&=c\cr}$$ $$a = b + c$$ $$a - b = c$$ | 69 |

| command | description | pp. |
|---|---|---|
| \eqalignno | math mode: macro to align numbered formulae | 70 |

\eqalign{ 1. part & 2. part   & nr \cr

. . .

   1. part & 2. part   & nr \cr}

the first parts are typeset flush right, the second flush left to the '&' positions.

Example:

$$\eqalignno{a&=b+c&(1)\cr a-b&=c&(2)\cr}$$

$$a = b + c \qquad\qquad (1)$$
$$a - b = c \qquad\qquad (2)$$

| command | description | pp. |
|---|---|---|
| * \eqno | math mode: generates a number on the right side of the page within a display style formula. | 70 |

$$ formula \eqno numbering part $$

(See also \leqno)

| command | description | pp. |
|---|---|---|
| \equiv | math mode: relation — $\equiv$ — | 72 |
| * \errhelp | stores within \errhelp{...information...} an additional help text, which the user can request as 'HELP'. The error announcing routines are invoked by \errmessage, see below. | |
| * \errmessage | forces the announcing of an error message, which is the parameter of this command: \errmessage{..text..} The TₑX program is in its usual error environment. A stored help text (see \errhelp) may be requested. | 111, *108* |
| * \errorstopmode | sets the *error stop mode*. If an error occurs, TₑX asks for additional input at the terminal. | |
| * \escapechar | defines the letter for the escape character, if a TₑX command is printed by \string. preset value: '\' (ASCII "5C) If you set \escapechar=-1, no escape character will be generated by \string. | 110ff |
| \eta | math mode: greek letter — $\eta$ — | 52 |
| * \everycr | by the command \everycr{..text..}, a set of commands is defined that will be executed automatically after every \cr command. | |
| * \everydisplay | by \everydisplay{..text..}, a set of commands is defined that will be executed automatically at the beginning of every *display style* formula (after '$$'). | 138 |
| * \everyhbox | by \everyhbox{..text..}, a set of commands is defined that will be executed automatically at the beginning of every *horizontal box*. That means each \hbox command invokes it. | |

| command | description | pp. |
|---|---|---|
| * \everyjob | by \everyjob{..text..}, a set of commands is defined that will be executed autmatically at the start of a TEX job. This is only usable in INITEX. The commands are part of the generated *format file*. | |
| * \everymath | by \everymath{..text..}, a set of commands is defined that will be executed autmatically at the start of each *text style* formula (after '$'). | 138 |
| * \everypar | by \everypar{..text..}, a set of commands is defined that will be executed at the beginning of each paragraph. | *37, 20* |
| * \everyvbox | by \everyvbox{..text..}, a set of commands is defined that will be executed automatically at the beginning of every *vertical box*. That means each \vbox command invokes it. | |
| ex | font specific unit of measure: *x-height*<br>This is the height of lowercase letters without ascenders (e.g., 'x'). It is stored as \fontdimen5 *\<font>*, e.g., \fontdimen5\tenrm | 12 |
| * \exhyphenpenalty | penalty for a line break after an explicit hyphen within a word, Example: 'mother-in-law'<br>preset value: \exhyphenpenalty=50 | |
| \exists | math mode: ordinary symbol — ∃ — | 73 |
| \exp | math mode: large operator — exp — | 64 |
| * \expandafter | changes the expansion order.<br>After \expandafter\one\two the command \two is expanded first. This can change potential macro parameters of \one. Maybe only a part of the expansion result is a macro parameter of \one afterwards. | 105,<br>*106,*<br>*108,*<br>*124,*<br>*132* |
| * \fam | is an internal register with the current font family for mathematical mode. It is reset automatically to the initial value −1 every time math mode starts.<br>It is changed by \fam *n* with $n = 0 \ldots 15$.<br>The commands \rm, \it, \bf ... change not only the current font but also the font family. All symbols with an entry of a *variable* family (7) in their \delcode, \delimiter, \mathcode or \mathchar fields will use the new family code (if it is greater than −1). | |
| * \fi | finishes an \if... or \ifcase construction.<br>syntax \if...  .. \else .. \fi<br>syntax \ifcase .. \or .. \or ... \else .. \fi | 100 |
| fil | internal measuring unit for dynamic space of first order \hskip 0pt plus 1fil is equivalent to \hfil.<br>Note: fil ≪ fill ≪ filll. | 125 |

| command | description | pp. |
|---|---|---|
| \filbreak | specifies a possible position for a page break. All text between two \filbreak commands is put onto the current page if there is enough space, otherwise onto the next page. | 31 |
| fill | internal measuring unit for dynamic space of second order<br>\hskip 0pt plus 2fill<br>is equivalent to \hfill\hfill.<br>Note: fil ≪ fill ≪ filll | 125 |
| filll | internal measuring unit for dynamic space of third order<br>Note: fil ≪ fill ≪ filll. | 125 |
| * \finalhyphendemerits | demerits for a hyphenation in the last line but one of a paragraph<br>preset value: \finalhyphendemerits=5000 | |
| * \firstmark | refers to the information which is stored by \mark<br>This produces the *first* mark text of the *current* page.<br>\firstmark may be used within \headline or \foot-line, that means within the *output routine*.<br>(See also \mark, \botmark, \topmark) | 157ff |
| \fiverm | change to 'roman' typeface in 5 point size | 42 |
| \fivebf | change to 'boldface' typeface in 5 point size | 42 |
| \fivei | change to 'math italic' font in 5 point size (cmmi5) for subcripts and superscripts, this is automatically done in mathematical mode. | 44 |
| \fivesy | change to 'math symbol font' in 5 point size (cmsy5) for subcripts and superscripts, this is automatically done in mathematical mode. | 44 |
| \flat | math mode: ordinary symbol — ♭ —<br>(See also \natural, \sharp — ♮ ♯ —) | 73 |
| * \floatingpenalty | internal register, counts penalty when an \insert command forces the partitioning of floating text (footnotes) across several pages. Some plain TeX macros automatically change this register, e.g. \footnote sets the value to 20000. | |
| \fmtname | is a plain TeX macro with the title of the format in use.<br>In plain TeX it is defined as \def\fmtname{plain}.<br>in LaTeX defined as \def\fmtname{lplain} | |
| \fmtversion | is an internal register with the version identifier of the format in use.<br>In plain TeX it is defined as, e.g.,<br>\def\fmtversion{2.95}. | |

| command | description | pp. |
|---|---|---|
| \folio | generates the page number for print<br>Negative page numbers are printed as lowercase roman numerals 'i, ii, iii, iv ...', otherwise '1, 2, 3, ...' is generated. | 32, *33ff*,<br>*155* |
| * \font | defines a new font (and reads the tfm file with the metric data of the font).<br>syntax: \font\\*name*=*filename*<br>(with an optional scaling value)<br>Example:<br>\font\largebold=cmbx10 scaled \magstep3<br>\font\mediumbold=cmbx10 at 12pt<br>\font\san=cmss10 | 43 |
| * \fontdimen | refers to one of the font specific register.<br>\fontdimen *number* \\*fontname*<br>\fontdimen parameters may be changed but all modifications are global. | |

**standard registers for text fonts**

1 *slant* factor for positioning of accents for slanted and italic typefaces

        17

2 normal interword space, may be overwritten by setting \spaceskip

        17

3 is the extra interword space, which may be overwritten by the 'plus' part of \spaceskip. This is the extra space TeX uses for justification of paragraph lines.

        17

4 is the extra interword shrinkable space, which TeX may reduce for justification. It will be overwritten by the 'minus' part of \spaceskip

5 *x-height*, height of lowercase letters without ascenders, e.g., 'a' 'o' or 'x'.

This is just the font specific measuring unit '1 ex'.

6 '\quad' is the font specific width of 'M', simultaneously the measuring unit '1 em'.

        17

7 additional interword space after punctuations;<br>\frenchspacing suppresses the use of it.<br>(A non zero value of \xspaceskip takes precedence over it.)

| command | description | pp. |
|---|---|---|

**additional registers for mathematical fonts**

8...12 corrective factors for the building of fractions

Depending on current style (text style, display style etc.) factors 8, 9, 10 (for numerators) or 11, 12 (for denominators) are used for vertical positioning.

13 minimal vertical shift of superscripts in *display style*

14 ditto for roots etc.

15 ditto for other cases

16 minimal distance between subscripts and baseline if there is no superscript

17 ditto, if there are subscripts. (If they both are present, the subscript will be typeset lower.)

18 standard displacement for superscripts

19 standard displacement for subscripts

20 minimal size for delimiters in *display style*

21 ditto for other styles

22 height of the horizontal math axis (Vertical centering (like \vcenter) is done with respect to this value.)

**registers for symbol fonts**

8 standard thickness for fraction rules etc.

9...13 displacement for subscripts and superscripts of large operators

* \fontname     produces the name of a defined font
After

    \font\tenrm=cmr10       (predefined)
    \font\bigbf=cmbx10 scaled \magstep1

the command \fontname\tenrm → 'cmr10'
yields        \fontname\bigbf → 'cmbx10 at 12pt'

\footins     is a number of an *insertion register* for footnotes.     154

| command | description | pp. |
|---|---|---|
| \footline | *token* register with the commands for the footline predefined as \footline={\hss\tenrm\folio\hss} (See also \headline for page headings) | 25, 33ff, 154 |
| \footnote | generates a footnote usage: \footnote{ symbol }{ text } (See also \vfootnote) | 36 |
| \footnoterule | is a macro which generates the footnote rule, it is used within the output routine. defined by \def\footnoterule{\kern -3pt \hrule width 2truein \kern 2.6pt } | 36 |
| \forall | math mode: ordinary symbol — $\forall$ — (See also \exists — $\exists$ —) | 73 |
| \frenchspacing | text mode: changes the style in which interword spaces are generated after punctuations. The interword spacing will be uniform. (Restore the old mode by \nonfrenchspacing) | 6 |
| \frown | math mode: relation — $\frown$ — (See also \smile — $\smile$ —) | 72 |
| * \futurelet | acts like a \let command, only the assigned information is not lost, but still kept in the 'input buffer'. syntax: \futurelet\cs $token_1$ $token_2$ acts like \let\cs=$token_2$ $token_1$ $token_2$ With the commands \futurelet\next\test\further you can check in \test the contents of \further, this information is assigned to \next. | 106 |
| \gamma | math mode: greek letter — $\gamma$ — | 52 |
| \Gamma | math mode: greek letter — $\Gamma$ — | 53 |
| \gcd | math mode: large operator — gcd — | 64 |
| * \gdef | is equivalent to \global\def, which generates a global definition of a macro independent from grouping. | 100 |
| \ge | math mode: relation — $\geq$ — | 72 |
| \geq | math mode: relation — $\geq$ — | 72 |
| \gets | math mode: relation — $\leftarrow$ — (equivalent with \leftarrow) | 72 |
| \gg | math mode: relation — $\gg$ — (See also \ll — $\ll$ —) | 72 |
| * \global | is a command which may precede assignments or definitions. The assignment or definition will be done 'globally' ignoring any grouping by braces. | 100 |
| * \globaldefs | is an internal TeX register, which governs the kind of assignments: preset value: \globaldefs=0 | |

| command | description | pp. |
|---|---|---|
| | 0 (standard) An assignment is global if it is preceded by \global. | |
| | < 0 All assignments are local. | |
| | \global will be ignored. | |
| | > 0 All assignments are global. | |
| \goodbreak | defines a good break position for a page break. If used within a paragraph, the paragraph will be finished. | 31 |
| \grave | math mode: mathematical accent<br>$\grave x$ yields — $\grave{x}$ —. | 55 |
| \H | text mode: *long Hungarian umlaut*<br>\H o yields — ő —. | 14 |
| * \halign | builds tables *(horizontal alignment)* with automatic sizing of column widths.<br>Syntax:<br>\halign{ *template line* \cr<br>        *row*$_1$ \cr<br>            . . .<br>        *row*$_n$ \cr}<br>In the input, the columns are separated by "&". | 81ff |
| \hang | is a macro which is used in combination with the \item command. It is defined as<br>\def\hang{\hangindent\parindent}<br>It changes \hangindent to \parindent.<br>(\hangindent is automatically restored at the beginning of any paragraph.) | |
| * \hangafter | in combination with \hangindent, governs the shape of a paragraph. If \hangafter≥ 0 the first \hangafter lines of a paragraph are shortened by \hangindent, otherwise the lines which follow. | 25, *26ff* |
| * \hangindent | governs the length of paragraph lines in combination with \hangafter. If \hangindent< 0 the lines are indented on the left side, otherwise on the right. The indentation amount is \| \hangindent \|. At the beginning of every paragraph T<sub>E</sub>X automatically sets<br>\hangindent=0pt, \hangafter=1<br>(Note: the indentation based on \parindent is done additionally.) | 25, *26ff* |
| \hat | math mode: mathematical accent<br>$\hat x$ yields — $\hat{x}$ —. | 55 |

| command | description | pp. |
|---|---|---|
| * \hbadness | is a limit for the badness of lines or boxes. If it is exceeded TeX generates a message.<br>preset value: \hbadness=1000 | |
| \hbar | math mode: ordinary symbol — $\hbar$ — | 73 |
| * \hbox | starts a *horizontal box*.<br>All the elements within the braces are put (horizontally) next to one another. An \hbox has a natural width, which is determined by its contents, but the width can also be externally declared.<br>\hbox to 10cm {...text...}<br>If the width is externally specified, the box has to be filled exactly, otherwise an error message will be generated. (This is usually done by dynamic space, e.g. \hfil.) An additional width (added to the natural width) may be specified by spread, as in<br>\hbox spread 2cm {...text...}<br>If an \hbox (or a \vbox) contains other boxes the innermost box governs the typesetting mode of the information contained in it. | *65, 71,*<br>114ff |
| \headline | is the *token* register with the contents of the running headline.<br>preset value: \headline={\hfil}<br>This means it is empty.<br>(See also \footline) | 25, 33ff,<br>152,<br>*158* |
| \heartsuit | math mode: ordinary symbol — $\heartsuit$ —<br>(See also \spadesuit, \clubsuit, diamondsuit) | 73 |
| height | is an optional keyword for the \hrule, \vrule commands to determine the height of a rule.<br>Example: \vrule height 4cm width0.4pt | 39 |
| * \hfil | generates dynamic horizontal space of first order. | *22*, 123 |
| * \hfill | generates dynamic horizontal space of second order. | *23, 78ff,*<br>125 |
| * \hfilneg | cancels a preceding \hfil (first order only!) There is no \hfillneg.<br>(See also \vfilneg). | |
| * \hfuzz | is the limit for announcing an 'overfull hbox'.<br>preset value: \hfuzz=0.1pt<br>(See also \vfuzz) | 40 |
| \hglue | generates horizontal space which does not disappear at a line break. (\nobreak and \vrule commands are used.)<br>Example: \hglue 3cm plus 1 cm<br>(See also \vglue) | |

| command | description | pp. |
|---|---|---|
| \hideskip | is an internal horizontal skip, defined by plain TEX as | 89 |
| | -1000pt plus 1fill | |
| | to get a specific skip amount. It is used by \hidewidth within \halign to generate elements of columns, whose width is not considered in the calculation of column widths, i.e. handled as 0 pt. | |
| \hidewidth | defined by \def\hidewidth{\hskip\hideskip} forces the current element of a \halign column to a logical width of zero. | 89 |
| * \hoffset | is the horizontal offset by which the printout is moved to the right side on the paper (if \hoffset > 0 else to the left). (Output drivers can usually override this value.) preset value: \hoffset=0pt (See also \voffset) | 25, *26* |
| \hom | math mode: large operator — hom — | 64 |
| \hookleftarrow | math mode: relation — ↩ — | 72 |
| \hookrightarrow | | 72 |
| | math mode: relation — ↪ — | |
| \hphantom | calculates the width of 'text' in \hphantom{text} but produces only horizontal skip of this value. The height is considered to be zero. (See also \vphantom, \phantom and \smash) | 74 |
| * \hrule | generates a horizontal rule. This instruction may only be used in *vertical* or *internal vertical* mode, application within a paragraph forces the end of the current paragraph. Syntax: \hrule width *dim* height *dim* depth *dim* \hrule has three optional parameters height, width and depth. \hrule without parameters generates a horizontal rule with the width of the surrounding box (of width \hsize between paragraphs) and a height (thickness) of 0.4 pt. | *36, 39,* 120 |
| \hrulefill | defined by \def\hrulefill{\leaders\hrule\hfill} fills a surrounding \hbox with a horizontal rule. Example: \hbox to 3cm{X\hrulefill X} yields X_____X See also \dotfill, \leftarrowfill, \rightarrowfill, \downbracefill, \upbracefill | 92 |
| * \hsize | internal register *horizontal size* It determines the length of paragraph lines. It may be changed within groups or within a \vbox to get paragraphs of different widths. preset value: \hsize=6.5 true in (See also \vsize) | 11, 25, *30, 119, 121* |

| command | description | pp. |
|---|---|---|
| * \hskip | generates horizontal space of a given length. For example \hskip 1cm generates a skip of exactly 1 cm. (See also \vskip) | 123 |
| * \hss | produces dynamic horizontal space, which is infinitely shrinkable (in contrast to \hfil, \hfill) and extendable. Often it is used to adjust overfull \hboxes to their external width, so that no complaining messages occur, but overprinting to left and right margins of the \hbox is possible. | *33ff*, 123 |
| * \ht | refers to the height of a box register $(0 \ldots 255)$. After \setbox0{\vrule height2cm width 0.4pt} you get \ht0 as 2 cm. It is even possible to change the height of a given box by an assignment of a new value to \ht *number*. (See also \wd for *width* and \dp for *depth*) | *112*, 118, *129* |
| * \hyphenation | generates an entry in the exception list for hyphenations. Example: \hyphenation{tut-anch-amun} The word must not contain accented letters; words without any hyphenation may also be entered. The exception list is limited in size, usually to about 300 words, but that is dependent on your implementation. (See also \showhyphens) | 38 |
| * \hyphenchar | is a font specific character that is used as hyphenating character. When a font is loaded by \font this value is preset to \defaulthyphenchar. By \hyphenchar\tenrm=-1 you can suppress the output of hyphenating characters at line breaks for the font \tenrm. Assignments of values greater than $-1$ override the preset value. (See also \defaulthyphenchar) | |
| * \hyphenpenalty | penalty for a single hyphenation at a line break. preset value: \hyphenpenalty=50 | 38 |
| \i | produces (dotless i) — ı—. math mode: $\vec\imath$ for — $\vec{\imath}$ — | 14 |
| \ialign | is an internal macro of plain TEX. It is just an abbreviation for an \halign command with a preceding \tabskip=0pt, additionally it clears \everycr. | |
| * \if | checks if the two following *tokens* agree. If the next tokens contain macros, these will be expanded until two *tokens* are found that are not expandable. | 101, *104*, *112* |

| command | description | pp. |
|---|---|---|
| * \ifcase | *case* construction | |

\ifcase *number or count register*
                commands for 0
    \or    *commands for 1*
    . . .
    \else *commands for other cases*
    \fi

| command | description | pp. |
|---|---|---|
| * \ifcat | tests if the category codes (See also \catcode) of the following two *tokens* do agree. As in \if, macros that follow \ifcat are expanded until two *tokens* are found which are not further expandable. | 101 |
| * \ifdim | compares dimensions, following the syntax of | 100, |

\ifdim *dimension*$_1$ < *dimension*$_2$
\ifdim *dimension*$_1$ = *dimension*$_2$
\ifdim *dimension*$_1$ > *dimension*$_2$
Any dimension may be a register or an explicitly given value like '12.34 pt'.

*112*

| command | description | pp. |
|---|---|---|
| * \ifeof | has to be followed by the number $(0 \ldots 15)$ of an open file. It tests if the end of the input file has been reached or if more information is available. | |
| \iff | math mode: relation — $\Longleftrightarrow$ — | 72 |
| * \iffalse | is an \if-command that is always *'false'*. This command is designed to be used within macros. Other commands which are defined by \newif expand to \iffalse or \iftrue. The advantage is that the usual form of if expression with an optional \else and \fi is available. | 103 |
| * \ifhbox | must be followed by the number of a box register. It results in *true*, if the contents of the box register are built by an \hbox command. | 103 |
| * \ifhmode | tests if currently *restricted horizontal mode* (just within an \hbox) or *horizontal mode* (building paragraphs) is active. | |
| * \ifinner | tests if *internal mode* is currently active. This is the mode within a \vbox *(internal vertical mode)* or within an \hbox *(restricted horizontal mode)*. | 102 |
| * \ifmmode | tests if mathematical mode is currently active. | 102 |
| * \ifnum | compares numbers or \count registers: | 100 |

\ifnum *zahl*$_1$ < *zahl*$_2$
\ifnum *zahl*$_1$ = *zahl*$_2$
\ifnum *zahl*$_1$ > *zahl*$_2$
Example: \ifnum\pageno>10
                \ifnum\count2<\count3

| command | description | pp. |
|---|---|---|
| * \ifodd | tests if the following number or the contents of a \count register is *odd*. | *34*, 101 |

Example: \ifodd\pageno, \ifodd\count7

| command | description | pp. |
|---|---|---|
| * \iftrue | is an \if-command that is always 'true'. This command is designed to be used within macros. Other commands which are defined by \newif expand to \iftrue or \iffalse. The advantage is that the usual form of if-expression with an optional \else and \fi is available. | 103 |
| * \ifvbox | must be followed by the number of a box register. It results in *true*, if the contents of the box register are built by a \vbox command. | 103 |
| * \ifvmode | tests if *vertical mode* (between paragraphs) or *internal vertical mode* (within a \vbox) is currently active. | 102 |
| * \ifvoid | must be followed by the number of a box register. It results in *true* if the given box is empty. | 103 |
| * \ifx | tests *without full expansion* whether the two following *tokens* are equal. If these are macros, it checks whether they have the same expansion (defining text). | 101, *104*, *105* |
| * \ignorespaces | ignores all spaces that follow this command. It is often used as the last command of a macro to gobble remaining spaces that follow at the position where the macro is called. | 92 |
| \Im | math mode: ordinary symbol — $\Im$ — | 73 |
| \imath | math mode: ordinary symbol — $\imath$ — produces "i" without dot $\vec\imath$ yields — $\vec\imath$ —. (See also \jmath) | 73 |
| \immediate | changes the execution time of the commands: \write, \openout, \closeout. Usually the information of these is stored and executed when the page they belong to is shipped out. This is done in the output routine. If the operations should not be delayed they have to be preceded by \immediate. | 176 |
| \in | math mode: produces — $\in$ —. (See also \ni — $\ni$ —) | 72 |
| * \indent | is normally used at the beginning of a paragraph. It starts the new paragraph with the paragraph indentation. The amount of indentation is determined by the paramenter \parindent. Two \indent commands give a duplicated indentation. (See also \noindent, which suppresses the paragraph indentation.) | 11 |
| \inf | math mode: large operator — inf — | 64 |
| \infty | math mode: ordinary symbol — $\infty$ — | 73 |
| * \input | reads further commands from another file, whose name has to be given next. Such an input file may contain further \input commands. Example: \input myfile | |

| command | description | pp. |
|---|---|---|

\* \insert — stores (vertical) material within an *insertion register*. It is an internal command used by \footnote and insertion commands like \topinsert.
Syntax: \insert $n$ { *vertical material* } Any insertion uses the other registers \box, \count, \dimen, \skip with the same number $n$. Therefore you should request a free insertion register by, e.g., \newinsert\myinsert. After \insert\myinsert{..information..} the stored text is available to the output routine in \box\myinsert. \dimen\myinsert puts a maximum limitation on the size of the insertion. \count\myinsert scales the insertion with respect to \pagegoal. A value of 1000 results in a factor of 1.0, like \magnification. \skip\myinsert produces extra space needed to put an insertion onto the page, e.g. for skip between text area and footnotes. — 35

\* \insertpenalties — while in the *output routine*, contains the number of insertions still stored. Otherwise it accumulates penalties when insertions like footnotes have to be broken across page boundaries. — 152

\int — math mode: large operator — $\int$ — (See also \smallint) — 59

\interdisplaylinepenalty — penalty for breaking formulae generated by \display-lines at page boundary.
preset value: \interdisplaylinepenalty=100

\interfootnotelinepenalty — penalty for breaking a footnote across a page boundary.
preset value: \interfootnotelinepenalty=100
(This is a count register of plain TeX macros that is defined by \newcount.)

\* \interlinepenalty — penalty for dividing a paragraph at a page boundary.
preset value: \interlinepenalty=0
(The \footnote command changes the value locally to \interfootnotelinepenalty.)

\iota — math mode: greek letter — $\iota$ — — 52

\it — changes to the *italic* typeface and changes the family to \itfam for mathematical mode. — 42

| command | description | pp. |
|---|---|---|
| \item | generates an itemized list with the indentation of the value of \parindent.<br>Example: \item{1.} first \item{2.} second<br>      \item{3.} third \item{4.} fourth<br>produces<br>1. first<br>2. second<br>3. third<br>4. fourth | 28ff |
| \itemitem | produces an itemized list with $2 \times$ \parindent as indentation. It is used like \item. | 28ff |
| \itfam | is the internal number of the *italic* font family.<br>(See also \newfam) | |
| \j | text mode: yields — ȷ —. | 14 |
| \jmath | math mode: yields — $\jmath$ —.<br>Example: $\vec\jmath$ produces — $\vec{\jmath}$ —.<br>(See also \imath) | 73 |
| * \jobname | is the name of the current TeX job, usually the name of the main input file. (This is dependent on the actual implementation you use.) | |
| \joinrel | is an internal macro of plain TeX to get 'long' arrows as in \longrightarrow. These arrows are built out of several parts. | |
| \jot | is a plain TeX dimen register, defined by<br>\newdimen\jot   \jot=3pt | |
| \kappa | math mode: greek letter — $\kappa$ — | 52 |
| \ker | math mode: large operator — ker — | 64 |
| * \kern | has to be followed by a dimension. Depending on the current mode, it generates vertical or horizontal *kern*, i.e. space. At this space no line or page break is possible. (The equivalent in math mode is \mkern.) | *36* |
| \l | text mode: (*Polish l*) yields — ł —. | *14* |
| \L | text mode: (*Polish L*) yields — Ł —. | *14* |
| \lambda | math mode: greek letter — $\lambda$ — | 52 |
| \Lambda | math mode: greek letter — $\Lambda$ — | 53 |
| \land | math mode: binary operator — $\wedge$ —<br>(\wedge is equivalent.) | 71 |
| \langle | math mode: opening delimiter — $\langle$ —<br>(See also \rangle) | 61 |

| command | description | pp. |
|---|---|---|
| * \lastbox | in *internal vertical mode* and in both *horizontal modes*, delivers the last \vbox or \hbox, if such a box is built just before this command. By an assignment instruction like \setbox0=\lastbox you can fetch back a box and store it into a box register for further inspection. This box is deleted from the current list. | |
| * \lastkern | If the last element of the current working list is a \kern, it produces this element. The element is *not* deleted from the list, in contrast to \lastbox. By \kern-\lastkern you can cancel this \kern, but this results in two \kern commands in sequence. By \unkern a preceding \kern is explicitly deleted. | |
| * \lastpenalty | If the last element of a list is a \penalty, it refers to just this value. By an assignment, e.g., <br> \count7=\lastpenalty <br> you can examine it, by \unpenalty you can explicitly delete it. | |
| * \lastskip | If the last element of a list is a \skip, it produces just this value. By an assignment, e.g., \skip6=\lastskip you can save it for further inspection. <br> By \unskip this element is deleted. | |
| \lbrace | math mode: opening delimiter — { — <br> It is adjusted in size in combination with \big.., \left, \right. <br> The command \{ is equivalent. <br> (See also \rbrace or \}) | 61, *62* |
| \lbrack | math mode: opening delimiter — [ — <br> It is adjusted in size in combination with \big.., \left, \right. The character [ is equivalent in mathematical mode. <br> (See also \rbrack) | 61, *62* |
| * \lccode | *(lowercase code)* This code is associated with any character code from 0 ... 127. It determines into which symbol a specific character has to be changed to get the associated lowercase symbol, if the command \lowercase is applied. There are the expected definitions from \lccode'\A='\a to \lccode'\Z='\z.) (See also \uccode for \uppercase) | |
| \lceil | math mode: opening delimiter — ⌈ — <br> (See also \rceil and \lfloor, \rfloor) | 61 |
| \ldotp | math mode: period as punctuation <br> (This is used within \ldots.) | |
| \ldots | math mode: *lower dots* subformula, yields — ... —. <br> (See also \vdots, \cdots, \ddots) | 66, *95* |
| \le | math mode: relation — ≤ — | 72 |

| command | description | pp. |
|---|---|---|
| * \leaders | repeats the following box or \hrule until the width of the following \hskip, \hfill is reached.<br>Example:<br>    \def\leaderfill{%<br>        \leaders\hbox to 1em{\hss.\hss}\hfill}<br>Boxes generated by \leaders in consecutive lines are adjusted so that they fit just one below the other.<br>(See also \cleaders *centered*, \xleaders *expanded*) | 91ff |
| \leavevmode | starts a paragraph if necessary.<br>It leaves the vertical mode between paragraphs. (This is done by a tricky \unhbox of an empty box. The paragraph is begun, but a \noindent will still suppress indentation.) | 164 |
| * \left | math mode: \left and \right are paired commands that surround a subformula. They are followed by a required delimiter. The given delimiters are adjusted in size according to the subformula. Additionally \left and \right begin and finish a group.<br>Example:<br>$$ \left( x \over x+1 \right) $$ yields $$\left(\frac{x}{x+1}\right)$$ | 63 |
| \leftarrow | math mode: relation, yields — ← —.<br>(\gets is equivalent.) | 72 |
| \Leftarrow | math mode: relation, yields — ⇐ —. | 72 |
| \leftarrowfill | text mode: fills a box with an arrow.<br>Example:<br>\hbox to 4cm{X \leftarrowfill\ Y}<br>    X ⟵——————————— Y<br>(See also \rightarrowfill,\hrulefill) | 92 |
| \leftharpoondown | <br>math mode: relation — ↽ — | 72 |
| \leftharpoonup | math mode: relation — ↼ — | 72 |
| \leftline | text mode: the contents of \leftline{..text..} are typeset flush left within a line. This command may only be used in vertical mode, i.e. not within a paragraph.<br>defined by<br>\def\line{\hbox to\hsize}<br>\def\leftline{\line#1{#1\hss}}<br>(See also \rightline, \centerline) | 8, 17, 40 |
| \leftrightarrow | <br>math mode: relation — ↔ — | 72 |
| \Leftrightarrow | <br>math mode: relation — ⇔ — | 72 |

| command | description | pp. |
|---|---|---|
| * \leftskip | is an internal register of TeX which determines the amount paragraph lines are shortened on the left side. The margin on the left side is enlarged if the value is greater than zero.<br>preset value: \leftskip=0pt<br>(See also \rightskip, \narrower) | *21*, 24ff |
| \leq | math mode: relation — $\leq$ —<br>(\le is equivalent) | 72 |
| \leqalignno | math mode: aligns formulae that are numbered on the left side:<br>\leqalign{ 1. part & 2. part & number \cr<br>··· <br>1. part & 2. part & number \cr}<br>The formula lines are adjusted horizontally at the "&" sign. The first parts are set flush right, the second parts flush left.<br>Example:<br>$$\leqalignno{a&=b+c&(1)\cr a-b&=c&(2)\cr}$$<br><br>(1) $\qquad\qquad a = b + c$<br>(2) $\qquad\qquad a - b = c$<br><br>(See also \eqalignno, \eqalign) | 70 |
| * \leqno | math mode: within a display style formula, generates a number on the left.<br>$$ formula \leqno number $$<br>(See also \eqno) | 70 |
| * \let | defines a new command by copying the definition of an old one. By<br>\let\bs=\bigskip<br>\def\bigskip{\vskip 24pt}<br>you can access the old version of \bigskip with \bs, but \bigskip is changed. | 98, *104, 105, 108* |
| \lfloor | math mode: opening delimiter — $\lfloor$ —<br>(See also \rfloor, \lceil and \rceil) | 61 |
| \lg | math mode: large operator — lg — | 64 |
| \lgroup | math mode: left opening — $\lgroup$ —<br>(May only be used in combination with \big.., \left, \right.)<br>(See also \rgroup) | 61 |
| \lhook | math mode: is a helper macro of plain TeX to build \hookrightarrow, \lhook yields — ↩ —.<br>(See also \rhook) | |
| \lim | math mode: large operator — lim — | 64 |

| command | description | pp. |
|---|---|---|
| \liminf | math mode: large operator — lim inf — | 64 |

\* \limits — math mode: changes positioning for superscripts and subscripts if it follows a mathematical operator. Lower and upper bounds are typeset just below and above the operator.
Example:
`$$\int\limits_0^\pi \sin x$$`

$$\int_0^\pi \sin x \qquad \text{normally} \qquad \int_0^\pi \sin x$$

60

(See also \nolimits, \displaylimits)

| \limsup | math mode: large operator — lim sup — | 64 |

\line — text mode: generates a line (of length \hsize).
It is used by \line{..text..}. By insertion of suitable dynamic space, e.g., \hfil, the generated box should be filled, otherwise TEX complains about an "underful hbox".
defined by \def\line{\hbox to \hsize}

\* \linepenalty — penalty for each line that is accumulated in the course of building paragraphs. This value is used to generate paragraphs with as small a line count as possible.
preset value: \linepenalty=10

\* \lineskip — is the new distance between the bottom edge of the previous box and the top edge of the next box which is generated if the original distance is less than the value of \lineskiplimit.
preset value: \lineskip=1pt

18

\* \lineskiplimit — is a threshold value for the distance between two boxes: If the top edge of the next box is closer to the bottom edge of the preceding box, the distance between them is corrected as \lineskip determines.
preset value: \lineskiplimit=0pt
As the preset value is zero a correction is only done if the two boxes would overlap.

18

\ll — math mode: relation — $\ll$ —
(See also \gg for — $\gg$ —)

72

\llap — *left lap*
prints information overlapping to the left, the current position is not changed.
Example: ooo\llap{//}uuu yields — o⁄⁄uuu —.
(See also \rlap for ooo⁄⁄u)

125

| command | description | pp. |
|---|---|---|
| \lmoustache | math mode: delimiter — ⎰ — | 61 |
|  | It may only be used in combination with \big.., \left and \right. (See also \rmoustache) |  |
| \ln | math mode: large operator — ln — | 64 |
| \lnot | math mode: ordinary symbol — ¬ — (\neg is equivalent.) | 73 |
| \log | math mode: large operator — log — | 64 |
| * \long | is a command that may precede a definition command \def, \gdef or \edef. The new definition is allowed to have parameters longer than a paragraph. Usually this is forbidden: TₑX reports an error message "runaway arguments? Paragraph ended ...". | 100, 112 |
| \longleftarrow | math mode: relation — ⟵ — | 72 |
| \Longleftarrow | math mode: relation — ⟸ — | 72 |
| \longleftrightarrow | math mode: relation — ⟷ — | 72 |
| \Longleftrightarrow | math mode: relation — ⟺ — | 72 |
| \longmapsto | math mode: relation — ⟼ — | 72 |
| \longrightarrow | math mode: relation — ⟶ — | 72 |
| \Longrightarrow | math mode: relation — ⟹ — | 72 |
| \loop | is a plain TₑX macro to generate program-like loops: Syntax: \loop α \if.. β \repeat α, β are any instructions but may also be empty. \if.. is any of the allowed \if-commands, \repeat determines the end of the loop. At the beginning α is interpreted. If the \if-condition results in *true* the β commands are read and the loop restarts at α when \repeat is encountered. If the \if-condition fails, the loop is terminated. | 111ff, 124 |
| * \looseness | is a parameter for building paragraphs. It is preset with zero. If it is changed to 1 or 2, the program tries to build paragraphs which are 1 or 2 lines longer. |  |
| \lor | math mode: binary operator — ∨ — (\vee is equivalent.) | 71 |
| * \lower | lowers a following box by a given dimension. This may be used in horizontal mode only. Example: Fau\lower3pt\hbox{X}pas yields     Fauₓpas (See also \raise, \moveleft, \moveright) | 126, 137 |

| command | description | pp. |
|---|---|---|
| * \lowercase | changes uppercase letters to lowercase letters in the input. By \lowercase{aBc} you get an input of abc. If a macro is included in the input, it is not expanded. The following recipe helps in this case: <br> \edef\next{...information...} <br> \lowercase\expandafter{\next} <br> (See also \uppercase) | |
| \lq | is a substitution command for — ' — (accent). <br> *left quote* | 6 |
| * \mag | is TEX's internal register for the global magnification. It is set by a \magnification command at the very beginning of the input and must *not* be changed later on. | |
| \magnification | determines the global scaling factor of the whole document. Usually the scaling factors generated by \magstep are used. (Values which are defined by a '**true**' dimension, e.g., \hsize and \vsize, are not changed.) | 12, 43 |
| \magstep | produces a series of predefined scaling values as power of 1.2 from \magstep0 ... \magstep5 as $(1000 * 1.2^n)$ | 13, 43 |
| \magstephalf | generates the scaling value of '1095' ($\sim \sqrt{1.2}$) | 43 |
| \makefootline | is a helper macro for the output routine. It generates the footline of the page. This is done by using the contents of the token register \footline. The default values build a line with a centered page number. | 154 |
| \makeheadline | is a helper macro for the output routine. It generates the headline of the page. This is done by using the contents of the token register \headline. If \headline is not changed an empty line is generated. | 152, *155* |
| \mapsto | math mode: relation — ↦ — | 72 |
| \mapstochar | is a helper macro of plain TEX to build \mapsto. It contains the symbol — ⊦—. | |
| * \mark | stores a text, e.g., \mark{current Author}, into a mark register. This register is controlled by page breaking. If several \mark commands are given, you can refer to the mark text with respect to the current page. \botmark produces the last entry of the current page, \topmark the last entry of the previous page and \firstmark the first entry of the current page. The usage is only meaningful when the stored information is referred to within the output routine, e.g., in \headline and \footline. (See also \botmark, \firstmark, \topmark) | 157ff |

| command | description | pp. |
|---|---|---|

* \mathaccent        is an internal TEX command to generate mathematical        55
accents.
Example: \ddot is defined by
\def\ddot{\mathaccent"707F }
Mathematical accents are done differently from accents
in text as they have to support style changes.

* \mathbin           math mode: forces the following information to be used        133,
with the function of a *binary operator*. In \mathbin= the        *137ff*
equals sign is used as a binary operator (instead of as
a relation). This is useful for producing spacing within
the formulae that reflects the intended functions.

* \mathchar          math mode: generates a mathematical symbol with a
specific function and determines the family number. It
is followed by a number. A hexadecimal notation is quite
understandable:
\mathchar"1350, divide the number in groups as
                          1 3 50,
produces the symbol "50, which is the summation sign.
It has to be used as a large operator (class 1) from the
fonts of family number 3.

Syntax: \mathchar"*cfhh*, with *c* for a class, *f* for a family
and *hh* for the position in the code table.
$(c,f,h \in 0\ldots9, A\ldots Z)$
There are eight possible classes:

0   ordinary symbol ($\alpha$)
1   large operator ($\sum$)
2   binary operator ($\star$)
3   relation ($>$)
4   left opening ($\{$)
5   right closing ($\}$)
6   punctuation ($.$)
7   like 0, with extra function:
    the family number will be substituted, if a family
    switch (by \fam) occurred in mathematical mode.
    (See also \delimiter, \delcode)

* \mathchardef        math mode: defines a name for a specific \mathchar
value. E.g., \mathchardef\sum="1350 defines the com-
mand \sum. The notation for the numeric value is as in
\mathchar.

| command | description | pp. |
|---|---|---|
| * \mathchoice | math mode: generates four variants of mathematical subformulae. \mathchoice{*display*}{*text*}{*script*}{*scriptscript*} The program chooses the variant depending on the current mathematical style as it is needed. The result is of the subformula type. If mathematical symbols are generated by combination and direct references to code tables, variants for all styles should be built. This allows use in all styles from display style up to scriptscript style. | 137 |
| * \mathclose | math mode: forces the following information to be used with the function of a *closing delimiter*. In \mathclose: the colon becomes a 'closing delimiter'. | 133ff |
| * \mathcode | math mode: defines how a single character of ASCII code, e.g. one of the letters "A" ... "Z" is to be interpreted in mathematical mode. Example: \mathcode'\<="313C assign the symbol "<" function 3 (relation), family 1 and position "3C" (in the code tables of the fonts in family 1) The syntax of the numeric values is further explained under \mathchar. Instead of '\< the numeric values decimal 60, hexadecimal "3C, or octal '74 may also be used. (See also \delimiter) | 133ff |
| \mathhexbox | math mode: is a helper macro of plain TₑX to generate \dag, \S, \P. They provide original mathematical symbols for text mode. | |
| * \mathinner | math mode: forces the following information to be used with the function of a *subformula*. | 74, 133ff |
| * \mathop | math mode: forces the following information to be used with the function of a *large operator*. | *64, 74*, 133ff |
| * \mathopen | math mode: forces the following information to be used with the function of an *opening delimiter*. | 74, 133ff |
| * \mathord | math mode: forces the following information to be used with the function of an *ordinary symbol*. | 74, 133ff |

| command | description | pp. |
|---|---|---|
| \mathpalette | math mode: | |

\mathpalette — math mode:

Syntax: \mathpalette{α}{β}

generates a \mathchoice command. It is defined by

```
\def\mathpalette#1#2{\mathchoice
        {#1\displaystyle{#2}}%
        {#1\textstyle{#2}}%
        {#1\scriptstyle{#2}}%
        {#1\scriptscriptstyle{#2}}}
```

The α part is used without modification, before the β parts style switching is inserted.

(This is used within the \root command.)

* \mathpunct — math mode: forces the following information to be used with the function of a *punctuation symbol*. — 74, 133ff

* \mathrel — math mode: forces the following information to be used with the function of a *relation*. — 74, 133ff

\mathstrut — math mode: generates an empty box with a specific height and depth. This is used to force a minimal distance between lines, e.g., in matrices.

defined by

`\def\mathstrut{\vphantom(}`

* \mathsurround — math mode: is an internal variable that determines how much additional space has to be generated before and after a formula within paragraphs (in *text style*, as used by ($..$)). — 133

preset value: `\mathsurround=0pt`

\matrix — math mode: generates a simple matrix without parentheses. — 65ff

Example:

```
$$\matrix{ 1 & 2 & 3 \cr
           4 & 5 & 6 \cr
           7 & 8 & 9 \cr}$$   yields
```

$$\begin{matrix} 1 & 2 & 3 \\ 4 & 5 & 6 \\ 7 & 8 & 9 \end{matrix}$$

(Note: internally \halign is used.)

\max — math mode: large operator — max — — 64

* \maxdeadcycles — is an internal register limiting the number of times the output routine may be called consecutively without doing a \shipout (real print of page).

preset value: `\maxdeadcycles=25`

* \maxdepth — is an internal register with the maximum box depth. — 153

preset value: `\maxdepth=4pt`

\maxdimen — internal dimen register of plain TₑX macros. It is preset with the maximum possible length.

preset value: `\maxdimen=16383.99999pt`

| command | description | pp. |
|---|---|---|
| * `\meaning` | is a command for debugging. It generates the meaning of characters or commands. | |

      `\meaning A` → 'the letter A'
      `\meaning\par` → '\par' (intrinsic)
      `\meaning\bigskip`
          → 'macro:->\vskip \biskipamount'

The output will be printed, for debugging on terminal use `\message{\meaning ... }`.
(See also `\show` and `\showthe`)

| command | description | pp. |
|---|---|---|
| `\medbreak` | text mode: determines a good position for page breaking and produces the same space as `\medskip`. It corresponds to `\smallbreak,\bigbreak` $(1:2:4)$. (See also `\smallbreak`, `\bigbreak`) | 32 |
| * `\medmuskip` | math mode: is the size of a medium mathematical space skip. It is used for spacing mathematical formulae. It is given in units of length of $mu = math\ units$ preset value: `\medmuskip=4mu plus 2mu minus 4mu` (See also `\thinmuskip`, `\thickmuskip`) | 64, 134ff |
| `\medskip` | text mode: produces vertical space with the size of `\medskipamount`. (See also `\smallskip`, `\bigskip`) `\medskip` is defined by `\def\medskip{\vskip\medskipamount}` | 15 |
| `\medskipamount` | is a skip register of plain TeX that contains the amount of vertical space that is generated by `\medskip`. preset value: `\medskipamount=6pt plus 2pt minus 2pt` (See also `\bigskipamount`, `\smallskipamount`) | |
| * `\message` | generates a message on the terminal and into the log file. Example: `\message{Here I am.. in chapter 1}` | |
| `\mid` | math mode: relation — \| — | 72 |
| `\midinsert` | is a command to insert information at the current position. But if there is not enough space on the current page, the information will be put on the top of the following page. This may be used for pictures. Syntax: `\midinsert` *vertical material* `\endinsert` (See also `\topinsert` and `\pageinsert`) | 35 |
| `\min` | math mode: large operator — min — | 64 |
| `minus` | is a keyword for dimensions of `\skip` command. It represents the skip part that can shrink. In `\hskip 3cm minus 1cm` the skip may shrink to 2 cm if there is not enough space. (See also `plus`) | |

| command | description | pp. |
|---|---|---|
| \mit | math mode: sets the "math italic font family" within mathematical mode. (This is the default for nearly every symbol.) | 44 |
| mm | unit of measure: millimeter<br>$1\,\text{mm} \approx 2.854\,\text{pt}$ | 12 |
| * \mkern | math mode: is the equivalent command to \kern in mathematical mode. It may only be used with one unit of length: "mu" *(math units)*. Depending on the current mode vertical or horizontal space is generated.<br>$18\,\text{mu} = 1\,\text{em}$<br>(See also \thinmuskip,\medmuskip,\thickmuskip) | *136* |
| \models | math mode: relation $- \models -$ | 72 |
| * \month | is an internal numeric register that is initialized with the month of the current date $(1\ldots 12)$.<br>It may be printed with \number\month or examined with \the\month, even a change is possible.<br>(See also \day, \year, \time) | |
| * \moveleft | may only be used in vertical mode when elements are arranged one below the other. It moves a box to the left.<br>Example:<br>\vbox{\hbox{AAAAA}%<br>    \moveleft8pt\hbox{BBBBB}\hbox{CCCCC}}<br>yields:<br><div align="center">AAAAA<br>BBBBB<br>CCCCC</div>(See also \moveright,\raise,\lower) | 126 |
| * \moveright | may only be used in vertical mode when elements are arranged one below the other. It moves a box to the right. A negative length may also be given.<br>(See also \moveleft,\raise,\lower) | 126 |
| \mp | math mode: binary operator $- \mp -$<br>(See also \pm for $- \pm -$) | 71 |
| * \mskip | math mode: generates skip within mathematical mode. It is measured in "mu" *(math units)*. | *130* |
| mu | unit of measure: *mathematical unit* only for mathematical mode<br>$18\,\text{mu} = 1\,\text{em}$ | |
| \mu | math mode: greek letter $- \mu -$ | 52 |

| command | description | pp. |
|---|---|---|
| * \multiply | general purpose command to multiply a quantity by an integer value.<br>Example:<br>`\multiply\count3 by 5`<br>`\multiply\bigskipamount by 2`<br>As all `\dimen` and `\skip` commands may be preceded with a (rational) factor this command is rarely used. | 92 |
| \multispan | is used while generating tables.<br>It is used if more than one column is to be considered as a single column element that spans several columns.<br>Example:<br>`\halign{\hfill#\hfill\quad&`<br>`          \hfill#\hfill\quad&`<br>`          \hfill#\hfill\quad&#\cr`<br>`  one  & two  & three &\cr`<br>`  four &\multispan2 \hfill together\hfill&\cr`<br>`  five & six  & seven  &\cr}` | 89, *91* |

one     two     three
four            together
five    six     seven

| command | description | pp. |
|---|---|---|
| * \muskip | math mode: refers to one of the 256 `\muskip` registers $(0\ldots 255)$.<br>`\muskip17`<br>After `\newmuskip\mymumu` you can refer to a free register with a name. | 130 |
| * \muskipdef | is an internal command to name `\muskip` registers.<br>After `\muskipdef\mymumu=17` the register 17 may be used by the name `\mymumu`. Then you can write<br>`    \muskip\mymumu`. | |
| \nabla | math mode: ordinary symbol — $\nabla$ — | 73 |
| \narrower | text mode: increases `\leftskip` and `\rightskip` by `\parindent`. The paragraphs are typeset with line length shortened on the right and left sides. If `\narrower` is used more than once it accumulates and the paragraphs can get very narrow. | 24, *119* |
| \natural | math mode: ordinary symbol — $\natural$ —<br>(See also `\flat` — $\flat$ —) | 73 |
| \ne | math mode: relation — $\neq$ —<br>(`\neq` is equivalent.) | 72 |
| \nearrow | math mode: relation — $\nearrow$ —<br>*(north east arrow)* | 72 |
| \negthinspace | generates a little backskip with the same amount as given by `\thinspace`: ‖. | 17 |
| \neq | math mode: relation — $\neq$ —<br>(`\ne` and `\not=` are equivalent.) | 72 |

| command | description | pp. |
|---|---|---|
| \newbox | reserves a free box register and names the number of this register. After "\newbox\mybox" you can refer to the box in commands like \setbox\mybox=\hbox{...}, \copy\mybox or \ht\mybox.<br>(Note: there is *no* \boxdef command, only the *number* of the box is named.) | 116 |

\newcount     reserves the next free \count register and assigns a name     130
to the register. This name may be used in further com-
mands.
Example:

| | |
|---|---|
| \newcount\inc | definition |
| \inc=13 | setting |
| \multiply\inc by 7 | changing |
| \advance\pageno by \inc | use |
| \number\inc | print |
| \romannumeral\inc | print |

\newdimen     reserves the next free \dimen register with a given name.     130,
This name may be used for further commands.     *138*
Example:

| | |
|---|---|
| \newdimen\len | definition |
| \len=4cm | setting |
| \advance\leftskip by\len | use |
| \rightskip=0.3\len | use |

\newfam     reserves the next free number of a family (one of 16).
The following font families are used in plain TₑX:

| | | |
|---|---|---|
| 0 | \rm (\rmfam) | 'roman' fonts |
| 1 | \mit | math italic fonts |
| 2 | \cal | math symbol fonts |
| 3 | | math extension fonts |
| 4 | \it (\itfam) | *italic* fonts |
| 5 | \sl (\slfam) | *slanted* fonts |
| 6 | \bf (\bffam) | **boldface** fonts |
| 7 | \tt (\ttfam) | typewriter fonts |

Each family consists of a \textfont, \scriptfont and
\scriptscriptfont which define the appropriate fonts
for the mathematical setting styles.
(Example: \textfont0=\tenrm)

\newif     generates a new \if command.     103
Example: After \newif\ifsecret you get the following
commands:

| | |
|---|---|
| \secrettrue | sets \ifsecret to \iftrue |
| \secretfalse | sets \ifsecret to \iffalse |
| \ifsecret | refers to the current value. |

The command that follows \newif must begin with the
letters "\if".

| command | description | pp. |
|---|---|---|
| \newinsert | reserves a free *insertion* register and the associated other TeX registers. By \newinsert\myins for \myins you get the number of the registers. These are<br>\box\myins   the box which contains the stored information during the output routine,<br>\count\myins a scaling value, which is used to calculate the amount of page requested by the insertion,<br>\dimen\myins the maximum length of an insertion put onto the page,<br>\skip\myins skip before an insertion.<br>(This is used by \footnote, \topinsert, \midinsert. See also \insert.) | |
| * \newlinechar | is an internal register with the ASCII code that represents the line end of input lines. This is usually preset with 13 (for 'CR'). | |
| \newmuskip | reserves the next free *muskip* register and assigns a name for futher use.<br>Example:<br>\newmuskip\mathskip<br>\mathskip=1.5mu<br>\advance\thickmuskip by \mathskip<br>\mskip\mathskip | 130 |
| \newread | reserves the next free number for an input file $(0 \ldots 15)$. By<br>    \newread\extrafile<br>    \openin\extrafile=UUDATA<br>    \read\extrafile to \inputdata<br>you open the file "UUDATA.TEX" and get the first line read to \inputdata. \read considers block structure and may possibly read more than one line if it is necessary.<br>If the input file contains the text 'abc' in its first line, the \read command above is equivalent to the instructions \def\inputdata{abc }. Notice the additional space generated by line end. | 174ff |
| \newskip | reserves the next free *skip* register and assigns a name for further use.<br>Example:<br>\newskip\skipreg<br>\skipreg=1.5cm plus 0.5cm minus 0.5cm<br>\hskip\skipreg | 130 |

| command | description | pp. |
|---------|-------------|-----|
| \newtoks | reserves the next free *token* register and assigns a name for further use.<br>Example: | 131 |

\newtoks\toktok      definition of name
\toktok={...data...}   changing
\the\toktok          use (output) of the register
\showthe\toktok     protocol

| command | description | pp. |
|---------|-------------|-----|
| \newwrite | reserves the next free number for an output file in the range of $(0 \ldots 15)$.<br>Example: | 174ff |

\newwrite\myoutfile          definition
\openout\myoutfile=PUUNCH    file opening
\write\myoutfile{...data...}  write into file
\closeout\myoutfile        close of file

| command | description | pp. |
|---------|-------------|-----|
| \next | is an often used helper macro in plain TEX. It is used to receive local definitions for further checking. | |
| \ni | math mode: relation — $\ni$ —<br>(\owns is equivalent.) | 72 |
| * \noalign | is used in setting tables, e.g., in \halign, \matrix.<br>\noalign{ *vertical material* }<br>puts the given information between two table rows.<br>Example:<br>    \noalign{\smallskip}<br>generates an extra skip between two table rows. | 82 |
| \nobreak | inhibits line and page break depending on the current mode. It is defined by<br>\def\nobreak{\penalty10000}<br>and generates a maximum amount of penalty if a break should occur at the current position. | 32 |
| * \noexpand | suppresses the expansion of the next *token*, e.g., a macro. It is typically used in combination with \edef *(expanded definition)*.<br>\edef builds a new macro by expanding all defining information when the \edef command is executed. For a single command within the macro, this may be suppressed by application of \noexpand.<br>Example:<br>\def\a{aaa}  \edef\b{\a\noexpand\a}<br>is equivalent to<br>\def\b{aaa\a}<br>If \b is called later, the current meaning of \a is inserted. | 99, 100,<br>*108,*<br>*177* |
| * \noindent | starts a new paragraph (if necessary) without an indentation.<br>(See also \indent, \parindent) | 11 |

| command | description | pp. |
|---|---|---|

\nointerlineskip                                                                   *152*

inhibits once the generation of vertical space between two consecutive boxes in vertical mode. The boxes are allowed to touch or even overlap each other.
\baselineskip, \lineskip and \lineskiplimit are not used, i.e. the depth of the preceding box is modified so that the parameters do not give a different effect. This is done by setting \prevdepth to
\prevdepth=-1000pt.
(See also \offinterlineskip)

* \nolimits                 math mode: changes the style of positioning subscripts      60, *64*
and superscripts to the preceding large operator. They are typeset beside the operator.
Example:
`$$\sum\nolimits_{i=1}^\infty$$`

yields $\sum\nolimits_{i=1}^{\infty}$   —   normally $\sum_{i=1}^{\infty}$   .

(See also \limits, \displaylimits)

\nonfrenchspacing                                                                     6

text mode: changes the style in which interword spaces are generated after punctuations. This change resets to the default where punctuation symbols are followed by extra space. The other mode is set by \frenchspacing.

* \nonscript                math mode: may precede a *skip* command in mathematical mode. The skip will not be done in scriptstyle and scriptscript style. This may save a \mathchoice command.
Example: \nonscript\;

* \nonstopmode              changes the stop mode of the TeX program: TeX will not stop if an error occurs. Error messages are written to the log file and the terminal.

\nopagenumbers   text mode: inhibits the generation of the footline below     33
the text area, i.e. the default page numbering is suppressed.
defined by
\def\nopagenumbers{\footline={\hfil}}

\normalbaselines

text mode: restores the register values of \lineskip, \lineskiplimit and \baselineskip to the saved values of the registers \normallineskip (1pt), \normallineskiplimit (0pt), \normalbaselineskip (12pt)

| command | description | pp. |
|---|---|---|

**\normalbaselineskip**
is a plain TeX register that stores the default skip between the lines of a paragraph, i.e. the distance of the baselines.
preset value: \normalbaselineskip=12pt

**\normalbottom**  text mode: restores from 'ragged bottom' which is set by \raggedbottom to the default where all pages are generated with the same height of the text area.

**\normallineskip**
is a plain TeX register that stores the default value of \lineskip. It is used by \normalbaselines.
preset value: \normallineskip=1pt

**\normallineskiplimit**
is a plain TeX register that stores the default value for \lineskiplimit. It is used by \normalbaselines.
preset value: \normallineskiplimit=0pt

**\not**  math mode: is used as a command that precedes a relation. This relation symbol is printed with a slash to give the negated form.          72
Example:
   \not= yields — $\neq$ —.
   \not\sim yields — $\not\sim$ —.

**\notin**  math mode: relation — $\notin$ —          72
(Is nearly equivalent to \not\in, but the slash is positioned a little more to the left.)

**\nu**  math mode: greek letter — $\nu$ —          52

**\null**  generates an empty \hbox
defined by \def\null{\hbox{}}

**\* \nulldelimiterspace**
math mode: is the width of an empty delimiter that is generated by \left. or \right.
preset value: \nulldelimiterspace=1.2pt

**\* \nullfont**  is the name of an internal empty font that is substituted if a font can not be found during execution of \font.

**\* \number**  prints the following number or the contents of a \count register.          112
Example:
\number1984       yields — 1984 —.
\number-007       yields — -7 —.
\count7=18
\number\count7 yields — 18 —.
(See also \romannumeral)

**\nwarrow**  math mode: relation — $\nwarrow$ —          72
(north west arrow)

| command | description | pp. |
|---|---|---|
| \o | text mode: yields — ø —. | 14 |
| \O | text mode: yields — Ø —. | 14 |
| \oalign | text mode: is a helper macro for plain TEX. It is used for construction of a *cedille* by the macro \c and by other accenting macros \d, \b. | |
| \obeylines | text mode: changes the meaning of a line end to an explicitly given \par command. Each input line generates a paragraph of its own. A line that does not fit the size of paragraph lines is broken into several lines. Example:<br>{\obeylines \it<br>  first line<br>    second line<br>   third line  \par}<br>is typeset as<br>   *first line*<br>   *second line*<br>   *third line*<br>(Note: each line is preceded by the usual paragraph indentation.) | 21ff |
| \obeyspaces | text mode: after the command \obeyspaces *all* spaces generate a space. Normally several spaces between words are treated as one. | |
| \odot | math mode: binary operator — ⊙ — | 71 |
| \oe | text mode: yields — œ —. | 14 |
| \OE | text mode: yields — Œ —. | 14 |
| \offinterlineskip | | 88ff, |
| | omits any interline space between the lines of a paragraph or between boxes in vertical mode.<br>defined by:<br>\def\offinterlineskip{\baselineskip=-1000pt<br>       \lineskip=0pt<br>         \lineskiplimit=\maxdimen}<br>(\normalbaselines restores the default values (12pt, 1pt, 0pt)) | *123* |
| \oint | math mode: large operator — $\oint$ — | 59 |
| \oldstyle | math mode: yields *oldstyle digits*<br>$\oldstyle 0123456789$ yields — 0123456789 — | 73 |
| \omega | math mode: greek letter — $\omega$ — | 52 |
| \Omega | math mode: greek letter — $\Omega$ — | 53 |
| \ominus | math mode: binary operator — ⊖ — | 71 |

| command | description | pp. |
|---|---|---|
| * \omit | is used within \halign for table generation. It may be given at the beginning of a table entry, where it suppresses the interpretation of the template element. The entry is typeset as if the template consists of a simple "#". | 89 |
| \ooalign | is a helper macro of plain TeX. It is used in the generation of \c and \copyright. | |
| * \openin | opens one of 16 possible input files that can be used to get external data by \read. It has to be followed by a number 0 ... 15.<br>Example:<br>\openin 7 = MYFILE<br>\read 7 to \mytext<br>opens the input file "MYFILE.TEX" with the associated number 7. By \read... a line of the file is given to \mytext.<br>(See also \read, \closein) | 174ff |
| * \openout | opens one of 16 possible output files that can receive additional output information generated by TeX.<br>Example:<br>\openout 7 = MYFILE<br>\write 7 {...information...}<br>opens the output file "MYFILE.TEX" with the associated number 7. By \write.. a line is written into the file.<br>(See also \write, \closeout, \immediate) | 174ff |
| \openup | enlarges the controlling values for the interline skip by a given value. These are \baselineskip, \lineskip and \lineskiplimit. Some macros of mathematical mode use \openup3pt to get extra spaced multiline formulae. | |
| \oplus | math mode: binary operator — $\oplus$ — | 71 |
| * \or | is a keyword within the \ifcase command.<br>Syntax:<br>\ifcase *number or register*<br>    *instructions for '0'*<br>  \or   *instructions for '1'*<br>  \or   *instructions for '2'*<br>  ...<br>  \else   *instruction for 'otherwise'*<br>\fi | |
| \oslash | math mode: binary operator — $\oslash$ — | 71 |
| \otimes | math mode: binary operator — $\otimes$ — | 71 |

| command | description | pp. |
|---|---|---|
| * \outer | is a command that may precede a \def, \edef or \gdef. It forces the macro thus defined not to be callable as a macro parameter or within a box. A call is only possible on the outer level.<br>Example: \bye is generated with use of \outer. | *23*, 100 |
| * \output | is an internal *token* register that contains the commands (or the name of another macro) for the output routine. The output routine is called when enough material is gathered to fill a page.<br>It is defined by<br>\output={\plainoutput} | 152ff |
| * \outputpenalty | within the output routine, contains the penalty of the chosen page break position. It is possible to examine this value and refuse the generated position, but this is quite complicated for beginners. | 151 |

* \over — math mode: generates a fraction.    57
$$ 1 \over { 2 \over x + 3 } + 1 $$
yields

$$\frac{1}{\frac{2}{x+3}+1}$$

(See also \atop,\above)

\overbrace — math mode: generates a brace above a fomula. Example:    68
$$ \overbrace{a + \cdots + a}^{\hbox{n times}}$$
yields

$$\overbrace{a + \cdots + a}^{\text{n times}}$$

(See also \underbrace and for text mode \downbrace-
fill, \upbracefill)

* \overfullrule — is the thickness of the error rule that is printed on the    40
right side of overfull lines or boxes.
By \overfullrule=0pt it can be suppressed.

\overleftarrow — math mode: generates an arrow from right to left above    56
the following parameter.
Example:
$\overleftarrow{A-B}$ yields

$$\overleftarrow{A - B}$$

(See also \overrightarrow)

* \overline — math mode: generates a rule above the information given    55
as a parameter. It is like a long accent.
Example:
$\overline{A/B}$ yields

$$\overline{A/B}$$

(See also \underline)

| command | description | pp. |
|---|---|---|
| \overrightarrow | | 56 |

math mode: generates an arrow from left to right above the following parameter.
Example:
$\overrightarrow{A-B}$ yields

$$\overrightarrow{A-B}$$

(See also \overleftarrow)

* \overwithdelims                                                                    63

math mode: generates a fraction-like expression that is delimited on the left and right sides by explictly specified symbols.
Example:
$$ f(G) \overwithdelims<> h(G) $$
yields

$$\left\langle \frac{f(G)}{h(G)} \right\rangle$$

| \owns | math mode: relation — $\ni$ — | 72 |
| | (\ni is equivalent) | |
| \P | text mode: *(paragraph/pilcrow)* yields — ¶ —. | 73 |
| \pagebody | is a helper macro for plain TEX in the *output routine*. The *output routine* is a macro that combines the page with headline, pagebody and footline. It writes the output information into the *dvi file*. | 153 |
| \pagecontents | is a helper macro for plain TEX in the output routine, called by \pagebody. | 153 |
| * \pagedepth | is an internal register with the *"depth"* of the current page. | |
| * \pagefilllstretch | | |
| | is an internal register for page breaking. It contains the accmulated *filll* units of the current page. | |
| * \pagefillstretch | | |
| | is an internal register for page breaking. It contains the accmulated *fill* units of the current page. | |
| * \pagefilstretch | | |
| | is an internal register for page breaking. It contains the accmulated *fil* units of the current page. | |
| * \pagegoal | is an internal register for page breaking. It contains the threshold value for the text area. If it is reached the output routine is called. The value is initialized with \vsize, but it changes when footnotes or other insertions occur. | |
| | The difference \pagegoal - \pagetotal determines the amount of free space on the current page. | |

| command | description | pp. |
|---|---|---|
| \pageinsert | text mode: may only be used in the combination \pageinsert ... \endinsert. The vertical information between the two commands is printed on its own page. (See also \midinsert, \topinsert) | 35 |
| \pageno | is the name of the register that contains the pagenumber, by convention. (It is the register \count0) By \pageno=17 the page counter is modified, at page breaks it is incremented automatically. The recommended command for printing is \folio. | 32ff |
| * \pageshrink | is an internal register for page breaking. It contains the accumulated shrink dimension of the current page. That is the amount by which the current page may be shortened. | |
| * \pagestretch | is an internal register for page breaking. It contains the accumulated stretch dimension of the current page. That is the amount by which the current page may be stretched. | |
| * \pagetotal | is an internal register for page breaking. It contains the accumulated size of gathered information for the text area. | |
| * \par | text mode: (finishes and) starts a new paragraph. (After \par TeX is in *horizontal mode*.) | 11 |
| \parallel | math mode: relation — $\parallel$ — (See also \Vert for an ordinary symbol or \| ) | 72 |
| * \parfillskip | text mode: internal register that holds the horizontal skip that is used to fill the last line of a paragraph with space. As it is preset with \parfillskip=0pt plus 1fil the last lines of paragraphs are typeset flush left. If it is changed to 0pt the last line of a paragraph is justified on the right side, but this can only be successfully done with large paragraphs. | 25 |
| * \parindent | text mode: is an internal register that contains the value of the usual indentation at the beginning of paragraphs. It is also used in the macros \item, \itemitem and \narrower. preset value: \parindent=20pt | 11, *28ff*, *37, 118* |
| * \parshape | text mode: defines the shape of a paragraph by specifying the desired size of each line. Syntax: \parshape = $n\ i_1\ l_1\ \ldots\ i_n\ l_n$ where $n$ means the number of lines, $i_j$ the indentation for the $j^{\text{th}}$ line and $l_j$ the residual length of the line. | 27 |
| \partial | math mode: ordinary symbol – $\partial$ — | 73 |

| command | description | pp. |
|---|---|---|
| * \parskip | text mode: is the additional skip generated between paragraphs. It should always contains a 'plus' part to allow justification of paragraphs during page building. Otherwise TeX will often complain about not entirely filled vboxes (pages).<br>preset value: \parskip=0pt plus 1pt | 15 |
| * \patterns | is only present in the INITEX variant of TeX. It constructs the patterns for hyphenation. | 173 |
| * \pausing | is an internal register for debugging. After changing \pausing=1 TeX will stop at every line when reading from an external file. | |
| * \penalty | generates 'penalties'. This effects line and page breaking depending on the current mode.<br>A command \penalty-100 defines quite a good break position.<br>(See also \break, \nobreak) | 38 |
| \perp | math mode: relation — $\perp$ — | 72 |
| \phantom | measures the size of information given as a parameter, e.g., \phantom{blablabla}, and generates empty space with the same horizontal and vertical size.<br>(See also \hphantom, \vphantom, \smash) | 17, 74 |
| \phi | math mode: greek letter — $\phi$ —<br>(See also \varphi for — $\varphi$ —) | 52 |
| \Phi | math mode: greek letter — $\Phi$ — | 53 |
| \pi | math mode: greek letter — $\pi$ —<br>(See also \varpi for — $\varpi$ —) | 52 |
| \Pi | math mode: greek letter — $\Pi$ — | 53 |
| \plainoutput | is the standard macro of plain TeX for the output routine. | 152ff |
| plus | is a keyword that is used when specifying skip values. This determines how much the skip may be enlarged to fit the size of an outer box.<br>Example:<br>\vskip 1cm plus 0.5cm minus 0.5cm<br>(See also minus) | 15, *19* |
| \pm | math mode: binary operator — $\pm$ —<br>(See also \mp for — $\mp$ —) | 71 |

| command | description | pp. |
|---|---|---|
| \pmatrix | math mode: *(parenthesized matrix)* produces a matrix with parentheses. | 65 |

Example:
```
$$\pmatrix{ 1 & 2 & 3 \cr
            4 & 5 & 6 \cr
            7 & 8 & 9 \cr}$$ yields
```

$$\begin{pmatrix} 1 & 2 & 3 \\ 4 & 5 & 6 \\ 7 & 8 & 9 \end{pmatrix}$$

Note: internally \halign is used.
(See also \matrix, \bordermatrix)

| \pmod | math mode: *parenthesized modulo* |
|---|---|

Example:
```
$ a \equiv b+1 \pmod m$ produces
```
$$a \equiv b + 1 \pmod m$$
(See also \bmod)

**\* \postdisplaypenalty**

are penalties that are used if a page break occurs after a display style formula.
preset value: \postdisplaypenalty=0

| \Pr | math mode: large operator — Pr — | 64 |
|---|---|---|
| \prec | math mode: relation — $\prec$ — | 72 |
| \preceq | math mode: relation — $\preceq$ — | 72 |

**\* \predisplaypenalty**

are penalties that are used if a page break occurs just before a display style formula.
preset value: \predisplaypenalty=10000

**\* \predisplaysize**

math mode: is an internal register that is used while generating display style formulae. It is initialized with the length of the preceding paragraph line.

| \preloaded | is a notation for 'preloaded' fonts whose font data is stored, but it is necessary to define the name by a new \font command. |
|---|---|

**\* \pretolerance**    text mode: controls paragraph building. It is an internal    39
register that contains the threshold value for penalties which may be accumulated during the first pass of paragraph building without hyphenation. If this value is not exceeded the result is accepted.
By changing \pretolerance=10000 hyphenation is suppressed as all paragraphs are accepted.
(See also \tolerance)

| command | description | pp. |
|---|---|---|
| * \prevdepth | is an internal register that contains the depth of the preceding box or of the last line of a preceding paragraph. It is used when measuring the distances between boxes before applying the rules for use of \lineskip, \lineskiplimit, \baselineskip. It may be changed to effect the spacing between boxes. (See also \nointerlineskip) | |
| * \prevgraf | text mode: is an internal counter that contains the number of lines in the previous paragraph up to the current position. (Changes are possible but are dangerous.) \prevgraf is applied in combination with \hangafter and \parshape. Is defined with a valid value every time the paragraph building is finished. This is done before a display style formula, just after a display style formula (the formula counts too) and after paragraph end. | |
| \prime | math mode: mathematical accent | 55 |

Example:
```
$ { f(x)=x^2 }\to {f^\prime(x)=2x}$
```
produces
$$f(x) = x^2 \to f'(x) = 2x$$
For ^\prime can write an apostrophe `$ ... f'(x)=2x}`
`$`.

| command | description | pp. |
|---|---|---|
| \prod | math mode: large operator — $\prod$ — | 59 |
| \propto | math mode: relation — $\propto$ — | 72 |
| \psi | math mode: greek letter — $\psi$ — | 52 |
| \Psi | math mode: greek letter — $\Psi$ — | 53 |
| pt | unit of measure: *point* <br> $1\,\text{pt} = 0.0351\,\text{cm}$ — $1\,\text{cm} = 28.54\,\text{pt}$ | 12 |
| \qquad | is horizontal skip. <br> It has the value $2\times$\quad or $2\,$em. <br> defined by <br> \def\qquad{\hskip2em\relax} <br> Here is the size of \qquad: ∣    ∣ | 16, 65 |
| \quad | is horizontal skip. <br> It has the value $0.5\times$\qquad or $1\,$em. <br> defined by \def\quad{\hskip1em\relax} <br> Here is the width of \quad: ∣ ∣ <br> Note: \quad is font dependent: <br>     in \tenrm (\rm) 10 pt <br>     in \tenbf (\bf) 11.5 pt   ← <br>     in \tensl (\sl) 10 pt <br>     in \tenit (\it) 10 pt | 6, 16, 65 |

| command | description | pp. |
|---|---|---|

**\* \radical**  is an internal command for TEX to generate \sqrt. It does quite a complex mapping into the symbol font to get the suitable sizes, it is used once in \def\sqrt{\radical"270370 }.

**\raggedbottom**  allows TEX to vary the length of the text area. Pages may be a line longer or shorter to keep paragraphs unbroken. The \footline is put at the same position of the page.
\normalbottom restores the default value.          *153*

**\raggedright**  text mode: allows unjustified margins on the right side of paragraphs. A line of a paragraph may be up to '2 em' shorter than \hsize, the target value for line breaking. The space between may not be stretched.
Is defined by
```
\def\raggedright{%
        \rightskip=0pt plus 2em
        \spaceskip=.3333em
        \xspaceskip=.5em}
```
21

**\* \raise**  raises a following box by a given dimension. This may be used in horizontal mode only.
Example: Fau\raise3pt\hbox{X}pas
yields      Fau$^{\text{X}}$pas
(See also \lower, \moveleft, \moveright)          126

**\rangle**  math mode: closing delimiter — $\rangle$ —
(See also \langle)          61

**\rbrace**  math mode: closing delimiter — } —
In combination with \big.., \left, \right it is adjusted in size.
\} is equivalent.
(See also \lbrace)          61

**\rbrack**  math mode: closing delimiter — ] —
In combination with \big.., \left, \right it is adjusted in size.
] is equivalent.
(See also \lbrack)          61

**\rceil**  math mode: closing delimiter — $\rceil$ —
In combination with \big.., \left, \right it is adjusted in size.
(See also \lceil and \lfloor, \rfloor)          61

**\Re**  math mode: ordinary symbol — $\Re$ —          73

| command | description | pp. |
|---|---|---|
| * \read | reads extra input from an external file. The input, usually one line of the file, is assigned to a command. Grouping with '{' and '}' is considered and will result in the reading of several lines to get matching braces.<br>Syntax: \read *n* to *name*<br>Example:<br>\openin 7 = DATA<br>\read 7 to \mydata<br>\mydata may be used for the input.<br>(See also \closein) | 174ff |
| * \relax | is a *continue* or *do nothing* command. But there is a noteworthy effect: it terminates number or dimension scanning of the previous command, which could inadvertently consume text. | *132* |
| \relbar | math mode: relation — – —<br>This plain TeX macro is internally used to build arrows. defined by \def\relbar{\mathrel-}) | |
| \Relbar | math mode: relation — = —<br>This plain TeX macro is internally used to build arrows. defined by \def\relbar{\mathrel=}) | |
| * \relpenalty | math mode: is the penalty for a break of a text style formula into two lines of a paragraph after a relation.<br>preset value: \relpenalty=500<br>(See also \binoppenalty) | |
| \removelastskip | removes a preceding skip that may be present. It may be used within vertical mode. | 15 |
| \repeat | is a command used in combination with the \loop command.<br>Syntax: \loop $\alpha$ \if.. $\beta$ \repeat<br>(See also \loop) | 111ff |
| \rfloor | math mode: closing delimiter — $\rfloor$ —<br>(See also \lfloor, \lceil and \rceil) | 61 |
| \rgroup | acts like a '}' — It closes a group or box. This group may be paired with '{' or '\bgroup'. This command is important for macros, which will close a group that they did not open. | |
| \rho | math mode: greek letter — $\rho$ —<br>(See also \varrho — $\varrho$ —) | 52 |
| \rhook | math mode: yields — ⸲ —.<br>It is a helper macro of plain TeX to build the command \hookleftarrow — $\hookleftarrow$ —. | |

| command | description | pp. |
|---|---|---|
| * \right | math mode: \left and \right are paired commands to surround a subformula. They are followed by a required delimiter. The given delimiters are adjusted in size according to the subformula. Additionally, \left and \right begin and end a group.<br>Example:<br>`$$ \left[ x \over x-1 \right]$$`<br>yields<br><br>$$\left[\frac{x}{x-1}\right]$$ | 63 |
| \rightarrow | math mode: relation — $\rightarrow$ —<br>(\to is equivalent.)<br>(See also \longrightarrow) | 72 |
| \Rightarrow | math mode: relation — $\Rightarrow$ —<br>(See also \Longrightarrow) | 72 |
| \rightarrowfill | text mode: fills a box with an arrow.<br>Example:<br>`\hbox to 3cm{A\rightarrowfill B}`<br>yields<br>A————————→B<br>(See also \leftarrowfill, \hrulefill) | 92 |
| \rightharpoondown | math mode: relation — $\rightharpoondown$ — | 72 |
| \rightharpoonup | math mode: relation — $\rightharpoonup$ — | 72 |
| \rightleftharpoons | math mode: relation — $\rightleftharpoons$ — | 72 |
| \rightline | text mode: the contents of \rightline{..text..} are typeset flush right within a line. This command may only be used in vertical mode, i.e. not within a paragraph.<br>defined by<br>`\def\line{\hbox to\hsize}`<br>`\def\rightline#1{\line{\hss#1}}`<br>(See also \leftline, \centerline) | 8, 17 |
| * \rightskip | is an internal register of TₑX which determines the amount paragraph lines are shortened on the right side. The margin on the right side is enlarged.<br>By changing \rightskip=1cm you get an extra margin of 1 cm on the right side.<br>preset value: \rightskip=0pt<br>(See also \leftskip, \narrower) | 24 |

| command | description | pp. |
|---|---|---|
| \rlap | *right lap* <br> prints information overlapping to the right, the current position is not changed. <br> Example: ooo\rlap{//}uuu yields — ooo//uu — <br> (See also \llap for o//uuu) | 125, *158* |
| \rm | switch to the 'roman' font family (Distinguish between the switch to a font and a family switch, which is important in mathematical mode!) The roman family is the standard font. | 42 |
| \rmoustache | math mode: closing delimiter — ⎱ — <br> May only be used in combination with \big.., \left, \right, it is adjusted in size. <br> (See also \lmoustache) | 61 |
| * \romannumeral | generates lowercase roman letters: <br> \romannumeral 1989   yields "mcmlxxxix". <br> To achieve capital letters you need the commands <br> \uppercase\expandafter{\romannumeral 1989} <br> This produces "MCMLXXXIX" <br> (For '1989' you may substitute \pageno or other count registers, like \count7.) | |
| \root | math mode: generates roots. <br> Example: <br> $$\root 3 \of {x+1}$$ yields <br> $$\sqrt[3]{x+1}$$ | 55 |
| \rq | is a substitute for *right quote* (apostrophe) | 6 |
| \S | yields — § — | 73 |
| \sb | math mode: is a *subscript* substitute for "_" | 5 |
| scaled | is a keyword used in combination with the \font command. It specifies the scaling value. The value is given as an integer, to obtain the desired factor it has to be divided by 1000. It is normally used in combination with \magstep. <br> Example: <br> \font\bigbf=cmbx10 scaled \magstep2 | 43 |
| * \scriptfont | register associated with each font family. It contains the command name for the *"scriptfont"*. This is the font that is used in mathematical mode for superscripts and subscripts of first order. <br> Some of the standard definitions are: <br>     \scriptfont0=\sevenrm      roman <br>     \scriptfont1=\seveni      math italic <br> The number following the command represents the family number. <br> (See also \fam, \newfam) | |

| command | description | pp. |
|---|---|---|

\* `\scriptscriptfont`

register associated with each font family. It contains the command name for the *"scriptscriptfont"*. This is the font that is used in mathematical mode for superscripts and subscripts of second order.
Some of the standard definitions are:
`\scriptscriptfont0=\fiverm`    roman
`\scriptscriptfont1=\fivei`    math italic
The number following the command represents the family number.
(See also `\fam`, `\newfam`)

\* `\scriptscriptstyle`    54, 56

math mode: forces the typesetting style of subscripts and superscripts of second order.

\* `\scriptspace`    math mode: is the additional space after a superscript or subscript.
preset value: `\scriptspace=0.5pt`

\* `\scriptstyle`    math mode: forces the typesetting style of subscripts    54, 56
and superscripts of first order.

\* `\scrollmode`    changes the interrupt mode of the TeX program when    145
an error occurs. The messages are logged to the screen but requests for additional input are suppressed. (This mode is also achieved by input of an "S" after an error message.)
(See also `\nonstopmode`, `\batchmode`)

`\searrow`    math mode: relation — $\searrow$ —    72
*(south east arrow)*

`\sec`    math mode: large operator — sec —    64

\* `\setbox`    defines the contents of a box register. It has to be fol-    112,
lowed by a number $(0\ldots255)$ or a name for a box num-    116,
ber.    117,
Example:    118,
`\setbox0=\hbox{abcdef}`    133
The box 0 contains a *horizontal box*. This may be used with `\box`, `\copy`, `\unhbox` or `\unhcopy`. (If a `\vbox` command is applied in combination with `\setbox`, the contents of the box are given by `\box`, `\copy`, `\unvbox` or `\unvcopy`.) The register numbers 0 to 9 are free. More box registers should be defined by `\newbox`.

`\setminus`    math mode: binary operator — $\setminus$ —    71
Example: `$A\setminus B$` yields $A \setminus B$.
(als ordinary symbol `\backslash`)

| command | description | pp. |
|---|---|---|
| \settabs | text mode: defines a set of tabbing positions for use with \+. You can define a number of even-sized columns or a template line: | 77 |

Example:

| \settabs 5 \columns | 5 equal columns |
|---|---|
| \settabs\+XXX&XXXXX&X\cr | The & signs define the tabbing positions. |

(See also \cleartabs, \+, \cr)

| command | description | pp. |
|---|---|---|
| \sevenbf | sets the **boldface** typeface in 7 point | 42 |
| \seveni | sets the 7 point *math italic* typeface | 44 |
| \sevensy | sets the 7 point *mathematical symbols* | 44 |
| \sevenrm | sets the 'roman' typeface in 7 point | 42 |
| * \sfcode | *space factor* — It determines whether additional space should be generated if this character precedes a space. This factor is assigned to each ASCII character. Based on its value extra spacing behind punctuation symbols is done. | |
| \sharp | math mode: ordinary symbol — ♯ — (See also \flat, \natural) | 73 |
| * \shipout | writes the contents of a box register (the page) to the dvi file. This is usually done during the output routine. | 152ff, *155* |
| * \show | is a command for debugging: it lists the meaning of the following command. | |

Example:

```
\show\pageno
\show\item
\show\centerline
```

yields

```
> \pageno=\count0.
> \item=macro:
->\par \hang \textindent.
> \centerline=macro:
#1-> \line {\hss #1\hss }.
```

After the \show command TₑX enters priority input mode (like error input mode).

| command | description | pp. |
|---|---|---|
| * \showbox | lists the contents of a box register. After \showbox0 the contents of the box register are written to the log file; if \tracingonline=1 has been set, they are also written to the terminal.<br>Example<br>    \setbox0=\hbox{abc}<br>    \showbox0<br>yields<br>    > \box0=<br>    \hbox(6.94444+0.0)x15.27782<br>    .\tenrm a<br>    .\tenrm b<br>    .\kern0.27779<br>    .\tenrm c | |
| * \showboxbreadth | determines the amount of information that is logged by \showbox. It limits the number of elements that are listed.<br>preset value: \showboxbreadth=5 | |
| * \showboxdepth | determines the amount of information that is logged by \showbox. It limits the depth of boxes that are still logged.<br>preset value: \showboxdepth=3 | |
| \showhyphens | lists possible hyphenating position in a given text, e.g., \showhyphens{panjandrum} produces pan-jan-drum. This is useful for checking hyphenation position of (unusual) words. | 38 |
| * \showlists | lists the internal list of vertical material. | |
| * \showthe | shows the *contents* of registers.<br>(But \show produces the meaning/definition.)<br>Example:<br>    \showthe\pageno<br>    \showthe\headline<br>produces<br>    > 1.  (If it is the first page.)<br>    > \hfil .<br>But<br>    \show\headline<br>yields<br>    > \headline=\toks10.<br>(See also \meaning) | |
| \sigma | math mode: greek letter — $\sigma$ —<br>(See also \varsigma — $\varsigma$ —) | 52 |
| \Sigma | math mode: greek letter — $\Sigma$ — | 53 |
| \sim | math mode: relation — $\sim$ — | 72 |

| command | description | pp. |
|---|---|---|
| \simeq | math mode: relation — $\simeq$ — | 72 |
| \sin | math mode: large operator — sin — | 64 |
| \sinh | math mode: large operator — sinh — | 64 |
| \skew | math mode: generates multiple accents.<br>Syntax:<br>\skew{*factor*}{*above*}{*below*}<br>The *factor* determines the amount of **mu** *(math units)* by which the accent is raised.<br>Example:<br>\$\skew 6 \hat {\bar A}\$ yields $\hat{\bar{A}}$ | |
| * \skewchar | math mode: is the code of the reference symbol to generate mathematical accents. | |
| * \skip | refers to one of the 256 *skip* registers $(0\ldots255)$ that may contain skip values. A skip value can include dimensions for stretch 'plus' and shrink 'minus'. (Normal \dimen registers refer to a simple length.) The registers with the numbers 0 to 9 are free. \newskip should be used to define a name for a free register. Use is demonstrated in the following example:<br>\skip0=3cm plus 1cm minus 1cm<br>\hskip\skip0 *or* \vskip\skip0<br>\newdimen\myskip   \myskip=3cm plus 1cm<br>\vskip\myskip | 130 |
| * \skipdef | this commands defines the name of a given skip register.<br>Example:<br>\skipdef\myskip=7<br>This command should not be used externally. It is much safer to use \newskip. | |
| \sl | sets the *slanted* font and the slanted family (for mathematical mode). | 42 |
| \slash | generates a "/" with possible hyphenation a this position.<br>Example:<br>    input\slash output<br>allows a hyphenation at the position of "/". | |
| \slfam | internal number of the *slanted* font family.<br>(See also \newfam) | |
| \smallbreak | text mode: determines a good position for page breaking and generates the same space as \smallskip. It corresponds to \medbreak,\bigbreak $(1:2:4)$.<br>(See also \medbreak and \bigbreak) | 32 |
| \smallint | math mode: large operator — $\int$ —<br>It contrasts to \int as a smaller variant. | 73 |

| command | description | pp. |
|---|---|---|

\smallskip — text mode: produces vertical space with the size of \smallskipamount. The following is valid:

$$2 \times \text{\smallskip} = \text{\medskip}$$
$$4 \times \text{\smallskip} = \text{\bigskip}$$

\smallskip is just defined by
\def\smallskip{\vskip\smallskipamount}

*(pp. 15)*

\smallskipamount — is a skip register of plain TeX that contains the amount of vertical space that is generated by \smallskip
preset value:
\smallskipamount=3pt plus 1pt minus 1pt
(See also \bigskipamount, \medskipamount)

\smash — generates the information given as parameter in
\smash{..text..}
But it is typeset with the logical height and depth of zero. The width is treated normally.
(See also \phantom, \vphantom, \hphantom)

*(pp. 74)*

\smile — math mode: relation — $\smile$ —
(See also \frown — $\frown$ —)

*(pp. 72)*

sp — internal unit of measure: *scaled point*
$1\,\text{pt} = 2^{16}\,\text{sp} = 65536\,\text{sp}$

*(pp. 12)*

\sp — math mode: is a *superscript* substitute for "^"
$x\sp 2$ yields — $x^2$ —

*(pp. 5)*

\space — generates a space.
defined by \def\space{ }

* \spacefactor — is an internal register that may override the character specific value of \sfcode, if it is not zero.

* \spaceskip — is an internal register that may override some of the \fontdimen parameters that govern the spacing between two words, if it is not zero.
(See also \xspaceskip, \fontdimen7 ...)

*(pp. 17, 21)*

\spadesuit — math mode: ordinary symbol — ♠ —
(See also \heartsuit, \diamondsuit, \clubsuit)

*(pp. 73)*

* \span — substitutes an "&" sign within \halign.
  1. use in an information line:
     Two elements are concatenated and processed as if they were one. The content of the template line is used.
  2. use in the template line:
     It forces the expansion of the following element (macro) during definition of the template line. The following macro may then contain '#' or '&' and may define further columns by its contents.
     (See also \multispan)

*(pp. 89, 93, 94)*

| command | description | pp. |
|---|---|---|
| * \special | is an implementation dependent command. It just writes text to the dvi file that is marked as 'special'. This information is interpreted by the output driver. | |
| * \splitbotmark | is an internal register that acts like \botmark but in combination with a \vsplit command. After a \vsplit, it produces the last \mark text that is contained in the split text. (See also \mark, \botmark, \splitfirstmark) | |
| * \splitfirstmark | is an internal register that acts like \firstmark in combination with a \vsplit command. After a \vsplit, it produces the first \mark text that is contained in the split text. (See also \mark, \botmark, \splitbotmark) | |
| * \splitmaxdepth | is an internal register that contains the maximum *depth* of a box that may be split with a \vsplit command. preset value: \splitmaxdepth=\maxdimen (arbitrary) | |
| * \splittopskip | is the skip that is generated to the beginning of a box that is built by a \vsplit command. preset value: \splittopskip=10pt (Note: this is the same value as \topskip.) | 129 |
| spread | is a keyword for a box creating command like \hbox, \vbox, \halign. It determines how much the created box is treated larger than its natural size. The natural size is accumulated by the contents of the box. Example: \hbox spread 1cm{\hfill abc\hfill} produces a box that is 1 cm wider than an \hbox{abc}. The text 'abc' will be surrounded at left and right side by 0.5 cm space. The box should contain dynamic space to fill the spread part. | 93, 118 |
| \sqcap | math mode: binary operator — $\sqcap$ — | 71 |
| \sqcup | math mode: binary operator — $\sqcup$ — | 71 |
| \sqrt | math mode: generates a square root Example: $$ \sqrt { \sqrt{x+1} - 1} $$ yields $$\sqrt{\sqrt{x+1}-1}$$ | 55 |
| \sqsubseteq | math mode: relation — $\sqsubseteq$ — | 72 |
| \sqsupseteq | math mode: relation — $\sqsupseteq$ — | 72 |
| \ss | text mode: yields — ß —. | 14 |
| \star | math mode: binary operator — $\star$ — | 71 |

| command | description | pp. |
|---|---|---|
| * \string | prints the following command as a string.<br>Example:<br>\tt\string\par produces "\par"<br>(Note: the escape character is printed as determined by \escapechar. In the wrong font you get an unexpected result: \rm\string\par yields ""par".) | *108,*<br>109ff,<br>*177* |
| \strut | generates an empty box, the dimensions of which agree with the normal line distances. This forces a minimal line skip especially if the generation of interline skip has been inhibited by \offinterlineskip. It forces a height of 8.5 pt and a depth of 3.5 pt. This is often used when generating tables that contain rules.<br>The number of the box used is stored in \strutbox.<br>(See also \mathstrut for mathematical mode) | 88ff |
| \strutbox | is the internal number of plain TEX for the box used in combination with the \strut command.<br>defined by<br>\newbox\strutbox (number of a free box)<br>\setbox\strutbox=\hbox{%<br>   \vrule height 8.5pt depth 3.5pt width0pt} | |
| \subset | math mode: relation — $\subset$ — | 72 |
| \subseteq | math mode: relation — $\subseteq$ — | 72 |
| \succ | math mode: relation — $\succ$ — | 72 |
| \succeq | math mode: relation — $\succeq$ — | 72 |
| \sum | math mode: large operator — $\sum$ — | 59 |
| \sup | math mode: large operator — sup — | 64 |
| \supereject | forces a call to the *output routine* by generating extremely many penalties.<br>defined by<br>\def\supereject{\par\penalty-20000}<br>The default output routine examines the penalty value and ships out stored insertions if a \supereject has been given. | 154 |
| \supset | math mode: relation — $\supset$ — | 72 |
| \supseteq | math mode: relation — $\supseteq$ — | 72 |
| \surd | math mode: ordinary symbol — $\surd$ — | 73 |
| \swarrow | math mode: relation — $\swarrow$ —<br>*(south west arrow)* | 72 |
| \t | text mode: *tie-after* accent: \t oo yields — o͡o — | 14 |
| \tabalign | is an internal plain TEX macro to generate tables by tabbing. It acts like '\+' but is not defined as '\outer' as '\+' is.<br>It may be used, e.g., for macro parameters. | |
| \tabs | is an internal plain TEX box number used by \settabs, \+, \cleartabs. | |

| command | description | pp. |
|---|---|---|
| \tabsdone | is an internal plain TₑX box number used by \settabs, \+, \cleartabs. | |
| \tabsyet | is an internal plain TₑX box number used by \settabs, \+, \cleartabs. | |
| * \tabskip | is the standard register that determines additional skip generated before, between and after columns that are built by an \halign command. The value of \tabskip that is valid before the \halign is used before the first column, the value that is valid at the end (\cr) of a template line is used for the skip after the last column. Between columns skip is generated that is determined by the values of \tabskip at the '&' positions. (preset value: \tabskip=0pt) | 85ff |
| \tan | math mode: large operator — tan — | 64 |
| \tanh | math mode: large operator — tanh — | 64 |
| \tau | math mode: greek letter — $\tau$ — | 52 |
| \tenex | changes to the font for large symbols in mathematical mode. This is done automatically by use of font families. | 44 |
| \tenbf | changes to the '**boldface**' typeface in 10 point. | 42, 44 |
| \teni | changes to the '*mathitalic*' typeface in 10 point. This is done automatically in formulae. | 44 |
| \tenit | changes to the '*italic*' typeface in 10 point. | 42, 44 |
| \tenrm | changes to the standard 'roman' typeface in 10 point. | 42, 44 |
| \tensl | changes to the '*slanted*' typeface in 10 point. | 42, 44 |
| \tentt | changes to the 'typewriter' typeface in 10 point. | 42, 44 |
| \tensy | changes to the symbol font in 10 point for mathematical formulae. This is automatically done in mathematical mode. | 44 |
| \TeX | produces the logo — TₑX —. | 14 |
| * \textfont | defines the *textfont* within a font family for typesetting formulae. Some predefined values are \textfont0=\tenrm \textfont1=\teni \textfont\bffam=\tenbf (See also \fam, \newfam) | |
| \textindent | is a helper macro in plain TₑX that is used by \item and \itemitem. defined by \def\textindent#1{\indent\llap{#1\enspace}% \ignorespaces} | 30 |

| command | description | pp. |
|---|---|---|
| * \textstyle | math mode: forces the building of a formula in *text style*, i.e., the formula is interpreted as if surrounded by $...$. <br> (See also \scriptstyle, \displaystyle and \scriptscriptstyle) | 56 |
| * \the | produces the contents of a register, e.g., \the\headline, \the\everypar or \the\skip5. <br> (See also \showthe which lists the contents to the log.) | 131ff |
| \theta | math mode: greek letter — $\theta$ — <br> (See also \vartheta — $\vartheta$ —) | 52 |
| \Theta | math mode: greek letter — $\Theta$ — | 53 |
| * \thickmuskip | math mode: is the size of a large mathematical space skip. <br> It is used for spacing mathematical formulae. It is given in units of length of mu = *math units* <br> preset value: \thickmuskip=5mu plus 5mu <br> (See also \thinmuskip, \medmuskip) | 64, 134ff |
| * \thinmuskip | math mode: is a thin mathematical space skip, in units of mu = *math units* <br> preset value: \thinmuskip=3mu <br> (See also \thickmuskip, \medmuskip) | 64, 134ff |
| \thinspace | text mode: generates a small space of $1/6$ *em* defined by <br> \def\thinspace{\kern.16667em }. <br> (See also \negthinspace) | 16 |
| \tilde | math mode: accent: $\tilde x$ yields — $\tilde{x}$ —. | 55 |
| * \time | is an internal integer register that contains the time, measured in minutes since midnight. This is a static value that is set at the time the TEX program starts. It may be examined or changed. <br> Use as in \the\time or \number\time <br> (See also \day, \month, \year) | |
| \times | math mode: binary operator — $\times$ — | 71 |
| to | is a keyword in \hbox, \vbox, \vtop ... commands. <br> Example: \hbox to 3cm{...} | 118 |
| \to | math mode: relation — $\rightarrow$ — <br> (\rightarrow is equivalent.) | 72 |

| command | description | pp. |
|---|---|---|
| * `\toks` | refers to one of 256 token registers ($0\ldots255$). Usually token registers are reserved and named by `\newtoks`. The most commonly used (named) token registers are `\headline` and `\footline`. *Token* registers are changed by an assignment like other registers.<br>Example:<br>    `\toks0={\bigskip\hrule\bigskip}`<br>    `\the\toks0`<br>better is<br>    `\newtoks\mytok`<br>    `\mytok={\bigskip\hrule\bigskip}`<br>    `\the\mytok` | 131ff |
| * `\toksdef` | assigns a name to a numbered token register.<br>After `\toksdef\mytoks=0` the token register may be used by the name `\mytoks` instead of `\toks0`. Usually `\newtoks` is used for definition and reservation. | |
| * `\tolerance` | is a threshold value for breaking lines into paragraphs. It is a limit for lines with hyphenations allowed. If it is enlarged more space between words is possible.<br>preset value: `\tolerance=200`<br>(See also `\pretolerance`) | |
| `\top` | math mode: ordinary symbol — ⊤ —<br>(See also `\bot` for — ⊥ —) | 73 |
| `\topins` | is a number of an *insertion register* to store insertions that are done with `\topinsert`.<br>It is defined by `\newinsert\topins`. | 153 |
| `\topinsert` | is a command to insert information at the top of the current page. But if there is not enough space on the current page, the information will be put onto the top of the following pages. This may be used to reserve space for pictures.<br>Syntax: `\topinsert` *vertical material* `\endinsert`<br>(See also `\midinsert` and `\pageinsert`) | 35 |
| * `\topmark` | produces the information which is stored by `\mark` This refers to the mark text that is valid before the current page, i.e. the `\botmark` of the preceding page. `\topmark` may be used within `\headline` or `\footline`, that means within the *output routine*.<br>(See also `\botmark`, `\mark`, `\firstmark`) | 157ff |
| * `\topskip` | is an internal register that is used for page breaking. It defines the minimal distance between the top of the text area and the baseline of the first line of a new page.<br>preset value: `\topskip=10pt`<br>(See also `\splittopskip`) | 25 |

| command | description | pp. |
|---|---|---|
| \tracingall | activates all protocol parameters. Afterwards you get a lot of logging stuff and lists. | 150 |

* \tracingcommands                                                                    150

  is a register that determines the logging of commands.
  preset value: \tracingcommands=0
  If you change
  \tracingcommands=1 you get all executed commands
  \tracingcommands=2 all commands including skipped
  parts of \if... instructions.

* \tracinglostchars

  is a register that determines whether the use of undefined characters should be logged. This is done if the
  value is greater than zero. (It is possible to generate
  fonts by Metafont and use them with TeX although they
  have incomplete code tables.)
  preset value: \tracinglostchars=1

| * \tracingmacros | is a register that determines whether the macro param- | 150 |
|---|---|---|
| | eters should be logged (if greater than zero). | |
| | preset value: \tracingmacros=0 | |

| * \tracingonline | determines whether 'tracing' output should be written | 150 |
|---|---|---|
| | to the terminal, done if greater than zero. | |
| | preset value: \tracingonline=0 | |

* \tracingoutput determines whether the contents of completed pages
  that are written to the dvi file by \shipout have to
  be logged.
  preset value: \tracingoutput=0

* \tracingpages  determines whether the mechanism for page breaking
  should be logged, done if greater than zero. For each box
  contributed to the current list the following information
  is logged:
  \pagetotal (t) accumulated amount of page
  \pagegoal   (g) target size
  *badness* (b) current weight
  *penalty* (p) weight of a break position
  *costs* (c) total ($c = p + b$)

* \tracingparagraphs

  If \tracingparagraphs=1 has been set TeX logs the
  control values for line breaking.

* \tracingrestores

  determines if restores of old values have to be logged.
  This is done after \tracingrestores=1. A restore happens if a value of a quantity has been locally changed
  within a '{...}' group and the group is closed.
  preset value: \tracingrestores=0

| command | description | pp. |
|---|---|---|
| * \tracingstats | determines whether statistics have to be generated at the end of the program run (for \tracingstats=1) or at the end of each page (for \tracingstats=2). The statistics look like | 150 |

```
Here is how much of TeX's memory you used:
159 strings   out of 8188
1307 string characters out of 28074
16708 words of memory out of 65001
1030 multiletter control
             sequences out of 7000
15815 words of font info for 53 fonts,
             out of 40000 for 150
14 hyphenation exceptions   out of 307
```

preset value: \tracingstats=0

| command | description | pp. |
|---|---|---|
| \triangle | math mode: ordinary symbol — $\triangle$ — | 73 |
| \triangleleft | math mode: binary operator — $\triangleleft$ — | 71 |
| \triangleright | math mode: binary operator — $\triangleright$ — | 71 |
| true | is a keyword that may be used in combination with units of measure. It precedes the unit that will not be scaled by the global value given by \magnification. Example: \vskip 10 true cm for a picture with fix size | *26, 36,* *44* |
| \tt | changes to typewriter font and to the typewriter font family if in mathematical mode. | 42 |
| \ttfam | contains the internal number for the typewriter font family. (See also \newfam) | |
| \ttraggedright | is a special form to get ragged right paragraphs that should be used in combination with the typewriter font. (See also \raggedright) | 21 |
| \u | text mode: accent: \u o yields — ŏ —. | 14 |
| * \uccode | *upper case code* This code is associated to any character code from 0 ... 127. It determines into which symbol a specific character has to be changed to get the associated uppercase symbol, if the command \uppercase is applied. These are the expected definitions from \uccode'\a='\A to \uccode'\z='\Z (See also \lccode for \lowercase) | |
| * \uchyph | is an internal parameter that determines if a word that begins with a capital letter may be hyphenated. If \uchyph > 0 hyphenation may happen. preset value: \uchyph=1 | |
| \underbar | text mode: generates a line below the parameter information. Note: descenders are crossed. Example: \underbar{top secret} produces — <u>top secret</u> —. | |

| command | description | pp. |
|---|---|---|
| \underbrace | math mode: generates a horizontal brace. | 68 |

Example:

`$$\underbrace{x+y+z}_{>0}$$` yields

$$\underbrace{x + y + z}_{>0}$$

(See also \overbrace)

| * \underline | math mode: underlines the information given as parameter. | 55 |

Example:

`$\underline{A+B}$` produces $\underline{A + B}$

(See also \overline)

| * \unhbox | produces the contents of the designated box register. The enclosing \hbox structure will be removed. This allows line breaking between the inner elements of the box. After \unhbox the box is empty. | 117 |

Example:

```
\setbox1=\hbox{AB}
\setbox2=\hbox{\unhbox1 C}
```

This is equivalent to

```
\setbox2=\hbox{ABC}
```

but

```
\setbox3=\hbox{\box1 C}
```

is equivalent to

```
\setbox3=\hbox{\hbox{ABC}
```

| * \unhcopy | acts like \unhbox, but the contents of the referenced box are not lost. | 117 |
| * \unkern | removes a preceding \kern value, if that is present. | |
| * \unpenalty | removes a preceding \penalty value, if that is present. | |
| * \unskip | removes a preceding \hskip or \vskip value, if that is present. | *92* |
| * \unvbox | produces the contents of the designated box register. The enclosing \vbox structure will be removed. This allows page breaking between the inner elements of the box. After \unvbox the specified box is empty. | 117, *112* |

Example:

```
\setbox1=\vbox{\hbox{AB}}
\setbox2=\vbox{\unvbox1\hbox{C}}
```

This is equivalent to

```
\setbox2=\vbox{\hbox{AB}\hbox{C}}
```

but

```
\setbox3=\vbox{\box1\hbox{C}}
```

is equivalent to

```
\setbox3=\vbox{\vbox{\hbox{AB}}\hbox{C}}
```

| * \unvcopy | acts like \unvbox, but the contents of the referenced box are not lost. | 117 |

| command | description | pp. |
|---|---|---|
| \uparrow | math mode: relation — ↑ — | 72 |
| \Uparrow | math mode: relation — ⇑ — | 72 |
| \upbracefill | fills a given box with a brace. This may be useful in generating tables. `\hbox to 3cm{\upbracefill}` yields | 92 |
| | (See also \downbracefill) | |
| \updownarrow | math mode: relation — ↕ — | 72 |
| \Updownarrow | math mode: relation — ⇕ — | 72 |
| \uplus | math mode: binary operator — ⊎ — | 71 |
| * \uppercase | changes lowercase letters to uppercase letters in the input. By `\uppercase{aBc}` you achieve an input of ABC. If a macro is included in the input, it is not expanded. The following recipe helps: `\edef\next{...information...}` `\uppercase\expandafter{\next}` (See also \lowercase) | |
| \upsilon | math mode: greek letter — $\upsilon$ — | 52 |
| \Upsilon | math mode: greek letter — $\Upsilon$ — | 53 |
| \v | text mode: accent: \v o yields — ŏ —. | 14 |
| * \vadjust | text mode: by `\vadjust{`*vertical material*`}` you store additional information that will be inserted after the paragraph has been built. The information will be inserted just after the line where the \vadjust command has been given. | 16, 127 |
| * \valign | text mode: corresponds to the \halign, but rows and columns are interchanged. | |
| \varepsilon | math mode: greek letter — $\varepsilon$ — (See also \epsilon — $\epsilon$ —) | 52 |
| \varphi | math mode: greek letter — $\varphi$ — (See also \phi — $\phi$ —) | 52 |
| \varpi | math mode: greek letter — $\varpi$ — (See also \pi — $\pi$ —) | 52 |
| \varsigma | math mode: greek letter — $\varsigma$ — (See also \sigma — $\sigma$ —) | 52 |
| \vartheta | math mode: greek letter — $\vartheta$ — (See also \theta — $\theta$ —) | 52 |
| * \vbadness | is a limit value, if it is exceeded bad \vboxes are logged. preset value: \vbadness=1000 (See also \hbadness) | |

| command | description | pp. |
|---|---|---|
| * \vbox | By \vbox{...information...} a vertical box is generated. All boxes and vertical material are set below one another. If horizontal material like ordinary text or \indent, \par is found, typesetting is switched to *horizontal mode* and line breaking with respect to \hsize occurs.<br>Vertically arranged, i.e. vertical materials, are<br>1. other boxes: \hbox, \vbox, \vtop, $\vcenter$<br>2. vertical skip: \vskip ..., \smallskip...<br>3. rules by \hrule.<br>The baseline and depth of a \vbox are determined by the baseline of the last line/box of the \vbox.<br>(See also \vtop and \vcenter) | *34, 80,* 114ff, *155* |
| * \vcenter | math mode: centers the following information vertically. (There is a slight correction to fit the mathematical axis (See also \fontdimen22\tensy).) | *115, 155* |
| \vdash | math mode: relation — ⊢ —<br>(See also \dashv — ⊣ —) | 72 |
| \vdots | math mode: *(vertical dots)* yields — ⋮ —<br>(See also \ldots, \ddots, \cdots — ... ⋱ ⋯ —) | 66 |
| \vec | math mode: mathematical accent<br>$\vec x$ yields — $\vec{x}$ — | 55 |
| \vee | math mode: binary operator — ∨ —<br>(\lor is equivalent.) | 71 |
| \vert | math mode: ordinary symbol — \| —<br>("\|" is equivalent.) | 73 |
| \Vert | math mode: ordinary symbol — ‖ —<br>("\\|", but a relation by \parallel) | 73 |
| * \vfil | generates dynamic vertical skip of first order. | 125 |
| * \vfill | generates dynamic vertical skip of second order. | 31, 125 |
| * \vfilll | generates dynamic vertical skip of third order.<br>Note: \vfilll ≫ \vfill ≫ \vfil | 125 |
| * \vfilneg | cancels a preceding \vfil (first order only!).<br>(See also \hfilneg) | 125 |
| \vfootnote | is a helper macro for plain TeX to generate footnotes. It is used in the same way as \footnote.<br>The difference is that the *footnote symbol* is *not* generated within the text but only within the footnote. This may be useful if a footnote should be generated out of a table, but that is not possible. So you can insert the symbol within the table in an ordinary fashion and use \vfootnote just before the table. | |

| command | description | pp. |
|---|---|---|
| * \vfuzz | limit for announcing an 'overfull vbox' <br> preset value: \vfuzz=0pt <br> (See also \hfuzz) | 40, *112* |
| \vglue | generates vertical space which does not disappear at the top of the page after a page break. (\nobreak and \hrule commands are used.) <br> Example: \vglue 3cm plus 1 cm <br> (See also \hglue) | 16 |
| * \voffset | is the vertical offset by which the printout is moved down on the paper (if \voffset> 0 else up). (Output drivers can usually override this value.) <br> preset value: \voffset=0pt | 25, 26 |
| \vphantom | measures the height and depth of the parameter. This will force the current line or box to be generated with at least these dimensions. The width is considered to be zero. <br> (See also \phantom, \hphantom, \smash) | 74 |
| * \vrule | generates a vertical rule. This command may only be used within horizontal mode. If \vrule is applied in vertical mode, e.g., within a \vbox, a switch to horizontal mode occurs. <br> Syntax: <br> \vrule width *dim* height *dim* depth *dim* <br> The parameters are optional, they determine width and height and depth of the desired rule. \vrule without any height specification generates a rule with the height of the surrounding box or line. The width is preset to 0.4 pt. | 39, 88ff, *120*, 125 |
| * \vsize | is the height of the text area. T<sub>E</sub>X uses this value as the initial value for page breaking. It may be changed locally. <br> preset value: \vsize=8.9 true in <br> (See also \hsize for the width.) | 11, 25, 26 |
| * \vskip | generates vertical skip. If given within a paragraph, the paragraph is finished and the skip is generated after it. <br> Example: \vskip 1 cm plus 0.5cm | 15, *16*, *67*, 125 |
| * \vsplit | generates the upper part of a \vbox considering a given length. The split operation is done the same way page breaking occurs. T<sub>E</sub>X searches for an optimal break position. | *112*, 128ff |

| command | description | pp. |
|---|---|---|
| | Example: | |

<br>

**command**     **description**     **pp.**

Example:
`\setbox0=\vsplit 1 to 5 cm`
The box with the number 1 is divided. The upper part
of length 5 cm is assigned to box 0, the remaing information is still stored in box 1. Furthermore, the first
line/box in box 0 is adjusted vertically with respect to
`\splittopskip`.
`\splitmaxdepth` is the maximum depth of the target
box.
preset value: `\splitmaxdepth=\maxdimen`

\* `\vss`  in vertical mode, generates dynamic skip that may stretch   125
or shrink as determined the surrounding `\vbox`. If a
`\vbox` contains a `\vss` command, there won't be any
message of 'overfull' or 'underfull' boxes.

\* `\vtop`  acts like `\vbox` with the following difference: the baseline   115,
of the whole box is generated by the baseline of the   *129*
first box element, but in `\vbox` by the last. Such a box
will hang down below the baseline of its surrounding
information. The depth is generated by the accumulated
size of the following information.

\* `\wd`  refers to the width of the contents of a box register. It   118
may be examined and even changed.
Example:
`\setbox0=\hbox{whole}`
`\wd0` contains the width of the text "whole".
(See also `\dp` and `\ht`)

`\wedge`  math mode: binary operator — $\wedge$ —   71
(`\land` is equivalent.)

`\widehat`  math mode: wide mathematical accent   56
`$\widehat{xyz}$` yields — $\widehat{xyz}$ —

`\widetilde`  math mode: wide mathematical accent   56
`$\widetilde{xyz}$` yields — $\widetilde{xyz}$ —

\* `\widowpenalty`  are penalties that are generated during page break, if
the last line of a paragraph is moved to the following
page.
preset value: `\widowpenalty=150`
(See also `\displaywidowpenalty`)

`width`  is an optional keyword in combination with `\hrule` and   39
`\vrule`
Example:
`\hrule width 10 cm`

`\wlog`  writes the information of its parameter to the log file
(only).

`\wp`  math mode: ordinary symbol — $\wp$ —   73

`\wr`  math mode: binary operator — $\wr$ —   71

| command | description | pp. |
|---|---|---|
| * \write | writes the information to an external output file. The output file must have been opened before by \openout. Syntax: \write *n* {...daten...} *n* is the number of the output file. Example: | 174ff |

| | |
|---|---|
| \openout 7=OUTFILE | open |
| \write 7{...daten...} | write |
| \closeout7 | close |

The information is internally stored and written during the output routine at \shipout, but is written at once if \write is preceded by \immediate.
(See also \read, \openin, \closein, \immediate)

| command | description | pp. |
|---|---|---|
| * \xdef | defines a global macro. The macro information is expanded during definition. \xdef is equivalent to \global\edef. (See also \edef,\def, \global) | 100, *178* |
| \xi | math mode: greek letter — $\xi$ — | 52 |
| \Xi | math mode: greek letter — $\Xi$ — | 53 |
| * \xleaders | repeats the following box or \hrule as often as determined by the following \hskip or \hfill. \hfill needs a surrounding box with a given width. Example: | |

```
\def\xleaderfill{
   \xleaders\hbox to 1em{\hss.\hss}\hfill}
```

The generated boxes are horizontally adjusted and remaining space is distributed between the boxes.
(See also \cleaders, \leaders)

| command | description | pp. |
|---|---|---|
| * \xspaceskip | is an internal register that may override some \fontdimen parameters that govern the spacing after punctuation symbols, if it is not zero. (See also \spaceskip, \fontdimen (7)). | 17, *21* |
| * \year | internal register, preset with the current year of the program start. It may be output by \the\year, \number\year or \romannumeral\year. (Change by assignment is also possible.) (See also \day, \month, \time) | |
| \zeta | math mode: greek letter — $\zeta$ — | 52 |

## 14.2 Key Words

## 14.3 Tables of Standard Fonts

## Command Table for Text Fonts

| 0 | 1 | 2 | 3 | 4 | 5 | 6 | 7 | |
|---|---|---|---|---|---|---|---|---|
| \Gamma | \i | | 0 | @ | P | ` | p | 0 |
| \Delta | \j | ! | 1 | A | Q | a | q | 1 |
| \Theta | \` | " | 2 | B | R | b | r | 2 |
| \Lambda | \' | \# | 3 | C | S | c | s | 3 |
| \Xi | \v | \$ | 4 | D | T | d | t | 4 |
| \Pi | \u | \% | 5 | E | U | e | u | 5 |
| \Sigma | \= | \& | 6 | F | V | f | v | 6 |
| \Upsilon | [\aa] | ' | 7 | G | W | g | w | 7 |
| \Phi | \c | ( | 8 | H | X | h | x | 8 |
| \Psi | \ss | ) | 9 | I | Y | i | y | 9 |
| \Omega | \ae | * | : | J | Z | j | z | A |
| ff | \oe | + | ; | K | [ | k | -- | B |
| fi | \o | , | !‘ | L | ‘‘ | l | --- | C |
| ffl | \AE | - | = | M | ] | m | \H | D |
| ffi | \OE | . | ?‘ | N | \^ | n | \~ | E |
| ffl | \O | / | ? | O | \. | o | \" | F |
| 0 | 1 | 2 | 3 | 4 | 5 | 6 | 7 | |

This table contains the calls for text symbols. For the following fonts these commands are valid and produce equivalent results:

| roman | 10 pt | \rm |
|---|---|---|
| | | \tenrm |
| | 7 pt | \sevenrm |
| | 5 pt | \fiverm |
| boldface | 10 pt | \bf |
| | | \tenbf |
| | 7 pt | \sevenbf |
| | 5 pt | \fivebf |
| slanted | 10 pt | \sl |
| | | \tensl |
| italic | 10 pt | \it |
| | | \tenit |

typewriter type

This font lacks some ligatures, furthermore the codes from 31 to 126 are used as in ordinary ASCII code tables.

### Organization of the Table

The first column contains uppercase greek letters and ligature symbols. The second column contains accents and national characters. The rest of the table corresponds to an ordinary ASCII code table, except for the characters "<", ">", and "\", "_", "{", "}", "|".

# Font Table for CMR10 — Roman

| | | | | | | | | |
|---|---|---|---|---|---|---|---|---|
| Γ | ı | ˘ | 0 | @ | P | ` | p | 0 |
| Δ | J | ! | 1 | A | Q | a | q | 1 |
| Θ | ˋ | " | 2 | B | R | b | r | 2 |
| Λ | ´ | # | 3 | C | S | c | s | 3 |
| Ξ | ˇ | $ | 4 | D | T | d | t | 4 |
| Π | ˘ | % | 5 | E | U | e | u | 5 |
| Σ | ¯ | & | 6 | F | V | f | v | 6 |
| Υ | ˚ | ' | 7 | G | W | g | w | 7 |
| Φ | ¸ | ( | 8 | H | X | h | x | 8 |
| Ψ | ß | ) | 9 | I | Y | i | y | 9 |
| Ω | æ | * | : | J | Z | j | z | A |
| ff | œ | + | ; | K | [ | k | – | B |
| fi | ø | , | ¡ | L | " | l | — | C |
| fl | Æ | - | = | M | ] | m | " | D |
| ffi | Œ | . | ¿ | N | ^ | n | ˜ | E |
| ffl | Ø | / | ? | O | ˙ | o | ¨ | F |
| 0 | 1 | 2 | 3 | 4 | 5 | 6 | 7 | |

\fontdimen parameter

| | |
|---|---|
| 1 | 0.00 pt |
| 2 | 3.33 pt |
| 3 | 1.67 pt |
| 4 | 1.11 pt |
| 5 | 4.31 pt |
| 6 | 10.0 pt |
| 7 | 1.11 pt |

Ligatures

| | |
|---|---|
| ff | ff |
| fi | fi |
| fl | fl |
| ffi | ffi |
| ffl | ffl |
| ! ` | ¡ |
| ? ` | ¿ |
| ' ' | " |
| ` ` | " |
| -- | – |
| --- | — |

**Use in plain TeX:** \tenrm  (\rm as \textfont0)

| size | tfm file | call (if defined) | |
|---|---|---|---|
| 5 point | CMR5 | \fiverm | (\scriptscriptfont0) |
| 6 point | CMR6 | | |
| 7 point | CMR7 | \sevenrm | (\scriptfont0) |
| 8 point | CMR8 | | |
| 9 point | CMR9 | | |
| 10 point | CMR10 | \tenrm | (\textfont0) |
| 12 point | CMR12 | | |
| 17 point | CMR17 | | |

# Font Table for CMBX10 — Bold Extended

| | | | | | | | | |
|---|---|---|---|---|---|---|---|---|
| Γ | ɪ | ˝ | 0 | @ | P | ` | p | 0 |
| Δ | ȷ | ! | 1 | A | Q | a | q | 1 |
| Θ | ` | ˝ | 2 | B | R | b | r | 2 |
| Λ | ´ | # | 3 | C | S | c | s | 3 |
| Ξ | ˘ | $ | 4 | D | T | d | t | 4 |
| Π | ˇ | % | 5 | E | U | e | u | 5 |
| Σ | ¯ | & | 6 | F | V | f | v | 6 |
| Υ | ˚ | ' | 7 | G | W | g | w | 7 |
| Φ | ¸ | ( | 8 | H | X | h | x | 8 |
| Ψ | ß | ) | 9 | I | Y | i | y | 9 |
| Ω | æ | * | : | J | Z | j | z | A |
| ff | œ | + | ; | K | [ | k | – | B |
| fi | ø | , | ¡ | L | " | l | — | C |
| fl | Æ | - | = | M | ] | m | ˝ | D |
| ffi | Œ | . | ¿ | N | ^ | n | ~ | E |
| ffl | Ø | / | ? | O | ˙ | o | ¨ | F |
| 0 | 1 | 2 | 3 | 4 | 5 | 6 | 7 | |

\fontdimen parameter

| | |
|---|---|
| 1 | 0.00 pt |
| 2 | 3.83 pt |
| 3 | 1.92 pt |
| 4 | 1.28 pt |
| 5 | 4.44 pt |
| 6 | 11.50 pt |
| 7 | 1.28 pt |

Ligatures

| | |
|---|---|
| ff | ff |
| fi | fi |
| fl | fl |
| ffi | ffi |
| ffl | ffl |
| !` | ¡ |
| ?` | ¿ |
| ') | " |
| ` ` | " |
| -- | – |
| --- | — |

**Use in plain TEX:**      \tenbf      (\bf as \textfont6)

| size | tfm file | call (if defined) | |
|---|---|---|---|
| 5 point | CMBX5 | \fivebf | (\scriptscriptfont6) |
| 6 point | CMBX6 | | |
| 7 point | CMBX7 | \sevenbf | (\scriptfont6) |
| 8 point | CMBX8 | | |
| 9 point | CMBX9 | | |
| 10 point | CMBX10 | \tenbf | (\textfont6) |
| 12 point | CMBX12 | | |

# Font Table for CMTI10 — Italic

| | | | | | | | | |
|---|---|---|---|---|---|---|---|---|
| Γ | ι | ˋ | 0 | @ | P | ' | p | 0 |
| Δ | ȷ | ! | 1 | A | Q | a | q | 1 |
| Θ | ` | " | 2 | B | R | b | r | 2 |
| Λ | ´ | # | 3 | C | S | c | s | 3 |
| Ξ | ˇ | £ | 4 | D | T | d | t | 4 |
| Π | ˘ | % | 5 | E | U | e | u | 5 |
| Σ | ¯ | & | 6 | F | V | f | v | 6 |
| Υ | ˚ | ' | 7 | G | W | g | w | 7 |
| Φ | ¸ | ( | 8 | H | X | h | x | 8 |
| Ψ | ß | ) | 9 | I | Y | i | y | 9 |
| Ω | æ | * | : | J | Z | j | z | A |
| ff | œ | + | ; | K | [ | k | – | B |
| fi | ø | , | ¡ | L | " | l | — | C |
| fl | Æ | - | = | M | ] | m | " | D |
| ffi | Œ | . | ¿ | N | ˆ | n | ˜ | E |
| ffl | Ø | / | ? | O | ˙ | o | ¨ | F |
| 0 | 1 | 2 | 3 | 4 | 5 | 6 | 7 | |

\fontdimen parameter

| | |
|---|---|
| 1 | 0.25 pt |
| 2 | 3.58 pt |
| 3 | 1.53 pt |
| 4 | 1.02 pt |
| 5 | 4.31 pt |
| 6 | 10.22 pt |
| 7 | 1.02 pt |

Ligatures

| | |
|---|---|
| ff | ff |
| fi | fi |
| fl | fl |
| ffi | ffi |
| ffl | ffl |
| !` | ¡ |
| ?` | ¿ |
| '' | " |
| `` | " |
| -- | – |
| --- | — |

**Use in plain TEX:**      \tenit      (\it as \textfont4)

| size | tfm file | call (if defined) |
|---|---|---|
| 7 point | CMTI7 | |
| 8 point | CMTI8 | |
| 9 point | CMTI9 | |
| 10 point | CMTI10 | \tenit   (\textfont4) |
| 12 point | CMTI12 | |

## Font Table for CMSL10 — Slanted

| | 0 | 1 | 2 | 3 | 4 | 5 | 6 | 7 | |
|---|---|---|---|---|---|---|---|---|---|
| | Γ | ı | ` | 0 | @ | P | ` | p | 0 |
| | Δ | J | ! | 1 | A | Q | a | q | 1 |
| | Θ | ` | " | 2 | B | R | b | r | 2 |
| | Λ | ´ | # | 3 | C | S | c | s | 3 |
| | Ξ | ˇ | $ | 4 | D | T | d | t | 4 |
| | Π | ˘ | % | 5 | E | U | e | u | 5 |
| | Σ | ¯ | & | 6 | F | V | f | v | 6 |
| | Υ | ° | ' | 7 | G | W | g | w | 7 |
| | Φ | ¸ | ( | 8 | H | X | h | x | 8 |
| | Ψ | ß | ) | 9 | I | Y | i | y | 9 |
| | Ω | æ | * | : | J | Z | j | z | A |
| | ff | œ | + | ; | K | [ | k | - | B |
| | fi | ø | , | i | L | " | l | — | C |
| | fl | Æ | - | = | M | ] | m | " | D |
| | ffi | Œ | . | ¿ | N | ^ | n | ˜ | E |
| | ffl | Ø | / | ? | O | ˙ | o | ¨ | F |
| | 0 | 1 | 2 | 3 | 4 | 5 | 6 | 7 | |

\fontdimen parameter

| | |
|---|---|
| 1 | 0.16 pt |
| 2 | 3.33 pt |
| 3 | 1.67 pt |
| 4 | 1.11 pt |
| 5 | 4.31 pt |
| 6 | 10.00 pt |
| 7 | 1.11 pt |

Ligatures

| | |
|---|---|
| ff | ff |
| fi | fi |
| fl | fl |
| ffi | ffi |
| ffl | ffl |
| ! ` | ¡ |
| ? ` | ¿ |
| ' ' | " |
| ` ` | " |
| -- | – |
| --- | — |

**Use in plain TEX:**      \tensl      (\sl as \textfont5)

| size | tfm file | call (if defined) |
|---|---|---|
| 8 point | CMSL8 | |
| 9 point | CMSL9 | |
| 10 point | CMSL10 | \tensl   (\textfont5) |
| 12 point | CMSL12 | |

# Font Table for CMTT10 — Typewriter Type

| | | | | | | | | |
|---|---|---|---|---|---|---|---|---|
| Γ | ı | ␣ | 0 | @ | P | ` | p | 0 |
| Δ | ȷ | ! | 1 | A | Q | a | q | 1 |
| Θ | ` | " | 2 | B | R | b | r | 2 |
| Λ | ´ | # | 3 | C | S | c | s | 3 |
| Ξ | ˘ | $ | 4 | D | T | d | t | 4 |
| Π | ˇ | % | 5 | E | U | e | u | 5 |
| Σ | ¯ | & | 6 | F | V | f | v | 6 |
| Υ | ˙ | ' | 7 | G | W | g | w | 7 |
| Φ | ¸ | ( | 8 | H | X | h | x | 8 |
| Ψ | ß | ) | 9 | I | Y | i | y | 9 |
| Ω | æ | * | : | J | Z | j | z | A |
| ↑ | œ | + | ; | K | [ | k | { | B |
| ↓ | ø | , | < | L | \ | l | \| | C |
| ' | Æ | - | = | M | ] | ɯ | } | D |
| ¡ | Œ | . | > | N | ^ | n | ˜ | E |
| ¿ | Ø | / | ? | O | _ | o | ¨ | F |
| 0 | 1 | 2 | 3 | 4 | 5 | 6 | 7 | |

\fontdimen parameter

| | |
|---|---|
| 1 | 0.00 pt |
| 2 | 5.25 pt |
| 3 | 0.00 pt |
| 4 | 0.00 pt |
| 5 | 4.31 pt |
| 6 | 10.49 pt |
| 7 | 5.25 pt |

Ligatures

!` ¡

?` ¿

**Use in plain TeX:**   \tentt   (\tt as \textfont7)

| size | tfm file | call (if defined) |
|---|---|---|
| 8 point | CMTT8 | |
| 9 point | CMTT9 | |
| 10 point | CMTT10 | \tentt (\textfont7) |
| 12 point | CMTT12 | |

# Font Table for CMMI10 — Math Italic

| Γ | ζ | ψ | o | ∂ | P | ℓ | p | 0 |
|---|---|---|---|---|---|---|---|---|
| Δ | η | ω | 1 | A | Q | a | q | 1 |
| Θ | θ | ε | 2 | B | R | b | r | 2 |
| Λ | ι | ϑ | 3 | C | S | c | s | 3 |
| Ξ | κ | ϖ | 4 | D | T | d | t | 4 |
| Π | λ | ϱ | 5 | E | U | e | u | 5 |
| Σ | μ | ς | 6 | F | V | f | v | 6 |
| Υ | ν | φ | 7 | G | W | g | w | 7 |
| Φ | ξ | ↼ | 8 | H | X | h | x | 8 |
| Ψ | π | ↽ | 9 | I | Y | i | y | 9 |
| Ω | ρ | ⇀ | . | J | Z | j | z | A |
| α | σ | ⇁ | , | K | ♭ | k | ı | B |
| β | τ | ˋ | < | L | ♮ | l | ȷ | C |
| γ | υ | ˊ | / | M | ♯ | m | ℘ | D |
| δ | φ | ▷ | > | N | ⌣ | n | → | E |
| ε | χ | ◁ | ⋆ | O | ⌢ | o | ⌢ | F |
| 0 | 1 | 2 | 3 | 4 | 5 | 6 | 7 |   |

\fontdimen parameter

| 1 | 0.25 pt |
|---|---|
| 2 | 0.00 pt |
| 3 | 0.00 pt |
| 4 | 0.00 pt |
| 5 | 4.31 pt |
| 6 | 10.00 pt |
| 7 | 0.00 pt |

**commands:**

greek letters,
                    see page 65
mathematical accents,
                    see page 65
special characters,
                    see page 83

**Use in plain TEX:**        \teni        (\mit as \textfont1)
**automatically in mathematical mode**

| size | tfm file | call (if defined) |
|---|---|---|
| 5 point | CMMI5 | \fivei (\scriptscriptfont1) |
| 6 point | CMMI6 | |
| 7 point | CMMI7 | \seveni (\scriptfont1) |
| 8 point | CMMI8 | |
| 9 point | CMMI9 | |
| 10 point | CMMI10 | \teni (\textfont1) |
| 12 point | CMMI12 | |

# Font Table for CMSY10 — Mathematical Symbols

| 0 | 1 | 2 | 3 | 4 | 5 | 6 | 7 | |
|---|---|---|---|---|---|---|---|---|
| − | ≍ | ← | ′ | ℵ | $\mathcal{P}$ | ⊢ | √ | 0 |
| · | ≡ | → | ∞ | $\mathcal{A}$ | $\mathcal{Q}$ | ⊣ | ⨿ | 1 |
| × | ⊆ | ↑ | ∈ | $\mathcal{B}$ | $\mathcal{R}$ | ⌊ | ∇ | 2 |
| ∗ | ⊇ | ↓ | ∋ | $\mathcal{C}$ | $\mathcal{S}$ | ⌋ | ∫ | 3 |
| ÷ | ≤ | ↔ | △ | $\mathcal{D}$ | $\mathcal{T}$ | ⌈ | ⊔ | 4 |
| ◇ | ≥ | ↗ | ▽ | $\mathcal{E}$ | $\mathcal{U}$ | ⌉ | ⊓ | 5 |
| ± | ⪯ | ↘ | / | $\mathcal{F}$ | $\mathcal{V}$ | { | ⊑ | 6 |
| ∓ | ⪰ | ≃ | ' | $\mathcal{G}$ | $\mathcal{W}$ | } | ⊒ | 7 |
| ⊕ | ∼ | ⇐ | ∀ | $\mathcal{H}$ | $\mathcal{X}$ | ⟨ | § | 8 |
| ⊖ | ≈ | ⇒ | ∃ | $\mathcal{I}$ | $\mathcal{Y}$ | ⟩ | † | 9 |
| ⊗ | ⊂ | ⇑ | ¬ | $\mathcal{J}$ | $\mathcal{Z}$ | \| | ‡ | A |
| ⊘ | ⊃ | ⇓ | ∅ | $\mathcal{K}$ | ∪ | ∥ | ¶ | B |
| ⊙ | ≪ | ⇔ | ℜ | $\mathcal{L}$ | ∩ | ↕ | ♣ | C |
| ○ | ≫ | ↖ | ℑ | $\mathcal{M}$ | ⊎ | ⇕ | ♢ | D |
| ∘ | ≺ | ↙ | ⊤ | $\mathcal{N}$ | ∧ | \\ | ♡ | E |
| • | ≻ | ∝ | ⊥ | $\mathcal{O}$ | ∨ | ℓ | ♠ | F |
| 0 | 1 | 2 | 3 | 4 | 5 | 6 | 7 | |

\fontdimen parameter

| | |
|---|---|
| 1 | 0.25 pt |
| 2 | 0.00 pt |
| 3 | 0.00 pt |
| 4 | 0.00 pt |
| 5 | 4.31 pt |
| 6 | 10.00 pt |
| 7 | 0.00 pt |
| 8 | 6.77 pt |
| 9 | 3.94 pt |
| 10 | 4.44 pt |
| 11 | 6.86 pt |
| 12 | 3.45 pt |
| 13 | 4.13 pt |
| 14 | 3.63 pt |
| 15 | 2.89 pt |
| 16 | 1.50 pt |
| 17 | 2.47 pt |
| 18 | 3.86 pt |
| 19 | 0.50 pt |
| 20 | 23.90 pt |
| 21 | 10.10 pt |
| 22 | 2.50 pt |

commands:

binary operators,
see page 81
relations,
see page 82
further symbols,
see page 83

**Use in plain TeX:** \tensy (in \textfont2)
**automatically in mathematical mode**

| size | tfm file | call (if defined) | |
|---|---|---|---|
| 5 point | CMSY5 | \fivesy | (\scriptscriptfont2) |
| 6 point | CMSY6 | | |
| 7 point | CMSY7 | \sevensy | (\scriptfont2) |
| 8 point | CMSY8 | | |
| 9 point | CMSY9 | | |
| 10 point | CMSY10 | \tensy | (\textfont2) |

| 0 | 1 | 2 | 3 | 4 | 5 | 6 | 7 | |
|---|---|---|---|---|---|---|---|---|
| ( | ( | ( | ( | \ | Σ | ∏ | √ | 0 |
| ) | ) | ) | \ | ) | Π | ⊔ | √ | 1 |
| [ | ( | [ | ⌈ | ı | ∫ | ⌢ | √ | 2 |
| ] | ) | ] | ⌉ | ı | ∪ | ⌢ | √ | 3 |
| ⌊ | [ | ⌊ | ⌊ | ⟨ | ∩ | — | \ | 4 |
| ⌋ | ] | ⌋ | ⌋ | ⟩ | ⊎ | ~ | \| | 5 |
| ⌈ | ⌊ | ⌈ | ı | ⊔ | ∧ | ⌣ | ⌈ | 6 |
| ⌉ | ⌋ | ⌉ | ı | ⊔ | ∨ | ⌣ | ‖ | 7 |
| { | ⌈ | { | ( | ∮ | Σ | [ | ↑ | 8 |
| } | ⌉ | } | ⟩ | ∮ | ∏ | ] | ↓ | 9 |
| ⟨ | { | ⟨ | ⌊ | ⊙ | ∫ | ⌊ | ⌐ | A |
| ⟩ | } | ⟩ | ⌋ | ⊙ | ∪ | ⌋ | ⌐ | B |
| \| | ⟨ | / | { | ⊕ | ∩ | ⌈ | ⌐ | C |
| ‖ | ⟩ | \ | } | ⊕ | ⊎ | ⌉ | ⌐ | D |
| / | / | / | · | ⊗ | ∧ | { | ⇑ | E |
| \ | \ | \ | ı | ⊗ | ∨ | } | ⇓ | F |

**Font Table for CMEX10 symbols**

\fontdimen parameter

| | |
|---|---|
| 1 | 0.00 pt |
| 2 | 0.00 pt |
| 3 | 0.00 pt |
| 4 | 0.00 pt |
| 5 | 4.32 pt |
| 6 | 10.00 pt |
| 7 | 0.00 pt |
| 8 | 0.40 pt |
| 9 | 1.11 pt |
| 10 | 1.67 pt |
| 11 | 2.00 pt |
| 12 | 6.00 pt |
| 13 | 1.00 pt |

**Use:**
\tenex
  in \textfont3
  automatically
size: only as CMEX10

**commands:**
operators,
     see page 69
delimiter,
     see page 71

## 14.4 Bibliography

Here you find a collection of different TeX resources, from the original *Computers and Typesetting* series and interesting conference reports to the TeX users group.

**Books**

DONALD E. KNUTH: *The TeXbook*
    Volume A *'Computers and Typesetting'*
    Reading, Massachusetts: Addison Wesley Publishing Company, 1986

DONALD E. KNUTH: *TeX: The Program*
    Volume B *'Computers and Typesetting'*
    Reading, Massachusetts: Addison Wesley Publishing Company, 1986

DONALD E. KNUTH: *The METAFONTbook*
    Volume C *'Computers and Typesetting'*
    Reading, Massachusetts: Addison Wesley Publishing Company, 1986

DONALD E. KNUTH: *METAFONT: The Program*
    Volume D *'Computers and Typesetting'*
    Reading, Massachusetts: Addison Wesley Publishing Company, 1986

DONALD E. KNUTH: *Computer Modern Typefaces*
    Volume E *'Computers and Typesetting'*
    Reading, Massachusetts: Addison Wesley Publishing Company, 1986

LESLIE LAMPORT: *LaTeX: A Document Preparation System*
    Reading, Massachusetts: Addison Wesley Publishing Company, 1985

MICHAEL D. SPIVAK: *The Joy of TeX*
    Providence, Rhode Island: The American Mathematical Society, 1986

**Reports**

PROCEEDINGS OF THE FIRST EUROPEAN CONFERENCE ON TeX FOR SCIENTIFIC DOCUMENTATION:
    Reading, Massachusetts: Addison Wesley Publishing Company, 1985

TeX FOR SCIENTIFIC DOCUMENTATION: *Second European Conference Strasburg, 1986*
    Berlin, Heidelberg, New York: Springer, 1986

PROCEEDINGS OF THE THIRD EUROPEAN CONFERENCE ON TeX FOR SCIENTIFIC DOCUMENTATION, *Exeter, England 1988*:
    To appear

PROCEEDINGS OF THE EIGHTH ANNUAL MEETING OF THE TEX USERS GROUP:
   Providence, Rhode Island: TEX Users Group, 1987

PROCEEDINGS OF THE NINTH ANNUAL MEETING OF THE TEX USERS GROUP:
   Providence, Rhode Island: TEX Users Group, 1988


**TUG**

TUGBOAT: THE COMMUNICATIONS OF THE TEX USERS GROUP:
   Providence, Rhode Island: TEX Users Group, quarterly


   The TEX Users Group can provide you with a host of TEX-related information,
membership includes subscription to TUGboat. For free information, contact

   TEX Users Group
   P. O. Box 9506
   Providence, RI 02940
   USA